MICROSOFT
InternetExplorer5

Introductory Concepts and Techniques

Gary B. Shelly
Thomas J. Cashman
Steven G. Forsythe

COURSE TECHNOLOGY

ONE MAIN STREET

CAMBRIDGE MA 02142

Thomson Learning™

SHELLY
CASHMAN
SERIES®

Australia Canada • Denmark • Japan • Mexico • New Zealand • Philippines
Puerto Rico • Singapore • South Africa • Spain • United Kingdom • United States

Asia (excluding Japan)
Thomson Learning
60 Albert Street, #15-01
Albert Complex
Singapore 189969

Japan
Thomson Learning
Palaceside Building 5F
1-1-1 Hitotsubashi, Chiyoda-ku
Tokyo 100 0003 Japan

Australia/New Zealand
Nelson/Thomson Learning
102 Dodds Street
South Melbourne, Victoria 3205
Australia

Latin America
Thomson Learning
Seneca, 53
Colonia Polanco
11560 Mexico D.F. Mexico

South Africa
Thomson Learning
Zonnebloem Building,
Constantia Square
526 Sixteenth Road
P.O. Box 2459
Halfway House, 1685
South Africa

Canada
Nelson/Thomson Learning
1120 Birchmount Road
Scarborough, Ontario
Canada M1K 5G4

UK/Europe/Middle East
Thomson Learning
Berkshire House
168-173 High Holborn
London, WC1V 7AA United Kingdom

Spain
Thomson Learning
Calle Magallanes, 25
28015-MADRID
ESPANA

TRADEMARKS
Course Technology and the Open Book logo are registered trademarks and CourseKits is a trademark of Course Technology.

SHELLY CASHMAN SERIES® and **Custom Edition®** are trademarks of Thomson Learning. Some of the product names and company names used in this book have been used for identification purposes only and may be trademarks or registered trademarks of their respective manufacturers and sellers. Thomson Learning and Course Technology disclaim any affiliation, association, or connection with, or sponsorship or endorsement by, such owners.

DISCLAIMER
Course Technology reserves the right to revise this publication and make changes from time to time in its content without notice.

PHOTO CREDITS: *Project 1, pages IE 1.2-3* Atom bomb, stars, Courtesy of Digital Stock; *Project 3, pages IE 3.2-3* Alphabet blocks, building blocks, children on Web sites, mother and child, Courtesy of PhotoDisc, Inc.

ISBN 0-7895-4646-9

1 2 3 4 5 6 7 8 9 10   BC   04 03 02 01 00

MICROSOFT
InternetExplorer5

Introductory Concepts and Techniques

C O N T E N T S

Preface

In just ten years since its birth, the World Wide Web, or Web for short, has grown beyond all expectations. During this short period of time, Web usage has increased from a limited number of users to more than 100 million users, accessing Web pages on any topic you can imagine. Schools, businesses, and the computing industry all are taking advantage of this new way of accessing the Internet to provide products, services and education electronically. Internet Explorer 5 provides the novice as well as the experienced user a window with which to look into the Web and tap an abundance of resources.

Objectives of This Textbook

Microsoft Internet Explorer 5: Introductory Concepts and Techniques is intended for use in combination with other books in an introductory computer concepts or applications course. This book also is suitable for use in a one-credit hour course or a continuing education course. Specific objectives of this book are as follows:

- To teach students how to use Internet Explorer 5 using the proven Shelly Cashman Series step-by-step, screen-by-screen pedagogy
- To expose students to various World Wide Web resources
- To acquaint student with the more popular search engines
- To show students how to do research using the World Wide Web
- To teach students how to communicate with other Internet users

Organization of This Textbook

Microsoft Internet Explorer 5: Introductory Concepts and Techniques consists of three projects and an Appendix. Each project ends with a large number of exercises to reinforce what students learn in the project. The projects and appendix are organized as follows:

Project 1 – Introduction to Internet Explorer In Project 1, students are introduced to the Internet, World Wide Web, and Internet Explorer. Topics include launching Internet Explorer; browsing the World Wide Web; stopping and refreshing a Web page; using the History list and the Favorites list to display Web pages; adding Web pages to and removing Web pages from the Favorites list; saving and printing a Web page; copying and pasting text and pictures from a Web page into WordPad; and using Internet Explorer Help.

Project 2 – Web Research Techniques and Search Engines In Project 2, students are introduced to the five Web page categories, techniques to search the Web using a search engine and the Search Assistant, and methods to evaluate a Web page. Topics include searching the Web using keywords or a directory; performing an advanced search; evaluating and recording relevant information about a Web source; using Search Assistant to search for an e-mail address, map, place, landmark, or encyclopedia article; and using the Address bar to display a Web page, search the Web, and display folder contents.

Project 3 – Communicating Over the Internet In Project 3, students learn to read and send an e-mail message, read and post an article to a newsgroup, place an Internet call, create and edit a Web page, and listen to a radio station. Topics include reading, replying to, and deleting an e-mail message; composing, formatting, and sending a new e-mail message; reading and posting a newsgroup article; subscribing and unsubscribing to a newsgroup; placing an Internet call and sending text messages; creating and editing a personal home page; displaying the Radio toolbar and radio station guide; and listening to a radio station.

Appendix A – Internet Explorer Options Appendix A explains how to change the settings for Internet options. Settings include changing the default home page; deleting the files in the Temporary Internet Files folder; setting the time that pages remain in the History list; changing the security level of a zone; controlling the type of content a computer can access on the Internet; modifying AutoComplete, Wallet, and personal profile settings; maintaining dial-up networking connections; modifying local area network (LAN) settings; and changing the programs Internet Explorer 5 uses as an editor, e-mail service, newsgroup reader, Internet call program, calendar program, and contact program.

Shelly Cashman Series Teaching Tools

A comprehensive set of Teaching Tools accompanies this textbook in the form of a CD-ROM. The CD-ROM includes an Instructor's Manual and teaching and testing aids. The CD-ROM (ISBN 0-7895-4659-0) is available through your Course Technology representative or by calling one of the following telephone numbers: Colleges and Universities, 1-800-648-7450; High Schools, 1-800-824-5179; and Career Colleges, 1-800-477-3692. The contents of the CD-ROM are listed below.

- **Instructor's Manual** The Instructor's Manual is made up of Microsoft Word files. The files include lecture notes, solutions, and a large test bank. The files allow you to modify the lecture notes or generate quizzes and exams from the test bank using your own word processing software.
- **Figures in the Book** Illustrations of the figures and tables in the textbook are available. Use this ancillary to create a slide show from the illustrations for lecture or to print transparencies for use in lecture with an overhead projector.
- **Course Test Manager** Course Test Manager is a powerful testing and assessment package that enables instructors to create and print tests from the large test bank. Instructors with access to a networked computer lab (LAN) can administer, grade, and track tests online. Students also can take online practice tests, which generate customized study guides that indicate where in the textbook students can find more information for each question.
- **Interactive Labs** Eighteen hands-on interactive labs that take students from ten to fifteen minutes each to step through help solidify and reinforce mouse and keyboard usage and computer concepts. Student assessment is available in each interactive lab by means of a Print button.

Acknowledgments

The Shelly Cashman Series would not be the leading computer education series without the contributions of outstanding publishing professionals. First, and foremost, among them is Becky Herrington, director of production and designer. She is the heart and soul of the Shelly Cashman Series, and it is only through her leadership, dedication, and tireless efforts that superior products are made possible. Becky created and produced the award-winning Windows series of books.

Under Becky's direction, the following individuals made significant contributions to these books: Doug Cowley, production manager; Ginny Harvey, series specialist and developmental editor; Ken Russo, senior Web designer; Mike Bodnar, associate production manager; Mark Norton, Web designer; Stephanie Nance, graphic artist and cover designer; Ellana Russo, Marlo Mitchem, Chris Schneider, and Hector Arvizu graphic artists, Jeanne Black and Betty Hopkins, Quark experts; Marilyn Martin copy editor; Katie Asling, proofreader; Cristina Haley, indexer; Sarah Evertson of Image Quest, photo researcher; and Susan Sebok and Ginny Harvey, contributing writers.

Special thanks go to Richard Keaveny, managing editor; Jim Quasney, series consultant; Lora Wade, product manager; Meagan Walsh, associate product manager; Francis Schurgot, Web product manager; Tonia Grafakos, associate Web product manager; Scott Wiseman, online developer; Rajika Gupta, marketing manager; and Erin Bennett, editorial assistant.

Gary B. Shelly
Thomas J. Cashman
Steven G. Forsythe

Internet Explorer 5

PROJECT

1

Introduction to Internet Explorer

You will have mastered the material in this project when you can:

O B J E C T I V E S

- Define Internet
- Describe hypermedia and browsers
- Define hyperlink, Uniform Resource Locator, and hypertext markup language
- Launch and quit Internet Explorer
- Describe the Internet Explorer features
- Use the History list, Favorites list, or URLs to browse the World Wide Web
- Use the Back, Forward, and Home buttons to display a Web page
- Add and remove a Web page from the Favorites list
- Save a picture or text from a Web page or an entire Web page on a floppy disk
- Stop the transfer of a Web page
- Refresh and print a Web page
- Copy and paste text or pictures from a Web page into WordPad
- Save and print a WordPad document
- Use Internet Explorer Help

A Remarkable Success

Web Designer's Innovation Skyrockets

Described as a revolutionary communications system requiring minimal technical understanding, the World Wide Web flourishes into the new millennium as the medium of choice for information sharing. At the helm of this innovation is Tim Berners-Lee, who in 1998, was awarded a $270,000 genius grant from the John D. and Catherine T. MacArthur Foundation for his pioneering efforts developing this system.

The impetus for the Internet occurred when Russia launched the first artificial Earth satellite, *Sputnik*, in 1957. In response, U.S. Department of Defense officials became alarmed about a possible nuclear attack. The Pentagon's Advanced Research Projects Agency developed ARPANET, a decentralized computer system that could reroute data if some transmission lines among the country's military, defense contractors, and research universities became obstructed. Four of these computers were networked in 1969; this number grew to fifteen two years later and to thirty-seven the following year.

Nonmilitary users connected to ARPANET in the 1970s, and some networks offered to allow the public to connect to the system in the 1980s. The Department of Defense then decided to create another private network for its nonclassified information. The department moved its files to its new military side, MILNET, and left ARPANET in place. More and more networks added information to ARPANET, which earned the new name, Internet, to reflect this community of connected computers.

At this point, Berners-Lee began his magic. When he was working as a scientist at the European Laboratory for Particle Physics in Geneva, Switzerland, he proposed the initial idea for the system that ultimately would evolve into the Web. He also set up the Internet's first Web server.

His creation, the World Wide Web, contains sites filled with multimedia. Internet users navigate clicking links, which connect the sites to each other. "I didn't know it was going to succeed the way it has," Berners-Lee said. Indeed, the size of the Web is expanding by an estimated one percent daily. Although it is impossible to count the number of people actually connected, some researchers theorize more than three million people in 200 countries use the Web. These numbers are expected to grow at a rate of ten percent monthly.

This is an exciting time in the history of Internet access and Web browsing. Internet Explorer is a popular Web browsing program that provides searching capabilities, allows you to link quickly to previously viewed Web pages via a History list, and keeps track of your favorite Web pages using the Favorites list.

People all over the world communicate via networks using online services for sharing information on computers. These services make it possible for you to send and receive electronic mail; talk to others in chat rooms; access the latest news, sports, weather, and financial information; and access the Internet. In addition, using the Web, you can carry out research, get a loan, shop for services and merchandise, and look for a job.

In this project, you are introduced to the worldwide system of networks, called the Internet; the software used to connect computers, called Transmission Control Protocol/ Internet Protocol (TCP/IP) that provides networking services; and the World Wide Web, which is the collection of hyperlinks throughout the Internet that creates an interconnected network of links. The links enable you to access the location of the computer on which text, graphics, video, sound, and virtual reality are stored.

Upon completing the project, you will join the millions of individuals worldwide successfully sharing networked information.

Internet Explorer 5

Introduction to Internet Explorer

P R O J E C T

1

CASE PERSPECTIVE

Although you are majoring in art history in college, your advisor recommends you take a short college course titled, Searching the Internet. Among the topics covered in the class are the basics of using Internet Explorer 5, searching the Internet for information, and how to save information you find on a Web page on your computer. You sign up and complete the course.

After completing the course, you ponder the idea of using the information you learned about Internet Explorer and searching the Internet to earn money by performing Internet research for college professors and local businesses. Instead of the usual resume/cover letter approach to obtaining a job, you decide to take out an advertisement in the local newspaper that advertises your Internet search skills.

Among the responses you receive from the advertisement is one from the manager of the Asian Art galleries. She hires you to identify the origin and authenticity of a piece of Asian art, titled Three Leaves, that the gallery recently purchased in China. You agree to search for information about the Asian art and supply the gallery with pictures or text associated with the art.

Introduction

Little known a few years ago, today the Internet is one of the more popular and faster growing areas in computing. Using the Internet, you can carry out research, get a loan, shop for services and merchandise, look for a job, conduct business, obtain pictures, movies, audio clips, and information from sites stored on computers around the world. You also are able to converse with people and listen to radio stations around the world.

Once considered mysterious, the Internet now is easily accessible to the public because user-friendly software and personal computers have reduced its complexity. The Internet, with its millions of connected computers, continues to grow with hundreds of thousands of new users coming online every month. An Intelliquest survey published in the spring of 1998 indicated that 66 million adults were online in the United States alone. One year later, in the spring of 1999, this number had jumped to 83 million. **Intelliquest** (www.intelliquest.com) is a computer market research firm.

You can find schools, businesses, newspapers, television stations, and government services on the Internet. Service providers throughout the country provide inexpensive access to the Internet, so the information provided by the various sites is readily available to anyone who has the use of a personal computer.

The Internet

The **Internet** is a worldwide system of networks, each of which is composed of a collection of smaller networks. A **network** is composed of several computers connected together for purposes such as resource and data sharing. For example, on a college campus, the network in the student lab can connect to the faculty computer network, which can connect to the administration network, and all of them can connect to the Internet (Figure 1-1).

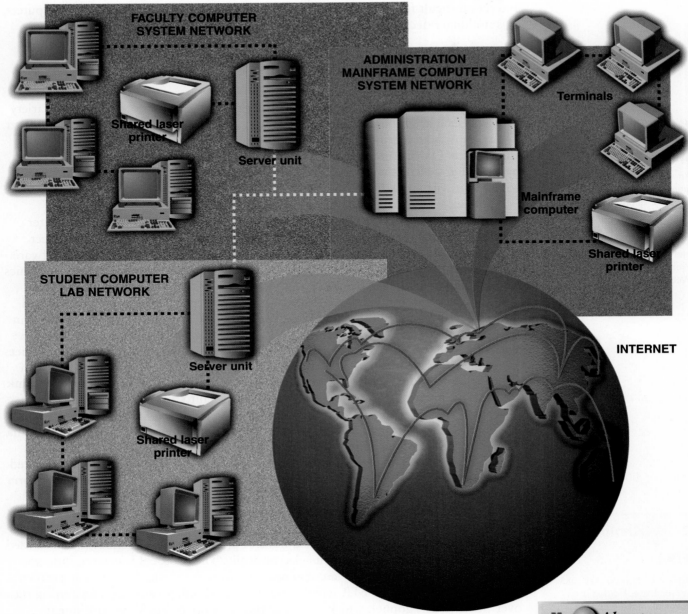

FIGURE 1-1

Networks connect with high-, medium- and low-speed data lines that allow data to move from one computer to another. For example an Internet connection from a home to an Internet service provider's computer may be over a low-speed telephone line. The provider's computer then accesses the Internet over a high-speed line to accommodate the many low-speed connections of its customers.

The software used to connect the computers, called **Transmission Control Protocol/Internet Protocol (TCP/IP)**, provides networking services such as remote terminal sessions and transferring files.

More About

The Internet

The Internet started as a government experiment for the military. The military wanted a communication technique that would connect different computers running different operating systems. This method had to survive one or more of the computers becoming unavailable. From this experiment, a communication technique originated called Transmission Control Protocol/Internet Protocol, or TCP/IP.

Before 1990, most computers were text-based. In other words, you had to know the set of available commands for each TCP/IP service program. This made using the Internet difficult for the casual user. Fortunately, with today's multimedia computers, it is no longer necessary to learn long lists of commands to use the Internet.

The World Wide Web

Modern computer systems have the capability of delivering information in a variety of ways, such as graphics, sound, video clips, animation, and, of course, regular text. Today, most advertisements for computers are for those that have these multimedia capabilities. On the Internet, this multimedia capability is available in a form called **hypermedia**, which is any variety of computer media, including text, graphics, video, sound, and virtual reality.

You access hypermedia using a **hyperlink**, or simply **link**, which is a special selectable connection that enables the user to access the location of the computer on which the hypermedia is stored and the hypermedia itself. A link can connect to hypermedia on any computer on the Internet that is running the proper software. Thus, clicking hyperlink on a computer in California could display text and graphics located on a computer in Illinois.

The collection of hyperlinks throughout the Internet creates an interconnected network of links called the **World Wide Web, Web,** or **WWW**. Each computer within the Web containing hypermedia that you can reference with a hyperlink is called a **Web site**. Millions of Web sites around the world are accessible through the Internet.

A picture, text file, and other hypermedia available at a Web site is stored in a file called a **hypertext document**, or **Web page**. Therefore, when you click a hyperlink to display a picture, read text, view a video, or listen to a song, you actually are viewing a Web page or part of a Web page that contains the hypermedia.

Figure 1-2 illustrates a Web page in the Disneyland Web site located in California. The Web page contains numerous hyperlinks. Clicking a hyperlink, such as the PLAN YOUR VISIT hyperlink, could display a Web page from a travel agency located on the other side of the world. Each Web page has a unique address, called a **Uniform Resource Locator (URL)**, which distinguishes it from all other pages on the Internet.

A typical URL is composed of three parts (Figure 1-3). The first part is the protocol. A **protocol** is a set of rules that computers follow. Most Web pages use the hypertext transfer protocol. **Hypertext transfer protocol (HTTP)** describes the rules used to transmit hypermedia documents electronically. The protocol is entered in lower-case (http) and is followed by a colon and two forward slashes (://). Other protocols used on the Web include FTP, which describes the simplest rules for transferring files over the Internet; gopher, which describes the rules for menu-driven document transfer over the Internet; and Telnet, which describes the rules for remote terminal sessions over the Internet.

The second part of a URL is the domain name. The **domain name** is the Internet address of the computer on the Internet where the Web page is located. Each computer on the Internet has a unique address, called an **Internet Protocol address**, or **IP address**. The domain name identifies where to forward a request for the Web page referenced by the URL. Most Web sites have a domain name that starts with www, such as www.uswest.com. The domain name in the URL in Figure 1-3 is www.scsite.com.

The last portion of the domain name indicates the type of organization responsible for the site. For example, com indicates a commercial organization, usually a business or corporation. Educational institutions have edu at the end of their domain names. Government entities use gov in their domain names. Table 1-1 shows the types of organizations and their extensions.

Web Sites

An organization can have more than one Web site. Separate departments may have their own Web computers, allowing faster response to requests for Web pages, and local control over the Web pages stored at that Web site.

HTML

HTML editing programs, such as FrontPage, Hotdog, and Hotmetal, make it easy to create Web pages without learning HTML syntax.

FIGURE 1-2

The optional third part of a URL is the file specification of the Web page. The **file specification** includes the file name and possibly one or more folder names. This information is called the **path**. If a URL does not contain a file specification, a default Web page, usually the Web site's home page, displays. This means you can display a Web page from a Web site even though you do not know the names of any files at the site. Simply supply the domain name of the Web site, and the default page will display.

You can find URLs that identify interesting Web sites in magazines and newspapers, on television, from friends, or even from just browsing the Web. In addition, you should visit the *Shelly Cashman Series Guide to the World Wide Web site* at www.scsite.com/ie5/app.html for a list of excellent sites. URLs of well-known companies and organizations usually contain the group's name within the domain name between the www and the extension; for example, www.ibm.com, or www.whitehouse.gov.

Because of the variety and number of URLs, you may find it useful to keep a directory of URLs. Internet Explorer has a feature that allows you to save and organize your favorite URLs so you can access them easily. Later in this project, you will save and retrieve URLs.

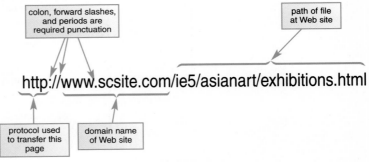

FIGURE 1-3

Table 1-1	
ORGANIZATION	*EXTENSION*
Commercial organizations	.com
Educational institutions	.edu
Government institutions	.gov
Military groups	.mil
Major network support centers	.net
Organizations not covered in other groups	.org
International organizations	.int
Individual countries/states	country code

Hypertext Markup Language

The Web page authors use a special formatting language called **hypertext markup language (HTML)** to create Web pages. Behind all that formatted text and eye-catching graphics is plain text. Special HTML formatting codes and functions that control attributes such as font size, colors, and centering surround the text and picture references. Figure 1-4 shows the hypertext markup language used to create the Web page shown in Figure 1-2 on the previous page. After viewing the document source, you can return to the Disneyland Web page by clicking the Close button in the upper-right corner of the window.

Close button

HTML format codes

```
<HTML>
<HEAD>

<!-- START META TAGS -- PARSER CREATED =) -->
<META name="KEYWORDS" content="DISNEYLAND SOUTHERN CALIFORNIA VACATIONS FAMILY VACATIONS CALIFORN
<META name="SBU" content="Disneyland">
<META name="REVISED" content="08/25/1998">
<META name="AUTHOR" content="Disney Online">
<META name="DESCRIPTION" content="Disneyland -- the official Web site of Disneyland Park and the
<META name="DATE" content="08/25/1998">
<META http-equiv="PICS-Label" content='(PICS-1.1 "http://www.rsac.org/ratingsv01.html" l gen true
<!-- STOP META TAGS -- PARSER CREATED -->

<TITLE>The Official Disneyland Web Site</TITLE>
</HEAD>

<BODY MARGINWIDTH=0 MARGINHEIGHT=0 TOPMARGIN=0 LEFTMARGIN=0 BGCOLOR="#003399" background="media/b
<TABLE WIDTH=600 CELLPADDING=0 CELLSPACING=0 BORDER=0><!--OVER-TABLE-->
<TR VALIGN=top>
        <TD WIDTH=100>
                <TABLE WIDTH=100 CELLPADDING=0 CELLSPACING=0 BORDER=0><!--BINDS TOP AND BOTTOM NA
                <TR VALIGN=top>
                        <TD ALIGN=center BGCOLOR="#003399">
                        <CENTER><A HREF="http://www.disney.com/index.html"><FONT FACE="Arial, Hel
                        <A HREF="/ddc_media/navigation/disneynav.map"><IMG SRC="/ddc_media/naviga
                        </TD>
                </TR>
                <TR VALIGN=top>
                        <TD ALIGN=center>
                                <TABLE WIDTH=100 CELLPADDING=0 CELLSPACING=0 BORDER=0><!--NAV TABL
                                <TR>
                                        <TD align=center valign=middle>
<!-- INSERT DISNEYLAND NAVIGATION HERE -->
```

Disneyland[1] - Notepad

File   Edit   Search   Help

Start   The Official Disneyland W...   Disneyland[1] - Notep...   12:28 PM

FIGURE 1-4

Though it looks somewhat cryptic, HTML is similar to a computer programming language. Using HTML, you can create Web pages and place them on the Web for others to see. Special software also has been developed to assist in creating Web pages. Internet Explorer's FrontPage is one of the many HTML authoring tools available. FrontPage will be discussed in more detail in Project 3.

Home Pages

No main menus or an official starting point exist in the World Wide Web. Although you can reference any page on the Web when you begin, most people start with specially designated Web pages called home pages or start pages. A **home page** is the introductory page for a Web site, whether it has been created by an organization or an individual. All other Web pages for that site usually are accessible from the home page. In addition, the home page is the default page that displays on a computer if you do not know the path of any other pages located at a particular Web site and use only the URL protocol and domain name. Your school or organization may allow you space to create your own home page and publish it on the World Wide Web.

More *About*

Home Pages

A Web site may consist of many home pages. A computer used by faculty members or students for their hypertext documents would have many home pages: one for each person.

Because it is the starting point for most Web sites, home pages try to make a good first impression and display attractive eye-catching graphics, specially formatted text, and a variety of links to hypermedia contained at that Web site as well as other interesting and useful Web sites.

Internet Browsers

Just as a **graphical user interface (GUI)** such as Microsoft Windows simplifies working with a computer by using a point-and-click method, a browser such as Internet Explorer makes using the World Wide Web easier by removing the complexity of having to remember the syntax, or rules, of commands used to reference Web pages at Web sites. A **browser** takes the URL associated with a hyperlink or the URL entered by a user, locates the computer containing the associated HTML codes, and uses the HTML codes to display a Web page.

What is Internet Explorer 5?

Internet Explorer 5 is a Web browsing program that allows you to search for and view Web pages, save pages you find for use in the future, maintain a list of the pages you visit, send and receive e-mail messages, edit Web pages, and listen to radio stations. The Internet Explorer 5 program is included with the Microsoft Windows 98 operating system software, Microsoft Office 2000 software, or you can download it from the Internet. The projects in this book illustrate the use of the Internet Explorer 5 browser.

Mouse Usage

In this book, the mouse is the primary way to communicate with Microsoft Internet Explorer. You can perform six operations with a standard mouse: point, click, right-click, double-click, drag, and right-drag. If you have a **Microsoft IntelliMouse™**, then you also have a wheel between the left and right buttons. You can use this wheel to perform three additional operations: rotate wheel, click wheel, or drag wheel.

Point means you move the mouse across a flat surface until the mouse pointer rests on the item of choice on the screen. As you move the mouse, the mouse pointer moves across the screen in the same direction. **Click** means you press and release the left mouse button. The terminology used in this book that directs you to point to a particular item and then click is, Click the particular item. For example, Click the Bold button means point to the Bold button and click.

Right-click means you press and release the right mouse button. As with the left mouse button, you normally will point to an item on the screen before right-clicking.

Double-click means you quickly press and release the left mouse button twice without moving the mouse. In most cases, you must point to an item before double-clicking. **Drag** means you point to an item, hold down the left mouse button, move the item to the desired location on the screen, and then release the left mouse button. **Right-drag** means you point to an item, hold down the right mouse button, move the item to the desired location, and then release the right mouse button.

If you have a Microsoft IntelliMouse™, then you can use **rotate wheel** to view parts of the Web page that are not visible. The wheel also can serve as a third button. When you use the wheel as a button, it is referred to as the **wheel button**. For example, dragging the wheel button causes some applications to scroll in the direction you drag.

The use of the mouse is an important skill to master when working with Microsoft Internet Explorer.

The Mouse

The mouse unit has been around for as long as the personal computer itself. It had little use with earlier operating systems, however, such as MS-DOS. Few used the mouse or even attached it to their computers until recently when Windows began to dominate the market. Even with Windows 98 some former MS-DOS users prefer to use the keyboard over the mouse.

The Internet Explorer Icon

The Internet Explorer icon displays automatically on the Windows desktop when you install Internet Explorer 5 or Windows 98. Another icon, designed by the Internet Service Provider, often replaces the Internet Explorer icon when you sign up with an Internet Service Provider.

Launching Internet Explorer

To launch Internet Explorer, the Windows desktop must display on the screen and the Internet Explorer icon must display on the desktop. The Internet Explorer icon displays when you install Internet Explorer or Windows 98. Some Internet service providers, however, must have their servers activated before you can launch Internet Explorer. Check with your instructor for information about how to launch Explorer. Perform the following steps to launch Internet Explorer.

 To Launch Internet Explorer

1 Point to the Internet Explorer icon on the desktop (Figure 1-5).

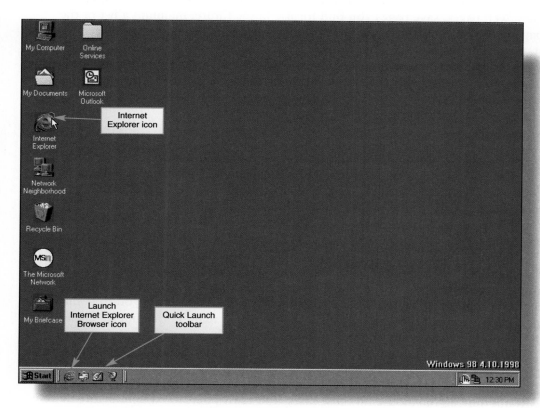

FIGURE 1-5

2 Double-click the Internet Explorer icon.

Windows launches Internet Explorer, maximizes the MSN.COM - Microsoft Internet Explorer window, adds the MSN.COM - Microsoft Internet Explorer button to the taskbar, displays the MSN.COM Web page title in the window title, and displays the MSN.COM home page in the display area (Figure 1-6). The home page may display differently on your computer.

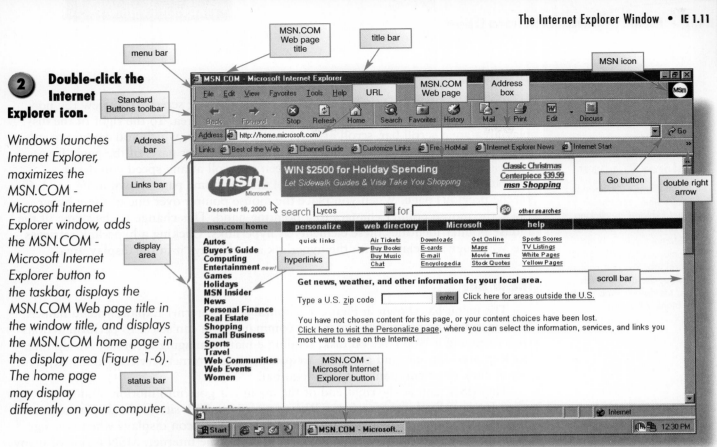

FIGURE 1-6

Normally, when Internet Explorer launches, the MSN.COM home page displays. Because it is possible to change the page that displays, the home page shown in Figure 1-6 may be different on your computer. Some computers display their own home pages when launching Internet Explorer. The title of the Web page (MSN.COM) displays on the title bar.

For an easy way to launch frequently used programs, a Quick Launch toolbar displays on the taskbar to the right of the Start button, as shown in Figure 1-5. It contains icons that provide quick access to Internet Explorer, Outlook Express, the Windows desktop, and Web Channels.

The Internet Explorer Window

The Internet Explorer window (Figure 1-6) consists of features to make browsing the Internet easy. It contains a title bar, a menu bar, the Standard Buttons toolbar, an Address bar, a Links bar, a scroll bar, the status bar, and a display area where pages from the World Wide Web may be viewed. The menu bar, Standard Buttons toolbar, Address bar, and Links bar display at the top of the screen just below the title bar. The status bar displays at the bottom of the screen.

Display Area

Only a portion of most pages will be visible on your screen. You view the portion of the page displayed on the screen in the display area. To the right of the display area are a scroll bar, scroll arrows, and a scroll box, which you can use to move the text in the display area up and down and reveal other parts of the page. If you are using the wheel, you can click the screen to scroll at any speed you desire.

Notice the hyperlinks on the Internet Explorer home page shown in Figure 1-6 on the previous page. When you place the mouse pointer over one of these hyperlinks, the mouse pointer changes to a pointing hand. This change in the shape of the mouse pointer identifies these elements as hyperlinks. Clicking a hyperlink retrieves the Web page associated with the hyperlink and displays it in the display area.

Menu Bar

The menu bar shown in Figure 1-6 contains the Internet Explorer menu names. Each menu name represents a menu of commands you can select to perform actions such as saving a Web page on disk, sending e-mail, managing favorites, setting Internet Explorer options, and accessing frequently used Internet services. To display a menu, click the menu name on the menu bar.

The MSN icon at the right end of the menu bar goes into motion (animates) when Internet Explorer transfers a Web page from a Web site to the display area and stops moving when the transfer is complete. The MSN icon displays when you sign up to use The Microsoft Network (MSN) to access the Internet. MSN is one of many online services available to computer users. Other popular online services include America Online, Prodigy, and CompuServe. Unlike other online services, access to MSN is a feature of Windows 98. Your computer may display the Internet Explorer icon, or an icon of another online service or Internet service provider (ISP) may display in place of the MSN icon on your computer. If the Internet Explorer icon displays, clicking the icon displays Microsoft Corporation's home page.

Standard Buttons Toolbar and Links Bar

The Standard Buttons toolbar and Links bar contain buttons that allow you to perform often-used tasks more quickly than using the menu bar allows. For example, to print the Web page in the display area, click the Print button on the Standard Buttons toolbar.

Each button on the Standard Buttons toolbar contains an icon and a text label describing its function. Table 1-2 illustrates the Standard Buttons toolbar and Table 1-3 illustrates the Links bar buttons. The tables also briefly describe the functions of the buttons. Each of the buttons will be explained in detail as it is used. The buttons on the Standard Buttons and Links toolbars may be different on your computer.

By right-clicking the Standard Buttons toolbar, you can customize its buttons. You can remove the text label on each button, or you can remove the entire toolbar by clicking the appropriate toolbar name on the shortcut menu.

Clicking the double right arrow at the right end of the Links bar (see Figure 1-6 on the previous page) displays a menu containing additional buttons that do not fit on the Links bar. Clicking the double right arrow a second time removes the menu.

More About

The Internet Explorer Window

You can change the page that displays when you launch Internet Explorer by clicking View on the menu bar, clicking Internet Options on the View menu, and clicking the General tab. You can choose to display the current Web page, the default Web page, or a blank Web page.

More About

Standard Buttons toolbar buttons

If the text label does not display on the buttons on your Standard Buttons toolbar, right-click the toolbar, click Customize, click the Text Options box arrow, click Show text labels, and then click the Close button. You also can change the size of the icons on the toolbar buttons using the Icon Options box arrow.

Table 1-2   Standard Buttons Toolbar

BUTTON	FUNCTION
Back	Retrieves the previous page (provided it was previously just viewed). To go more than one page back, click the Back button arrow, and then click a Web page title on the list.
Forward	Retrieves the next page. To go more than one page forward, click the Forward button arrow, and then click a Web page title on the list.
Stop	Stops the transfer of a Web page.
Refresh	Requests the Web page in the display area be retrieved from the Web site again.
Home	Requests the default home page be displayed.
Search	Displays the Explorer bar containing search categories.
Favorites	Displays the Explorer bar containing the Favorites list.
History	Displays the Explorer bar containing the History list.
Mail	Displays a menu containing commands to access e-mail messages and Internet newsgroups.
Print	Prints the Web page shown in the display area.
Edit	Edits the Web page shown in the display area.
Discuss	Adds or edits a discussion server.

Table 1-3   Links Toolbar

BUTTON	FUNCTION
Best of the Web	Displays links to interesting, unusual Web pages.
Channel Guide	Displays an up-to-date list of available channels.
Customize Links	Displays links to pages that describe how to better organize the way you browse the Web.
Free HotMail	Displays the Hotmail Web site to set up and access free e-mail accounts.
Internet Explorer News	Displays links to announcements and current news stories about Internet Explorer and its components.
Internet Start	Displays the home page.

Address Bar

The Address bar illustrated in Figure 1-6 on page IE 1.11 contains the Address box, which holds the Uniform Resource Locator (URL) for the page currently shown in the Internet Explorer display area, and the Go button. The URL updates automatically as you browse from page to page over the World Wide Web. To connect to another Web site, you can select the current URL in the Address box, type the new URL, and click the Go button.

Status Bar

If you position the mouse pointer over a hyperlink, the status bar displays the URL of the Web page that is associated with the link. In addition, while Internet Explorer transfers a Web page from a Web site to the display area, the status bar provides information about the progress of the transfer.

More About

The Address Bar

To move the insertion point to the Address box when the box is empty or to highlight the URL in the Address box, press ALT+D.

Browsing the World Wide Web

More About

The Display Area

You can increase the size of the display area by moving and resizing the Standard Buttons toolbar, Address bar, or Links bar, or by removing a toolbar. To practice removing, moving, and sizing a toolbar, perform In the Lab Assignment 8 at the end of this project.

The MSN.COM home page (see Figure 1-6 on page IE 1.11) provides a starting point for browsing the World Wide Web. You can display some of the more interesting or newer pages by taking advantage of the Links bar buttons, Best of the Web and Internet Explorer News. If you click the Best of the Web button, Internet Explorer displays a page with links to fascinating, excellent Web pages organized by topics such as business, entertainment, and news. If you click the Internet Explorer News button, Internet Explorer displays a page that contains announcements and current news stories about Internet Explorer and its components.

Microsoft Corporation updates the Best of the Web and Internet Explorer News pages often as new Web pages become available, so links that display one day may be gone the next, having been replaced with new offerings.

On the Standard Buttons toolbar, the Search button allows you to browse the World Wide Web and search for topics in which you may be interested. The Search button will be discussed in detail in Project 2.

The most common way to browse the World Wide Web is to obtain the URL of a Web page you wish to visit and then enter it into the Address box. If you type an incorrect letter or symbol in the URL in the Address box and notice the error before you click the Go button, you can use the BACKSPACE key to erase all the characters back to and including the one that is incorrect and then continue typing.

It is by visiting various Web sites that you can begin to understand the enormous appeal of the World Wide Web. The following steps show you how to contact a Web site provided by Web Art Publishing from Santa Fe, New Mexico and visit the Web page titled Asian Arts, which contains information and pictures of artwork from various countries of Asia. The URL for the Asian Art page is:

www.scsite.com/ie5/asianart.htm.

You are not required to provide the leading http:// protocol when initially typing the URL in the Address box because the default protocol used with the browser is http. Internet Explorer will insert http:// automatically if you do not supply it.

To Browse the World Wide Web by Entering a URL

1 **Click the Address box.**

The URL in the Address box is highlighted and the mouse pointer changes to an I-beam (Figure 1-7).

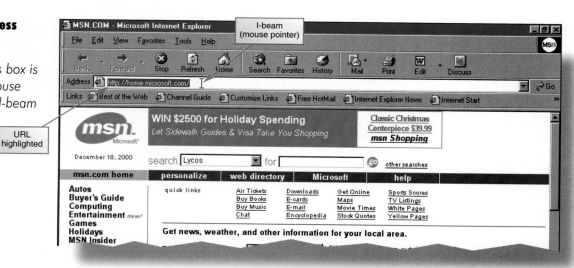

FIGURE 1-7

2 Type
www.scsite.com/
ie5/asianart.htm **in the
Address box and then point
to the Go button.**

*The new URL displays in the
Address box (Figure 1-8). A
ScreenTip displays below the
Go button.*

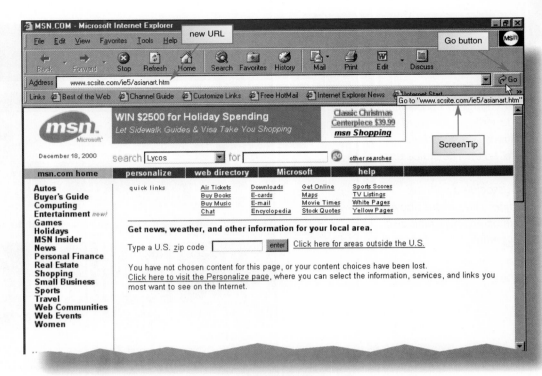

FIGURE 1-8

3 Click the Go button.

*While Internet Explorer trans-
fers the Asian Arts page from
the Web site, the MSN icon
moves (animates), a message
displays on the status bar
providing information about
the progress of the transfer.
When the transfer is com-
plete, the motion of the MSN
icon stops, the message dis-
appears, the Asian Arts Web
page title displays on the title
bar and on the button on the
taskbar, and the Asian Arts
Web page displays (Figure
1-9).*

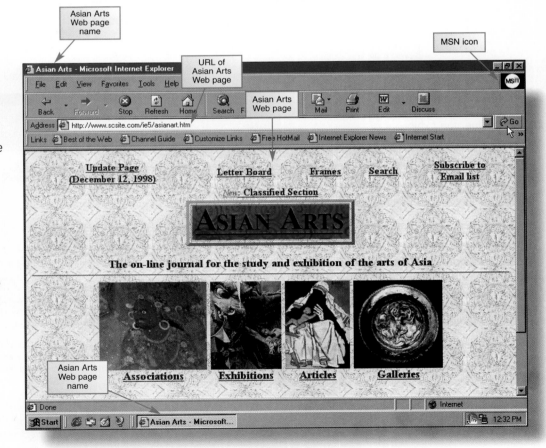

FIGURE 1-9

4 **Point to the Exhibitions hyperlink.**

The shape of the mouse pointer changes to a pointing hand to indicate the word Exhibitions is a hyperlink (Figure 1-10). The status bar contains the URL of the Web page associated with the hyperlink. The picture above the Exhibitions hyperlink also is a hyperlink.

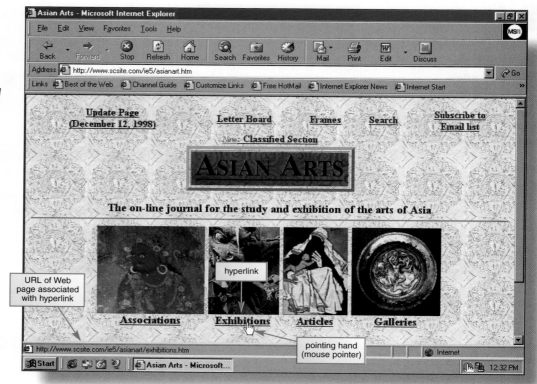

FIGURE 1-10

5 **Click Exhibitions.**

In a short time, the Exhibitions page displays (Figure 1-11). The Exhibitions Web page title displays in the title bar and a vertical scroll bar in the display area indicates the Web page is larger than the display area. You will have to scroll down to view additional information and pictures on the Web page.

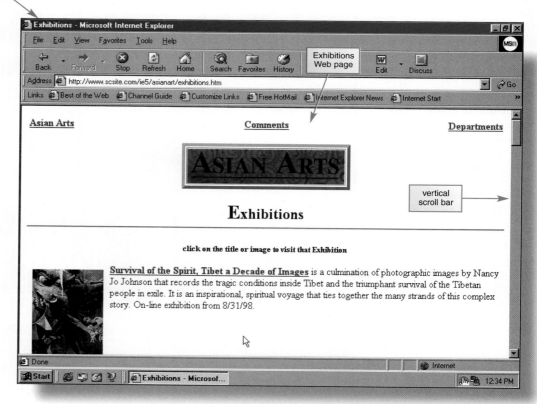

FIGURE 1-11

6 Scroll the display area to display the hyperlink, The Splendors of Imperial China: Treasures from the National Palace Museum, Taipei, and then point to the hyperlink.

The display area scrolls, mouse pointer changes to a pointing hand icon, and the URL of the Web page associated with the hyperlink displays on the status bar (Figure 1-12). The picture to the right of the display area also is a hyperlink.

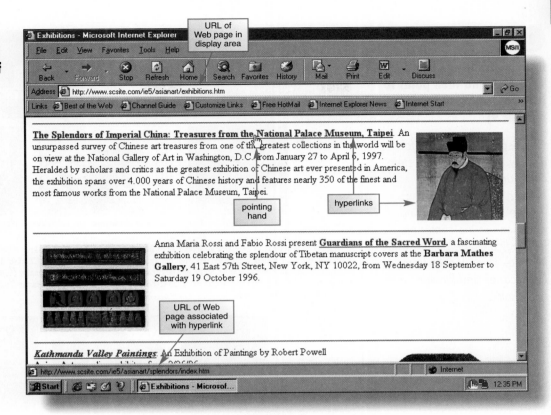

FIGURE 1-12

7 Click the hyperlink.

After a brief interval, the Web page, The Splendors of Imperial China, displays and the Splendors of Imperial China Web page title displays on the title bar (Figure 1-13). The Web page contains pictures and descriptions of the Chinese art located in the National Place Museum in Taipei, China.

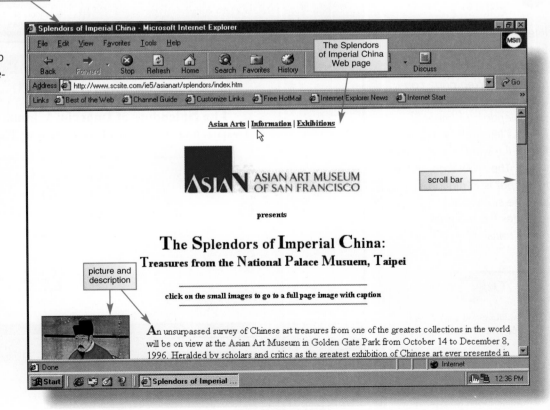

FIGURE 1-13

8 **Scroll the display area to view the three pictures numbered 8, 9, and 10 and then point to the center picture (picture number 9).**

The display area scrolls to display the pictures of a stem cup, various leaves and flowers, and a globe vase (Figure 1-14). The pointing hand icon in the center picture indicates the picture with the title, Three leaves from Landscapes and Flowers, is a hyperlink.

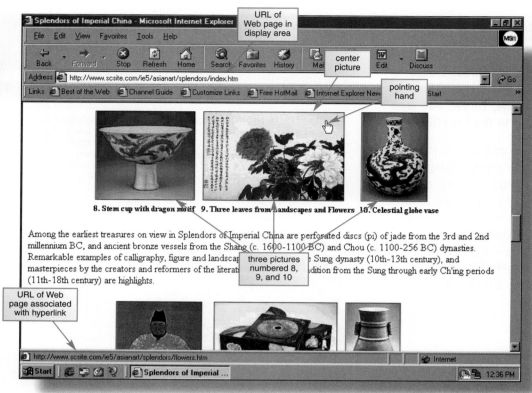

FIGURE 1-14

9 **Click the center picture.**

Internet Explorer begins to display the Web page containing the picture and places the Splendors of Imperial China - Image 9 Web page title in the window title (Figure 1-15). The MSN icon on the menu bar is in motion, and the status bar indicates the progress of the transfer.

Other Ways

1. On File menu click Open, type URL in Open box, click OK button
2. Press CTRL+O, type URL in Open box, click OK button
3. Press ALT+F, press o key, type URL in Open box, press ENTER key

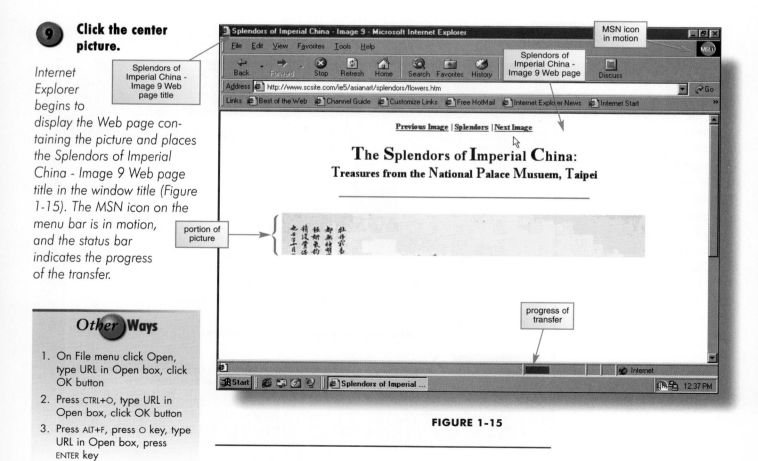

FIGURE 1-15

The preceding steps illustrate how simple it is to browse the World Wide Web. Displaying a Web page associated with a hyperlink is as easy as clicking a text or picture hyperlink.

Stopping the Transfer of a Page

If a Web page you are trying to view is taking too long to transfer or if you clicked the wrong hyperlink, you may decide not to wait for the page to finish transferring. The Stop button on the Standard Buttons toolbar allows you to stop the transfer of a page while the transfer is in progress. You will know the transfer is still in progress if the MSN icon is moving. The following steps show how to interrupt the transfer of the Web page containing the three leaves picture. If the icon on your menu bar is no longer moving, the transfer is complete and you should read the following steps without performing the steps.

More About

Pictures

Some Web page authors note the size of an image to assist you in deciding to display or save the picture. If an image is several megabytes in size, you might decide not to select the link because of the time it would take to transfer the picture from the Web site to your display area.

Steps To Stop the Transfer of a Web Page

1 **Point to the Stop button on the Standard Buttons toolbar (Figure 1-16).**

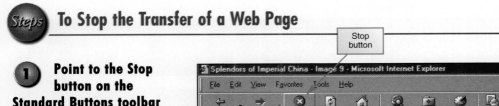

FIGURE 1-16

2 **Click the Stop button.**

The motion of the MSN icon stops and a portion of the picture displays (Figure 1-17).

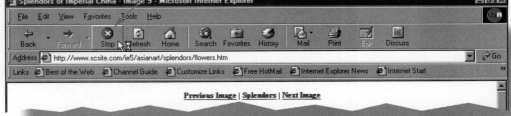

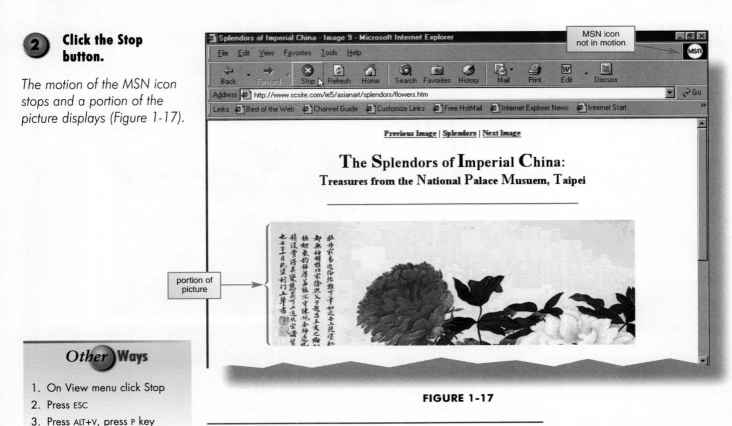

Other Ways

1. On View menu click Stop
2. Press ESC
3. Press ALT+V, press P key

FIGURE 1-17

Stopping the transfer of a Web page will leave a partially transferred Web page in the display area. Pictures or text displaying before the Stop button is clicked remain visible in the display area and any visible hyperlinks can be clicked to display the associated Web pages.

Refreshing a Web Page

In Figure 1-17 on the previous page, only a portion of the picture displays in the display area. If you decide you want to see the complete Web page, you can reload the page using the Refresh button on the Standard Buttons toolbar. Perform the following steps to refresh the Web page.

Steps **To Refresh a Web Page**

1 **Point to the Refresh button on the Standard Buttons toolbar (Figure 1-18).**

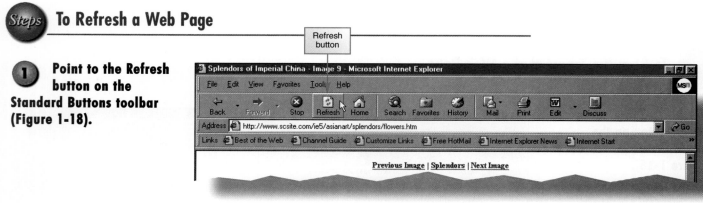

FIGURE 1-18

2 **Click the Refresh button and then scroll the page down to display the complete picture.**

The complete Web page containing the picture of the leaves and flowers displays (Figure 1-19).

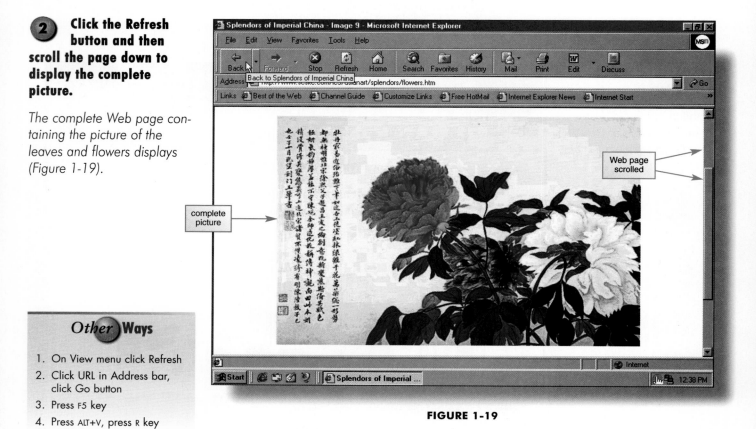

FIGURE 1-19

Other Ways

1. On View menu click Refresh
2. Click URL in Address bar, click Go button
3. Press F5 key
4. Press ALT+V, press R key

In the event the connection to the Web site where a Web page is located becomes broken and the transfer of the Web page does not finish, you can use the Refresh button to request the Web page again. In addition, you also can use the Refresh button to refresh a Web page that contains information that changes frequently, such as stock quotes or sports scores.

Using the steps and techniques previously shown to browse the World Wide Web, you entered a URL and displayed a Web page, clicked a hyperlink to display another Web page, stopped the transfer of a Web page, and refreshed a Web page. As you browse the World Wide Web, Internet Explorer keeps a list of the Web pages you visit, so you can quickly return to those pages in the future. The next section explains how to use this list to recall previously viewed Web pages.

History List

When you enter a URL and click the Go button or click a hyperlink, Internet Explorer adds the URL for that Web page to the History list. To again display a Web page from the History list, you can click the Back button or Forward button on the Standard Buttons toolbar.

When you launch Internet Explorer, the dim arrows on the Back and Forward buttons indicate the buttons are inactive and cannot be clicked. When you visit the first Web page after launching Internet Explorer, the arrow on the Back button changes to a solid white color, and pointing to the button changes the color of the arrow from white to blue, indicating the button is active and the History list contains the URL of the Web page.

You can use the Back and Forward buttons to display a previously viewed Web page if Internet Explorer places its URL on the History list during the current Internet Explorer session. However, you cannot rely on the History list for permanent storage of Web pages you frequently visit because Internet Explorer clears the History list after a specified number of days.

Just as Internet Explorer stores URLs in the History list for quick retrieval, it also stores the Web pages you display in the Temporary Internet Files folder on the hard disk. When you display a previously displayed Web page, the page displays quickly because Internet Explorer is able to retrieve the page from the Temporary Internet Files folder on the hard disk instead of from a Web site on the Internet.

Perform the following steps to use the Back and Forward buttons to display Web pages from the History list.

 To Move Back and Forward in the History List

1 **Point to the Back button on the Standard Buttons toolbar (Figure 1-20).**

The ScreenTip indicates the Splendors of Imperial China Web page will display when you click the Back button.

FIGURE 1-20

More About

Redisplaying Web Pages

Web pages retrieved from a Web site and displayed in the display area are stored in the Temporary Internet File folder on the hard disk. If you request the same Web page again, Internet Explorer will retrieve the page from the folder on your hard disk instead of having to contact the Web site again to retrieve the page. This can result in a considerable time saving.

More About

The History List

You can clear the History list by clicking Tools on the menu bar, clicking Internet Options, clicking the Clear History button in the Internet Options dialog box, and clicking the OK button. In the Options dialog box, you also can change the setting for the number of days Internet Explorer keeps a Web page in the History list before deleting the page.

2 **Click the Back button.**

The Splendors of Imperial China Web page redisplays and the arrow in the Forward button is solid to indicate the Splendors of Imperial China Web page is not the last Web page in the History list (Figure 1-21).

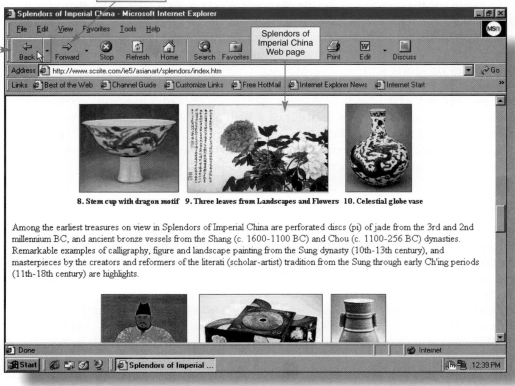

FIGURE 1-21

3 **Click the Back button again and then point to the Forward button on the Standard Buttons toolbar.**

The Exhibitions Web page redisplays and the link, The Splendors of Imperial China: Treasures from the National Palace Museum, Taipei, changes color to indicate you previously visited that Web page (Figure 1-22). The ScreenTip indicates the Splendors of Imperial China Web page will display the next time you click the Forward button.

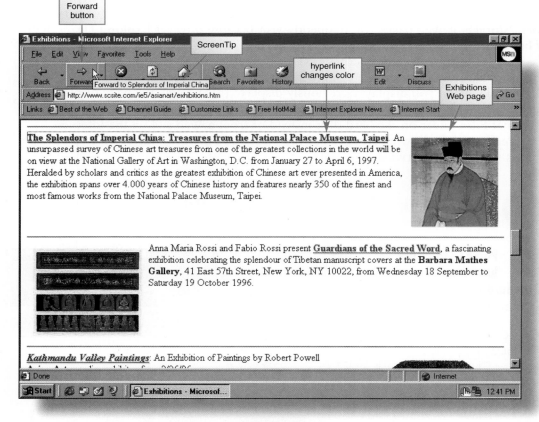

FIGURE 1-22

Click the Forward button.

The Splendors of Imperial China Web page displays again (Figure 1-23).

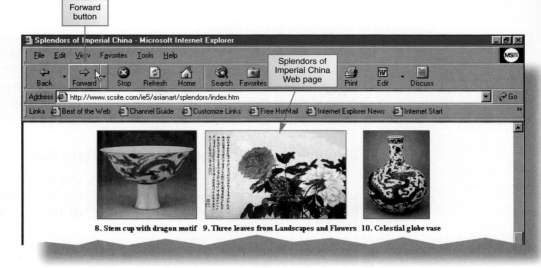

FIGURE 1-23

5 **Click the Forward button again.**

The Splendors of Imperial China - Image 9 Web page redisplays (Figure 1-24). The Forward button is now inactive to indicate there are no additional pages to which you can move forward.

FIGURE 1-24

You can continue to page backward until you reach the beginning of the History list. At that time, the Back button becomes inactive, which indicates that no additional pages to which you can move back are contained in the History list. You can, however, move forward by clicking the Forward button.

Other Ways

1. Press ALT+LEFT ARROW (to display previous Web page)
2. Click down arrow on Back button, click Web page title
3. Press ALT+RIGHT ARROW (to display next Web page)
4. Click DOWN ARROW on Forward button, click Web page title

You can see that traversing through the History list is easy using the Back and Forward buttons. Notice that each previously viewed page can be redisplayed as you click the Back or Forward button on the Standard Buttons toolbar. The buttons automatically become active or inactive as you move through the History list. Because many pages may display before the one you want to view, this method can be time-consuming.

Displaying a Web Page Using the History List

Using the History list, you can return directly to any of the Web pages you have visited. To display the History list, click the History button to display the Explorer bar and the History list. When the Explorer bar is visible, the display area contains two frames. The Explorer bar displays on the left, and the current Web page on the right. The Explorer bar will remain on the screen until you close it. To redisplay a Web page using the History list, first display the entire History list, and then click the desired Web page title, as shown in the following steps.

Steps ▶ **To Display a Web Page Using the History List**

1 Point to the History button on the Standard Buttons toolbar (Figure 1-25).

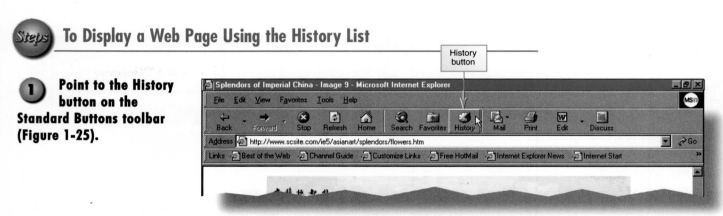

FIGURE 1-25

2 Click the History button and then point to Asian Arts.

The Explorer bar and History title display (Figure 1-26). Indented below the Today icon are the scsite and home.microsoft folders. Indented below the scsite folder are the Web pages you viewed in the scsite Web site and the title of the Web page that displays in the right frame is highlighted. A ScreenTip contains the URL for the Asian Arts Web page.

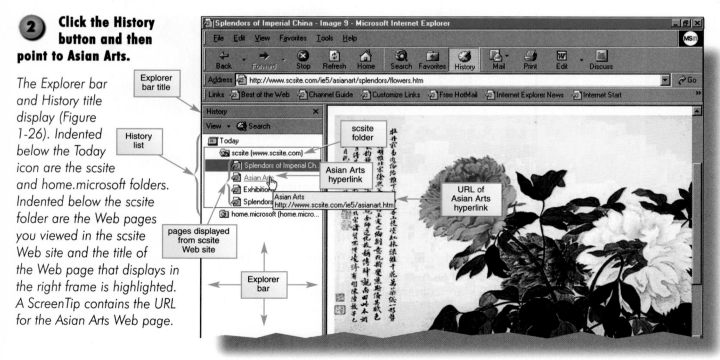

FIGURE 1-26

3 **Click Asian Arts and then point to the Close button on the Explorer bar.**

The Asian Arts Web page redisplays (Figure 1-27). The Asian Arts title in the History list is highlighted and the Web page title on the title bar and URL in the Address box change.

4 **Click the Close button.**

The Explorer bar closes.

FIGURE 1-27

If you have a small History list or the page you want is only one or two pages away, you can traverse the History list more quickly using the Back and Forward buttons than bringing up the Explorer bar and then selecting individual pages. If you have visited a large number of Web pages, however, your History list will be long, and you may find it easier to use the History list in the Explorer bar to select the precise page to redisplay.

History lists are useful for returning to a Web page you have visited recently. You can set the number of days Internet Explorer keeps the URLs in the History list by using the Internet Options command on the Tools menu. Because the History list occasionally is cleared, you should not use the History list to store the URLs of your favorite or frequently visited pages permanently.

You can see from the previous figures that URLs can be long and cryptic (see Figure 1-26 on the previous page). It is easy to make a mistake while entering such URLs. Fortunately, Internet Explorer has the capability of keeping track of your favorite Web pages. You can store the URLs of your favorite Web pages permanently in an area appropriately called the Favorites list.

Keeping Track of Your Favorite Web Pages

The Favorites feature of Internet Explorer allows you to save the URLs of your favorite Web pages in the Favorites list. A **favorite** consists of the title and URL of a Web page. Think of the Favorites list as an electronic address book containing the URL and page title of Web pages that are important to you. You can add new favorites and remove favorites you no longer want. Perform the steps on the following page to add the Asian Arts Web Page to the Favorites list.

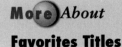

Other Ways

1. On View menu point to Explorer bar, click History
2. Press ALT+V, press E key, press H key
3. Press F4

More About

Favorites Titles

Internet Explorer allows you to change the title that identifies a favorite. Using Organize favorites on the Favorites menu, right-click a favorite in the Organize favorites dialog box and then click Rename.

To Add a Web Page to the Favorites List

1 **Click Favorites on the menu bar and then point to Add to Favorites.**

The Favorites menu displays (Figure 1-28). The Add to Favorites command adds the title of the page and the URL in the Address box to the Favorites list, the Organize Favorites command allows you to manage the Favorites list, and the folders and favorites in the Favorites list display at the bottom of the menu. The folders and favorites in the Favorites list may be different on your computer.

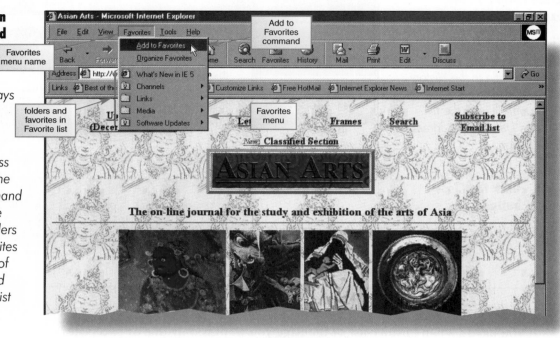

FIGURE 1-28

2 **Click Add to Favorites and then point to the OK button in the Add Favorite dialog box.**

The Add Favorite dialog box displays (Figure 1-29). The Name text box contains the title of the Asian Arts Web page, and the Address box contains the URL.

3 **Click the OK button.**

Although not visible in the Asian Arts - Microsoft Internet Explorer window in Figure 1-29, the Asian Arts title will display in the Favorites list when you click the Favorite button.

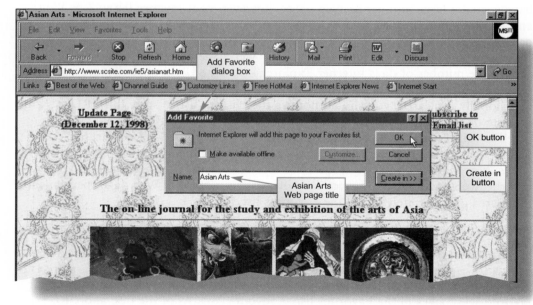

FIGURE 1-29

 Other Ways

1. Click Favorites button on Standard Buttons toolbar, click Add button in Explorer bar, click OK button
2. Press CTRL+D
3. Press ALT+A, press A key, press ENTER key

In Figure 1-29, clicking the Create in button expands the Add Favorite dialog box, displays a hierarchy of the folders in the Favorites list, and allows you to select a folder in which to store a favorite. You also can change the name of a favorite by double-clicking the Name text box and typing the new name.

Using the Home Button to Display a Web Page

At any time, you can display the home page (MSN home page) in the display area using the Home button on the Standard Buttons toolbar. Perform the following steps to display the MSN home page.

More About

Favorites

You can re-arrange the order of your favorites by dragging a favorite to another location on the Explorer bar and then releasing it.

 Steps To Display the Home Page Using the Home Button

1 **Point to the Home button on the Standards Buttons toolbar (Figure 1-30).**

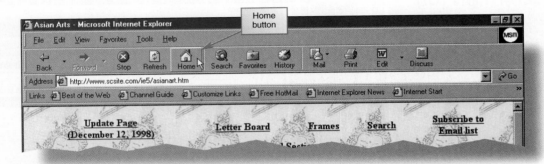

FIGURE 1-30

2 **Click the Home button.**

The MSN home page displays in the MSN.COM - Microsoft Internet Explorer window and the URL for the home page displays in the Address box (Figure 1-31).

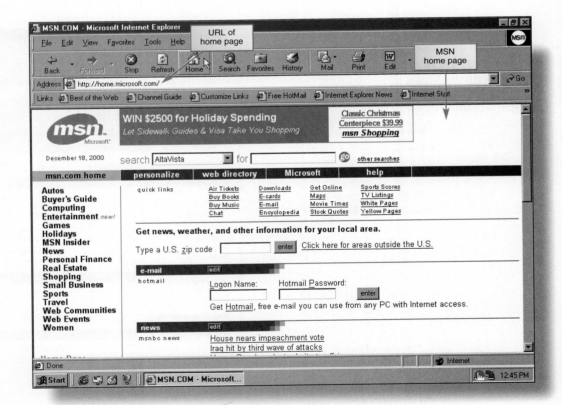

FIGURE 1-31

Displaying a Web Page Using the Favorites List

You can use favorites to display frequently accessed Web pages quickly without having to navigate through several unwanted pages. Using a favorite to display a Web page is similar to using the History list to view a Web page. Perform the following steps to use the Favorites list to display the Asian Arts Web page.

Steps To Display a Web Page Using the Favorites List

1 Point to the Favorites button on the Standards Buttons toolbar (Figure 1-32).

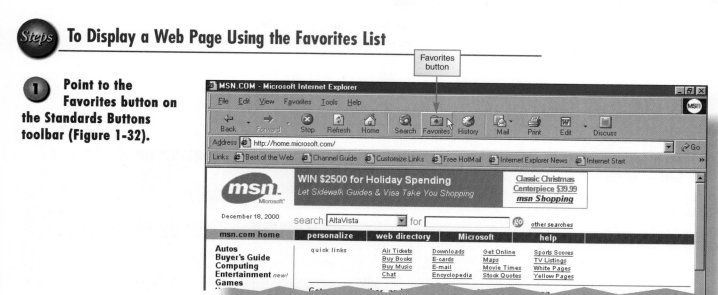

FIGURE 1-32

2 Click the Favorites button and then point to Asian Arts in the Favorites list.

The Explorer bar and Favorites title display (Figure 1-33). The MSN home page displays and the newly added favorite (Asian Arts) displays in the Favorites list.

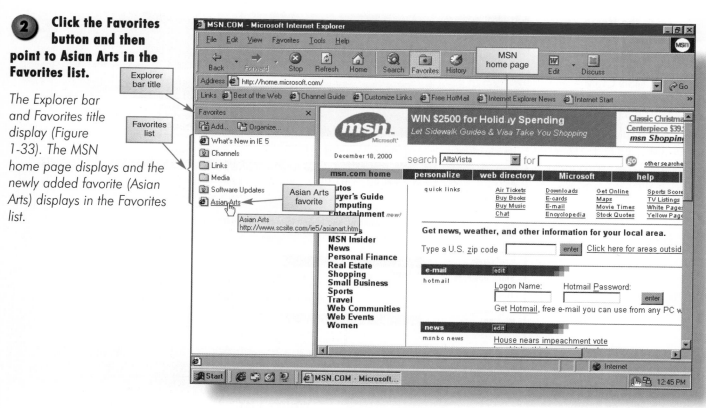

FIGURE 1-33

3 Click Asian Arts.

The Asian Arts Web page is again visible (Figure 1-34). The Asian Arts title and its URL again display in their respective locations.

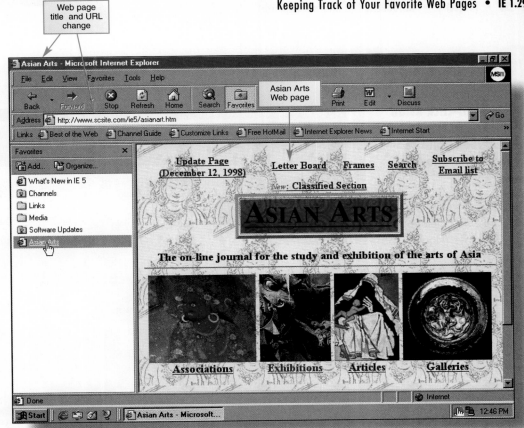

FIGURE 1-34

Additional favorites display in the Favorites list in Figure 1-33. Among the favorites are the Channels folder that includes a list of available channels you can select, the Links folder that contains entries corresponding to the buttons on the Links bar, the Media folder that contains a list of interesting media sources (news, sports, music, and so on), and the Software Updates folder that contains links to a Web site where you can obtain updates for the software on your computer. Other folders may display in the Favorites list on your computer.

You have learned how to add a URL to the Favorites list and how to retrieve a Web page using the Favorites list. As you gain experience and continue to browse the World Wide Web and add pages to your Favorites list, it is likely that in time you will want to remove unwanted favorites from the list.

Removing Favorites

Several reasons are valid for wanting to remove a favorite. With the World Wide Web changing every day, the URL that worked today may not work tomorrow; or perhaps you simply no longer want a particular favorite on your list. The steps on the next two pages show how to remove a favorite from the Favorites list.

Other Ways

1. On Favorites menu click favorite.

Steps: To Remove a Web Page from the Favorites List

1 **Right-click Asian Arts in the Favorites list and then point to Delete on the shortcut menu.**

A shortcut menu containing the highlighted Delete command displays (Figure 1-35).

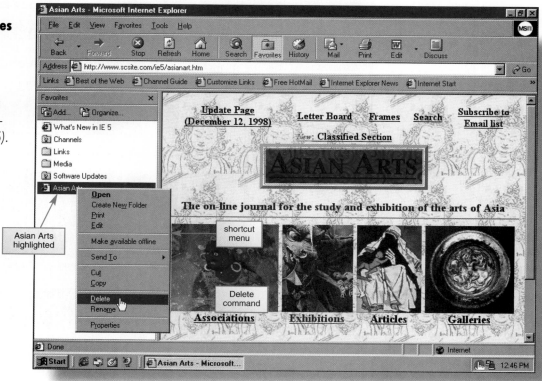

FIGURE 1-35

2 **Click Delete and then point to the Yes button in the Confirm File Delete dialog box.**

The Confirm File Delete dialog box displays (Figure 1-36). A question asks if you are sure you want to send Asian Arts to the Recycle Bin.

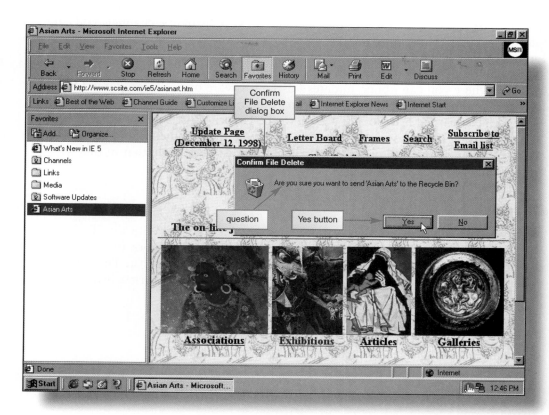

FIGURE 1-36

3 **Click the Yes button and then point to the Close button in the Explorer bar.**

The Confirm File Delete dialog box closes and the Asian Arts favorite is removed from the Favorites list (Figure 1-37).

4 **Click the Close button.**

The Explorer bar closes.

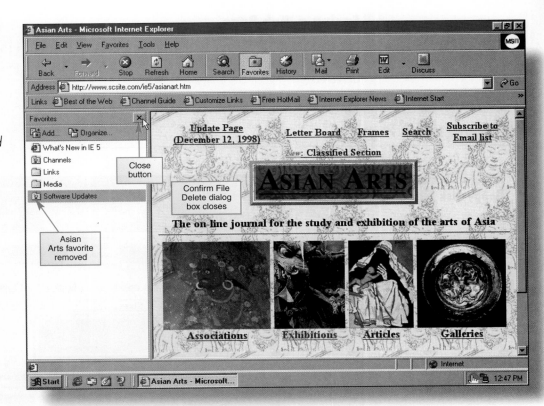

FIGURE 1-37

Using the commands on the shortcut menu can help you manage your favorites. Internet Explorer also provides advanced features for handling favorites. For example, you can create folders that allow you to organize your Favorites list into categories. In Figure 1-33 on page IE 1.28, Internet Explorer created four folders (Channels, Links, Media, and Software Updates) to help you to organize your favorites. Your can create additional folders using the Organize Favorites command on the Favorites menu.

Using the commands on the shortcut menu can help you manage your favorites. Internet Explorer also provides advanced features for handling favorites. For example, you can create folders that allow you to organize your Favorites list into categories. In Figure 1-33 on page IE 1.28, Internet Explorer created four folders (Channels, Links, Media, and Software Updates) to help you to organize your favorites. Your can create additional folders using the Organize Favorites command on the Favorites menu.

You have learned to create, use, and remove favorites. Saving URLs in the Favorites list is not the only way to save information you obtain using Internet Explorer. Some of the more interesting text and pictures you locate while displaying Web pages also are worth saving.

Saving Information Obtained with Internet Explorer

Many different types of Web pages are available on the World Wide Web. Because these pages help you accumulate information, you may wish to save the information you discover for future reference. The different types of Web pages and the different ways you may intend to use them require different methods of saving the pages.

Internet Explorer allows you to save pictures or text from a Web page or the entire Web page. The following pages illustrate how to save an entire Web page, how to save a single picture, and how to save text.

Other **Ways**

1. On Favorites menu click Organize Favorites, click title, click Delete button
2. Click Organize button in Explorer bar, click title, click Delete button

---

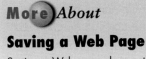

More **About**

Saving a Web Page

Saving a Web page does not automatically save any images or pictures on the page. You must save pictures separately.

Saving a Web Page

One method of saving information on a Web page is to save the entire Web page. Perform the following steps to save the Asian Arts Web page on a floppy disk in drive A.

 To Save a Web Page

1 **Insert a formatted floppy disk into drive A.**

2 **Click File on the menu bar and then point to Save As.**

The File menu displays (Figure 1-38). The highlighted Save As command displays on the File menu.

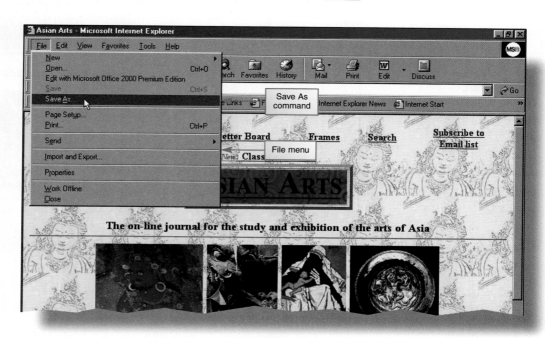

FIGURE 1-38

3 **Click Save As and then point to the Save in box arrow.**

The Save in box in the Save Web Page dialog box contains the Desktop entry, the list box contains a list of the folders on the desktop, and the File name text box contains the highlighted Web page title (Asian Arts) and insertion point (Figure 1-39). The file name in the File name box can be changed by typing a new file name from the keyboard. The Desktop entry in the Save in box may be different on your computer.

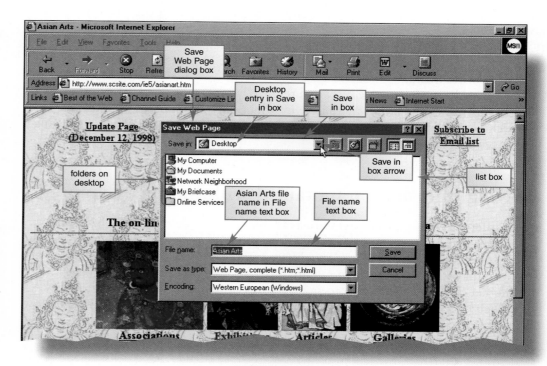

FIGURE 1-39

4 Click the Save in box arrow and then point to 3½ Floppy [A:] in the Save in list.

The Save in list contains various components of your computer with the 3½ Floppy [A:] drive name highlighted (Figure 1-40).

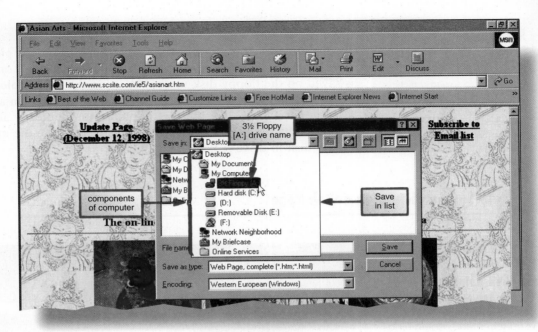

FIGURE 1-40

5 Click 3½ Floppy [A:] and then point to the Save button.

The highlighted 3½ Floppy [A:] drive name displays in the Save in box (Figure 1-41). The entry in the Save as type box (Web Page, Complete (.htm; *.html) determines how the Web page is saved.*

6 Click the Save button.

The Save Web Page dialog box closes and a smaller Save Web Page dialog box displays while the Asian Arts Web page is saved using the file name, Asian Arts.htm, on the floppy disk in drive A.

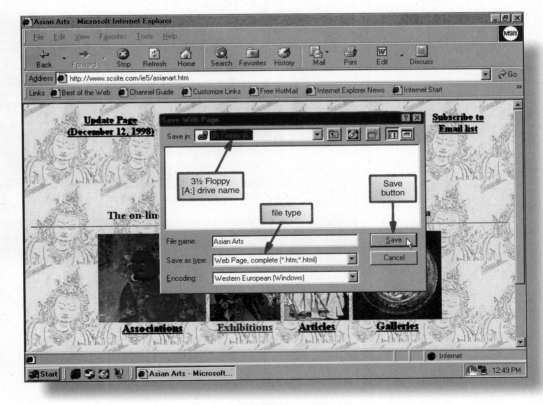

FIGURE 1-41

The Asian Arts.htm file contains the HTML codes that describe to a browser how to display the Web page (see Figure 1-4 on page IE 1.8). The graphics, frames, and formatted text are included in the file. If you want to save the pictures on a Web page, you must save each one as a separate entry.

Other Ways

1. Press CTRL+S
2. Press ALT+F, press A key

More About

Setting a Picture

In addition to saving a picture, you also can set a picture as wallpaper on your desktop by right-clicking the image and clicking Set as Wallpaper. The image displays on the desktop.

Saving a Picture on a Web Page

A second method of saving information is to save a picture located on a Web page. In the following steps, the image06[1] file located on the Asian Arts Web page is saved on the floppy disk in drive A using the **Joint Photographic Experts Group (JPEG)** format. JPEG is a method of encoding pictures on a computer. When you save a picture as a JPEG file, Internet Explorer automatically adds the .jpg file extension to the file name. Perform the following steps to save the image06[1] picture on a floppy disk in drive A using the JPEG format.

 To Save a Picture on a Web Page

1 **Right-click the Galleries picture and then point to Save Picture As.**

A shortcut menu, containing the highlighted Save Picture As command, displays (Figure 1-42).

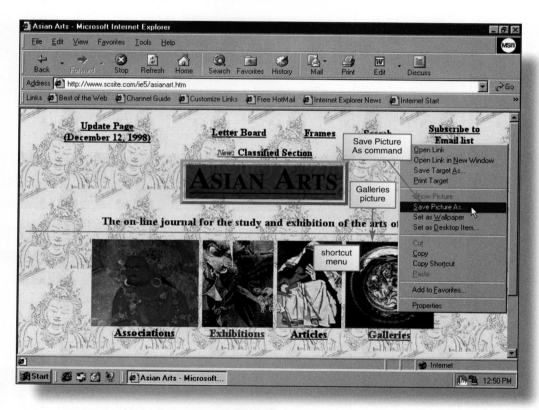

FIGURE 1-42

2 **Click Save Picture As, click the Save in box arrow, click 3½ Floppy [A:], and then point to the Save button.**

The Save Picture dialog box displays (Figure 1-43). The Save in box contains the 3½ Floppy [A:] drive name, the File name text box contains the image06[1] file name, and the Save as type text box contains the JPEG (.jpg) file type.*

3 **Click the Save button.**

The picture is saved using the image06[1].jpg file name on the floppy disk in drive A and the Save Picture dialog box closes.

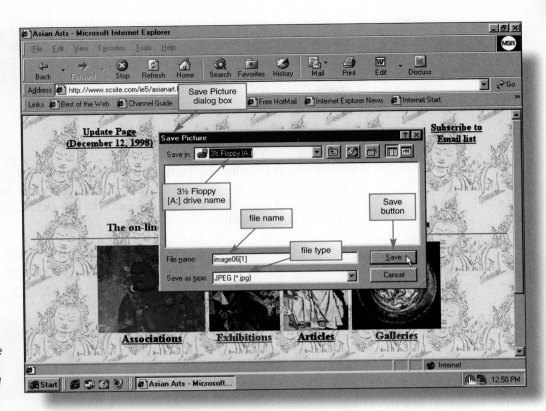

FIGURE 1-43

The image 06[1] name, given to the Galleries picture to identify the picture among the hundreds of pictures on the Web site, is used to save the picture on disk. To change this file name, type another file name in the File name box before clicking the Save button.

Copying and Pasting Using the Clipboard

A third method of saving information, called the **copy (cut) and paste method**, allows you to copy an entire Web page, or portions thereof, and insert the information in any Windows document. The **Clipboard**, which is a temporary storage area in main memory, temporarily holds the information being copied. The portion of the Web page you select is **copied** from the Web page to the Clipboard and then **pasted** from the Clipboard into the document. Information you copy to the Clipboard remains there until you add more information or clear it. You can copy and paste both text and pictures from a Web page into a document. You cannot copy text and pictures in one copy and paste operation. You must copy them in separate operations.

To demonstrate how to copy text and pictures from a Web page to another Windows document, you will use the Clipboard as a holding area when you insert a picture and text from the Exhibitions Web page into a WordPad document.

To begin the operation, you will launch WordPad using the Start button. Next, you will switch back to Internet Explorer and copy to the Clipboard the portion of the text you wish to paste into the WordPad document. Finally, you will switch back to WordPad and paste the contents from the Clipboard into the document. These steps are shown in the following sections.

Launching WordPad

Before you can use the copy and paste method to copy text or pictures, you must launch WordPad using the Start button on the taskbar. Launching WordPad displays the active Document - WordPad window (dark blue title bar) on top of the inactive Asian Arts - Microsoft Internet Explorer window (light blue title bar). Perform the following steps to launch WordPad.

Steps | **To Launch WordPad**

1 Click the Start button on the taskbar, point to Programs on the Start menu, point to Accessories on the Programs submenu, and then point to WordPad on the Accessories submenu.

The Start menu, Programs submenu, and Accessories submenu display (Figure 1-44). The highlighted WordPad command displays on the Accessories submenu.

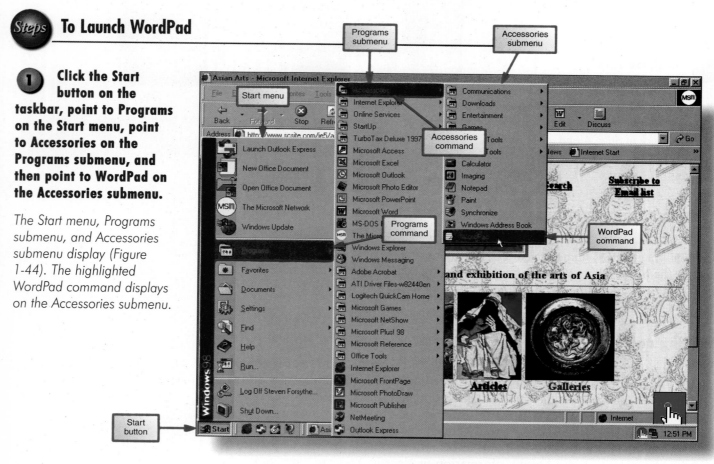

FIGURE 1-44

2 Click WordPad.

Windows launches WordPad, displays the active Document - WordPad window on top of the inactive Asian Arts - Microsoft Internet Explorer window, and displays the Document - WordPad button on the taskbar (Figure 1-45). An empty WordPad document, into which the text can be pasted, displays in the Document - WordPad window. An insertion point and the I-beam mouse pointer display in the empty document.

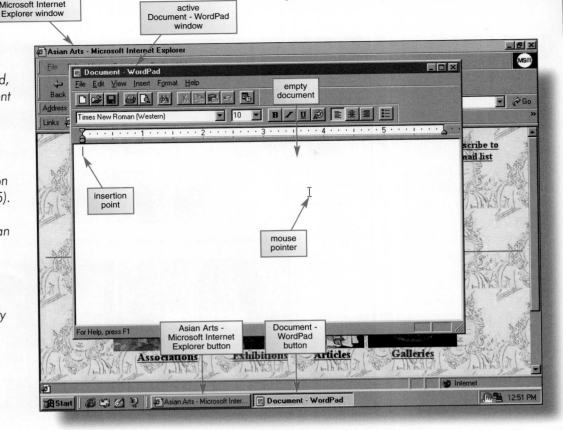

FIGURE 1-45

Other Ways

1. Click Start button, click Run, type wordpad, click OK button
2. Click Start button, click Help, click Index tab, type wordpad, click Display button, click the Click here link

Displaying the Exhibitions Web Page

After launching WordPad and before copying text from a Web page to the Clipboard, display the Asian Arts - Microsoft Internet Explorer window and then display the Exhibitions Web page. Complete the following steps to display the Exhibitions Web page.

 To Display the Exhibitions Web Page

1 Point to the Asian Arts - Microsoft Internet Explorer button on the taskbar (Figure 1-46).

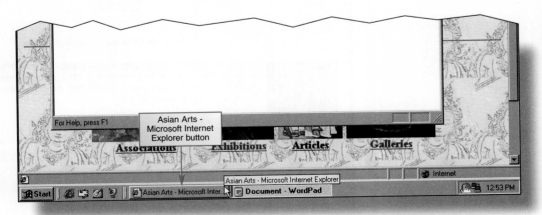

FIGURE 1-46

2 **Click the Asian Arts - Microsoft Internet Explorer button and then point to the Exhibitions hyperlink.**

The Asian Arts - Microsoft Internet Explorer window displays on top of the Document - WordPad window on the desktop (Figure 1-47). The display area contains the Asian Arts Web page.

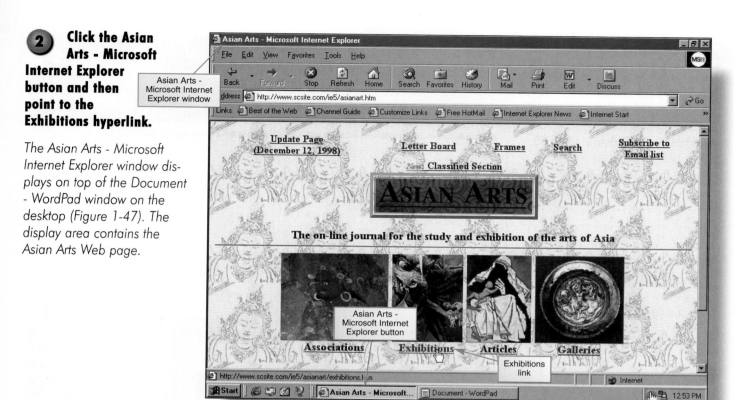

FIGURE 1-47

3 **Click the Exhibitions link.**

The Exhibitions Web page displays in the Exhibitions - Microsoft Internet Explorer window (Figure 1-48). The window title and button name change.

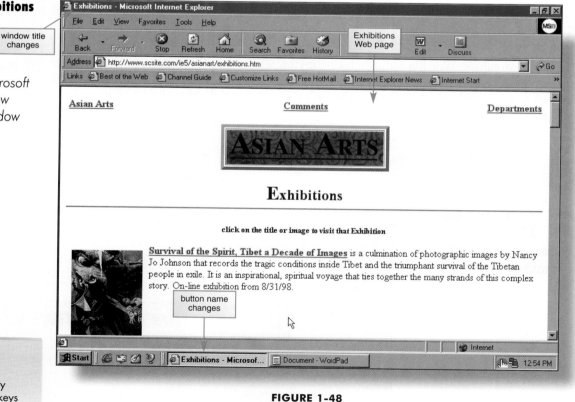

FIGURE 1-48

Other Ways

1. Press ALT+TAB to display window title, release keys
2. If visible, click window title bar

With the Document - WordPad window open and the text you wish to copy contained on the Exhibitions Web page, the next steps are to scroll the display area to display the text to be copied, copy the text from the Exhibitions Web page to the Clipboard, and then paste the text into the WordPad document.

Copying Text from a Web Page and Pasting It into a WordPad Document

The following steps show how to copy the text about the Splendors of Imperial China to the Clipboard, switch to WordPad, and paste the text on the Clipboard into the WordPad document.

 To Copy and Paste Text from a Web Page into a WordPad Document

1 **Scroll the Exhibitions Web page to display The Splendors of Imperial China: Treasures from the National Palace Museum, Taipei hyperlink, and then position the mouse pointer (I-beam) at the beginning of the text that follows the hyperlink text.**

The text description of The Splendors of Imperial China: Treasures from the National Palace Museum, Taipei displays (Figure 1-49).

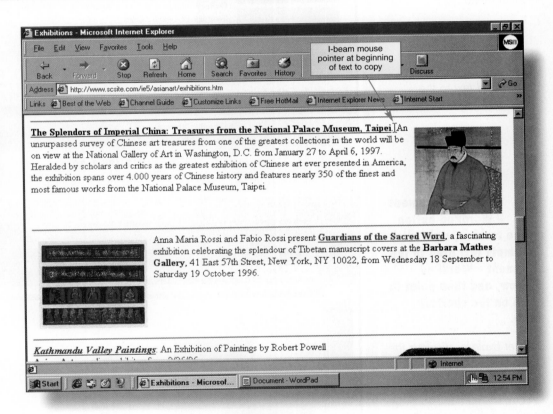

FIGURE 1-49

Drag through the text to select the text that follows the hyperlink text, right-click the highlighted text, and then point to the Copy command.

Internet Explorer highlights the selected text and displays a shortcut menu (Figure 1-50). The highlighted Copy command displays on the shortcut menu.

 Click Copy.

Internet Explorer copies the selected text to the Clipboard.

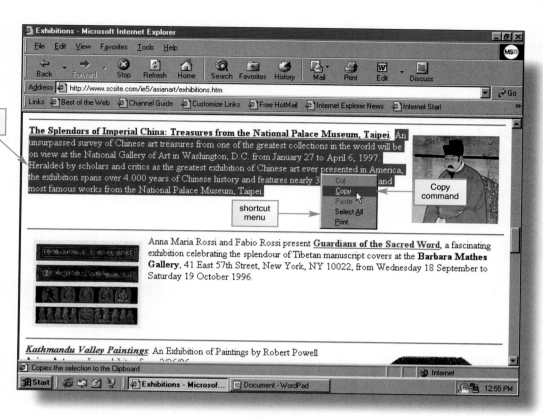

FIGURE 1-50

 Click the Document - WordPad button on the taskbar, right-click the empty text area in the Document - WordPad window, and then point to Paste on the shortcut menu.

Internet Explorer displays the Document - WordPad window and a shortcut menu (Figure 1-51). The highlighted Paste command displays on the shortcut menu.

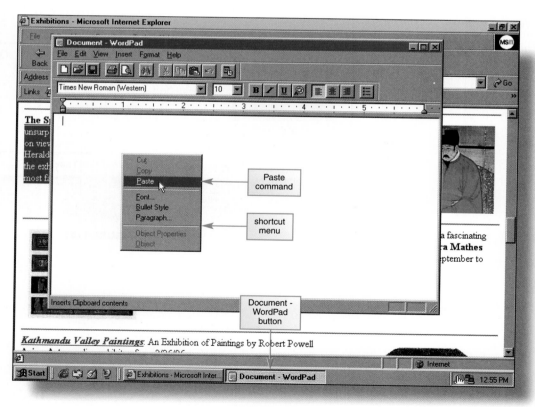

FIGURE 1-51

Click Paste.

Internet Explorer pastes the contents of the Clipboard into the Document - WordPad window (Figure 1-52).

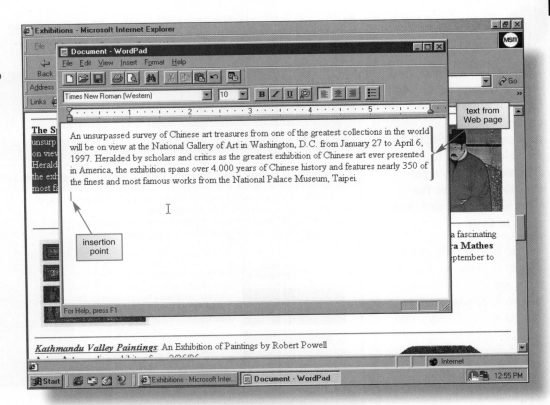

FIGURE 1-52

The text portion of the copy and paste operation is complete. The WordPad document contains a paragraph of text you retrieved from a Web page. You also can use the copy and paste operation to insert a URL that displays in the Address box into a document or e-mail message. The next step is to copy and paste a picture from the Web page into the WordPad document.

Copying a Picture from a Web Page and Pasting it into WordPad

The steps to copy a picture from a Web page are similar to those used to copy and paste text. The steps on the following two pages show how to copy and then paste a picture from a Web page into a WordPad document.

Other Ways

1. Select text, on Edit menu click Copy, position insertion point, on Edit menu click Paste

2. Select text, press CTRL+C, position insertion point, press CTRL+V

Steps **To Copy and Paste a Picture from a Web Page into a WordPad Document**

1 **Click the Exhibitions - Microsoft Internet Explorer button on the taskbar, click outside the selected text to deselect the text, right-click the picture to the right of the text, and then point to Copy.**

The Exhibitions - Microsoft Internet Explorer window displays, the selected text in the window is deselected, a shortcut menu displays, and the Copy command is highlighted (Figure 1-53).

2 **Click Copy.**

Internet Explorer closes the shortcut menu and copies the picture to the Clipboard.

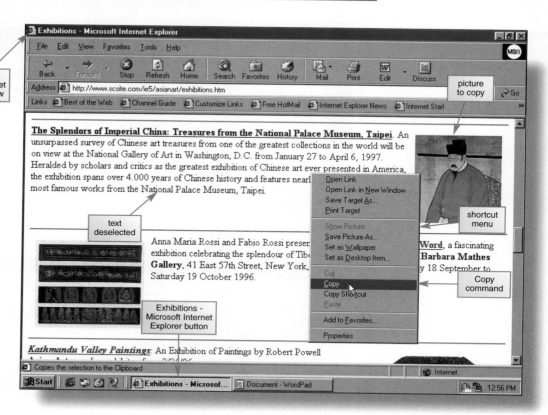

FIGURE 1-53

 3 **Click the Document - WordPad button on the taskbar, right-click an area below the insertion point in the Document - WordPad window, and then point to Paste.**

The Document - WordPad window and a shortcut menu display (Figure 1-54). The highlighted Paste command displays on the shortcut menu.

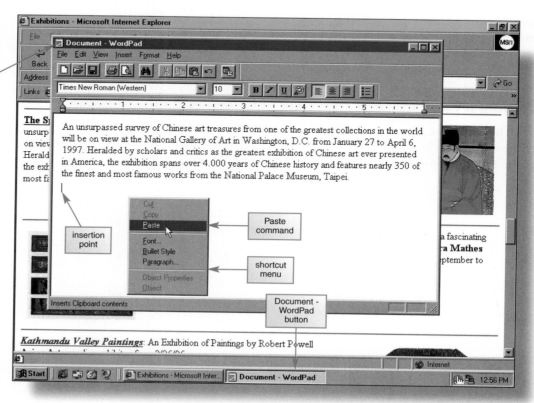

FIGURE 1-54

4 **Click Paste.**

Internet Explorer pastes the contents of the Clipboard in the Document - WordPad window at the location of the insertion point (Figure 1-55). You can resize the picture in the window by dragging the corners of the picture in toward the center of the picture to make it smaller or outward from the center to make it larger.

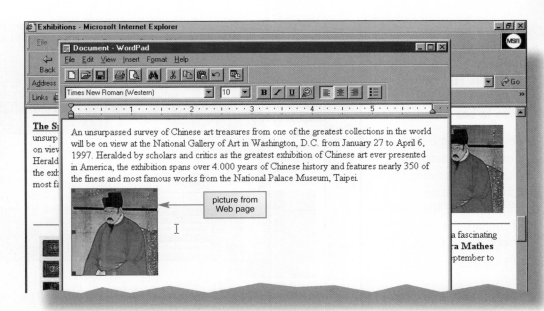

FIGURE 1-55

The copy and paste operations are complete. The WordPad window contains text and a picture retrieved from the Exhibitions Web page. You now can use the tools provided with WordPad to manipulate the picture and text.

Saving the WordPad Document and Quitting WordPad

When you have completed the WordPad document, you can save it on a floppy disk and quit WordPad. Perform the following steps to save the WordPad document using the Splendors of Imperial China file name and then quit WordPad.

Other **Ways**

1. Right-click picture, click Copy, position insertion point, click CTRL+V

More *About*

WordPad

WordPad can save a file as a Microsoft Word document, RTF or Rich Text Format, or as a plain text file.

 To Save the WordPad Document and Quit WordPad

1 **Point to the Save button on the toolbar in the Document - WordPad window (Figure 1-56)**

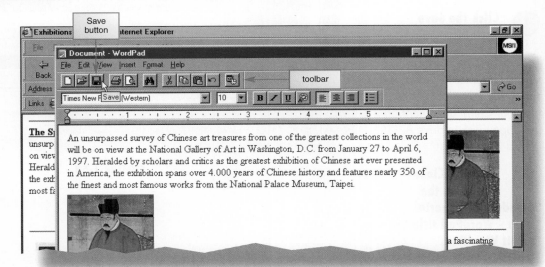

FIGURE 1-56

Click the Save button, type Splendors of Imperial China **in the File name text box, and then point to the Save in box arrow.**

The Save As dialog box displays and the Splendors of Imperial China file name is typed in the File name text box (Figure 1-57). The Save in box contains the My Documents folder name.

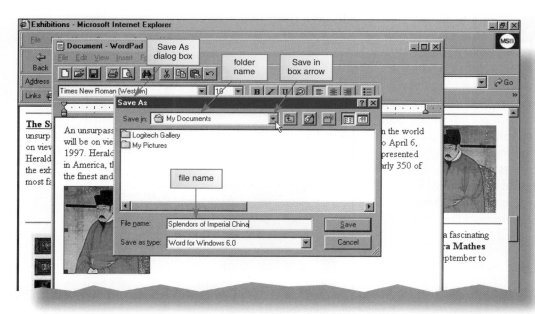

FIGURE 1-57

 Click the Save in box arrow, click 3½ Floppy [A:] in the Save in list, and then point to the Save button.

The Save in list displays, the 3½ Floppy [A:] drive name is selected, the Save in list closes, and the 3½ Floppy [A:] drive name displays in the Save in box (Figure 1-58).

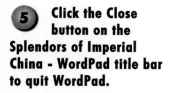 **Click the Save button.**

The Save As dialog box closes and Internet Explorer saves the Splendors of Imperial China document on the floppy disk in drive A.

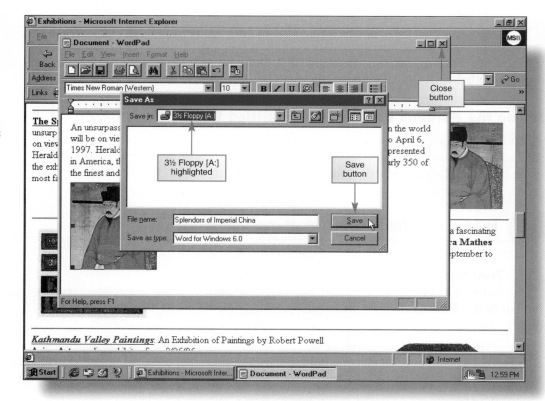

FIGURE 1-58

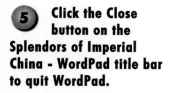 **Click the Close button on the Splendors of Imperial China - WordPad title bar to quit WordPad.**

The WordPad window closes and the Internet Explorer window is visible on the desktop.

Other Ways

1. Press ALT+F, press A key, type file name, select folder, press ENTER key
2. Press CTRL+S, type file name, select folder, press ENTER key

Computer users commonly search for and save text and pictures found on the World Wide Web to a disk for use in the future. Previously in this project, you copied text and a picture from the Exhibitions Web page to a blank WordPad document, and then saved the document on a floppy disk using the file name, Splendors of Imperial China.

After saving the Splendors of Imperial China document and before closing the Splendors of Imperial China — WordPad window, you may want to print the document. To print the Splendors of Imperial China document, click File on the menu bar, click Print on the File menu, and click the OK button.

To print the Splendors of Imperial China document after closing the WordPad window, you must launch WordPad and open the document prior to printing the document. To launch WordPad, click the Start button, point to Programs, point to Accessories, and click WordPad. To open the Splendors of Imperial China document, click File on the menu bar, click Open, select the Splendors of Imperial China file name, and click the Open button. After opening the document, you can print the document using the Print command on the file menu.

Printing a Web Page in Internet Explorer

Internet Explorer's printing capability allows you to print both the text and picture portions of a Web page. The easiest way to print is to use the Print button on the Standard Buttons toolbar. In the following steps, you will print the Exhibitions Web Page and four pieces of paper will print on the printer (see Figure 1-60 on page IE 1.46.) Perform the following steps to print the Exhibitions Web page.

 To Print a Web Page

1 **Point to the Print button on the Standard Buttons toolbar (Figure 1-59).**

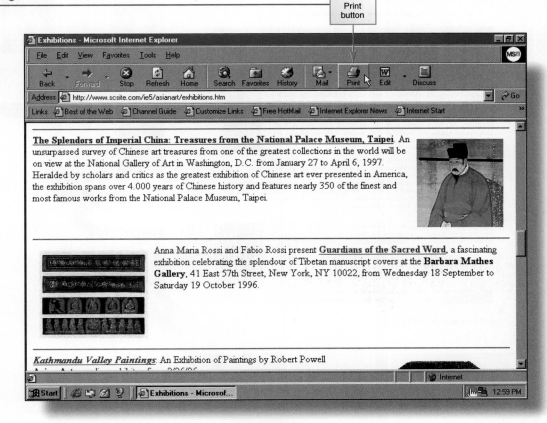

FIGURE 1-59

Click the Print button. When the printer stops, retrieve the printout.

The URL of the Web page prints as a footer in the lower-left corner of each page (Figure 1-60). The Web page title displays in the upper-left corner of each page and the page number and total number of pages in the Web site display in the upper-right corner of each page.

Exhibitions   Page 4 of 4

Heavens' Embroidered Cloths: One Thousand Years of Chinese Textiles:
Hong Kong Museum of Art, June 23rd - September 17th. 6/20/95

Exhibitions   Page 3 of 4

Mustang: An Exhibition of Paintings and Photographs in Nepal
Patan Museum, Nepal, commentary by Mary Slusser. 12/20/95

Departments

Sculpture from a Sacred Realm An Exhibition of Indian Sculpture From 2nd century
B.C. to 13th century A.D. **Rossi & Rossi**, London, England. 11/17/95

Exhibitions   Page 2 of 4

 royal palaces of the former Malla kings of the Kathmandu Valley. Its gilded door
and window face one of the most beautiful squares in the world. The residential
palace compound of Keshav Narayan Chowk which houses the museum dates from
1734, displacing a Buddhist monastery that is still remembered in an annual public
rite on the palace doorstep. The Museum opened to the public in July 1997.

Kathmandu Portfolio + 1. An Exhibition of Photographs of
scenes from Kathmandu, 1970-1974, by Ira Cohen, photographer
and poet. The photographs are accompanied by his *Kathmandu
Dream Piece.* On-line exhibition from 6/04/97.

title of
Web page

page
numbers

Exhibitions ←   → Page 1 of 4

Asian Arts   **Comments**   **Departments**

d by the **Indigo**
for the first time the
lation of Nepal's
s located in the
isolation of the
millennia they
of adjacent India,
bition from

ASIAN ARTS

Exhibitions

click on the title or image to visit that Exhibition

September 30th.

Survival of the Spirit, Tibet a Decade of Images is a culmination of photographic
images by Nancy Jo Johnson that records the tragic conditions inside Tibet and the
triumphant survival of the Tibetan people in exile. It is an inspirational, spiritual
voyage that ties together the many strands of this complex story. On-line exhibition
from 8/31/98.

s of the Sacred
ur of Tibetan
l East 57th Street,
r to Saturday 19

Himalayan Visions. An exhibition of drawings from the Himalaya that visually and
metaphysically explores its profoundly spiritual geography, both natural and human.
"In the Himalaya and on the Tibetan Plateau, one is confronted in a profound way
with the enigmatic nature of being alive... and as an artist, this experience is
important in the process of creation; after all, emptiness is the womb from which
form becomes manifest and through which the aesthetic experience becomes aware
of itself" - from the Artist's Statement. On-line exhibition from 6/12/98.

Treasures of the Chinese Scholar, a new exhibition at the University of
Pennsylvania Museum of Archaeology and Anthropology opening March 14, 1998,
features 160 selections of extraordinary "scholar art"-calligraphy, painting, and
works of art in wood, lacquer, ivory, stone, horn and metal-from as early as the
Zhou Dynasty (770-256 B.C.) through the Qing Dynasty (1644-1911 A.D.). The
exhibition, drawn from collection of Ji Zhen Zhai ("Studio of Accumulated
Treasures"), is on view through January 3, 1999.

Tibet: Tradition and Change is an important exhibition of Tibetan art opening at
the Albuquerque Museum, Albuquerque New Mexico USA on October 18th. The
curator of the exhibition is Dr. Pratapaditya Pal, who has chosen a variety of
previously unseen and important works of art.

URL of
Web page

 The Patan Museum displays the traditional sacred art of Nepal in an illustrious
architectural setting. Its home is an old residential court of Patan Darbar, one of the

http://www.asianart.com/exhibitions.html   3/29/00

3/29/00

3/29/00

3/29/00

3/29/00

FIGURE 1-60

Other Ways

1. On File menu click Print,
   click OK button
2. Press CTRL+P, press ENTER

You also can click Print on the File menu to print a Web page. When you do this, a Print dialog box displays. The printing options available in the Print dialog box allow you to print the entire document, print selected pages of a document, print to a disk file, print multiple copies, change the printer properties, and cancel the print request.

Internet Explorer Help

Internet Explorer is a program with many features and options. Although you will master some of these features and options quickly, it is not necessary for you to remember everything about each one of them.

Reference materials and other forms of assistance are available using **Internet Explorer Help**. You can display these materials and print them or copy them to other Windows documents. To use the Help feature to learn more about the topic of searching for text within the currently displayed Web page, complete the following steps.

More About

Printing

You can choose to print a table containing a list of all links on the Web page you are printing or all documents with links on the Web page. Click the Print all linked documents check box or Print table of links check box to print the table or documents.

More About

Help

A tour of the Internet Explorer Help system is available by clicking the Tour command on the Help menu. Also available on the Help menu is the Online Support command, which allows you to obtain current product support over the Internet.

 To Access Internet Explorer Help

1 **Click Help on the menu bar and then point to Contents and Index.**

The Help menu, containing the Contents and Index command, displays (Figure 1-61).

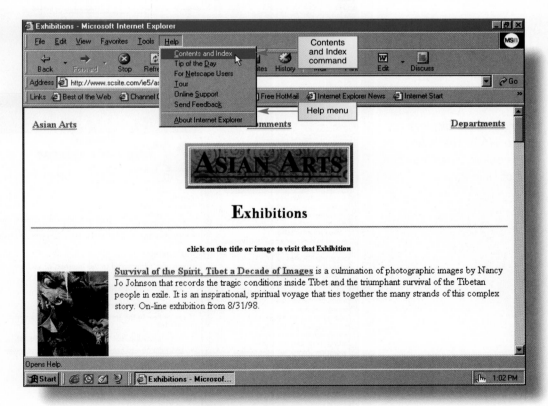

FIGURE 1-61

2 **Click Contents and Index and then point to the Index tab.**

The Microsoft Internet Explorer Help window displays (Figure 1-62). The window contains the Help toolbar and two panes. The navigation pane contains three tabs (Contents, Index, and Search) and the display pane contains Help information. The Contents sheet shown in the navigation pane, contains topics organized into categories. The Index sheet contains an index of Help topics. The Search sheet allows you to search for specific Help topics.

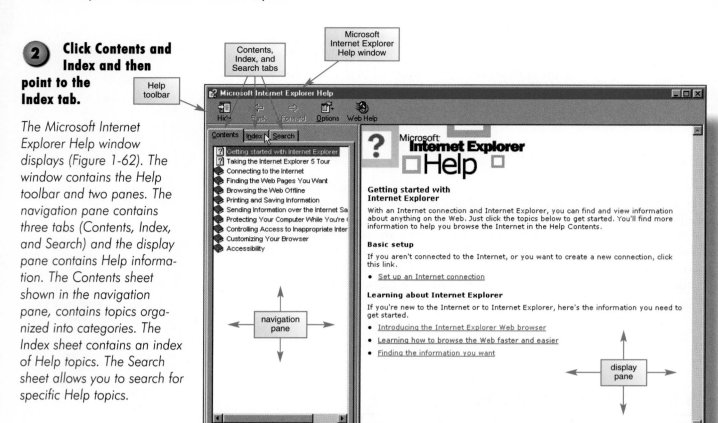

FIGURE 1-62

3 **Click the Index tab.**

The Index sheet displays (Figure 1-63). The Index sheet contains a text box and a list of Help topics.

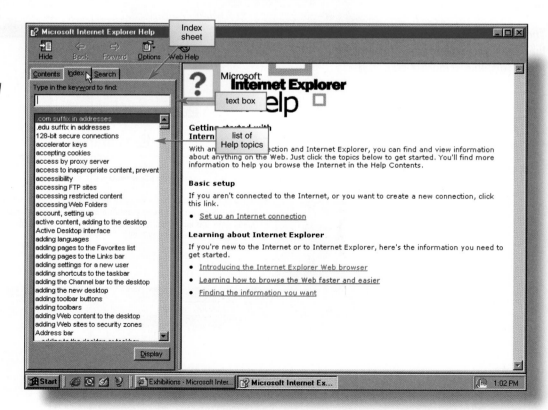

FIGURE 1-63

4 **Type find in the text box and then point to finding text on a Web page.**

When you type the word find, the list automatically scrolls and the first entry beginning with the characters, f-i-n-d, is highlighted (Figure 1-64). To see additional entries, use the scroll bar at the right of the list. To highlight an entry in the list, click the entry.

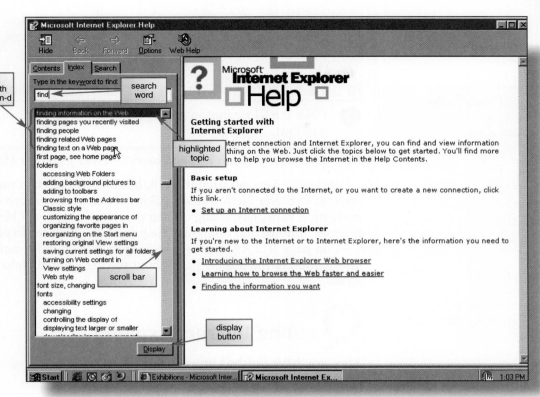

FIGURE 1-64

5 **Double-click finding text on a Web page.**

Information about finding information on the Web and two related topics display in the display pane (Figure 1-65).

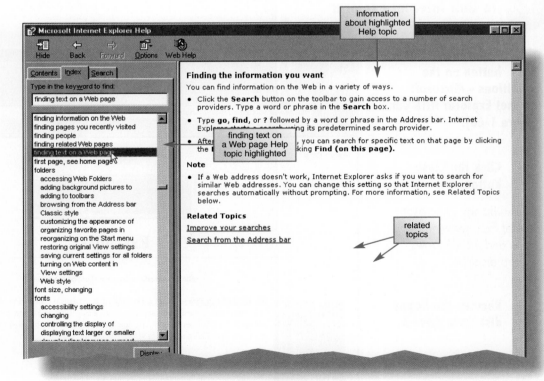

FIGURE 1-65

Other Ways

1. Press F1 key
2. Press ALT+H, press C key

After viewing the index entries, normally you will close the Internet Explorer Help window. To close the Internet Explorer Help window, complete the following step.

1. Click ALT+F4

TO CLOSE THE MICROSOFT INTERNET EXPLORER HELP WINDOW

1 Click the Close button on the title bar of the Microsoft Internet Explorer Help window.

Internet Explorer closes the Microsoft Internet Explorer Help window.

In Figure 1-62 on page IE 1.48, buttons on the Help toolbar in the Microsoft Internet Explorer Help window allow you to perform activities such as hiding the navigation pane, navigating among previously displayed Help topics, changing Internet options, and obtaining Help from the Internet Explorer Web site. In Figure 1-64 on page IE 1.49, clicking the Display button in the navigation pane displays information in the display pane about the highlighted Help topic in the navigation pane.

Quitting Internet Explorer

After you have finished browsing the World Wide Web, quit Internet Explorer. Perform the following steps to quit Internet Explorer.

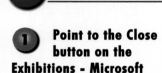 **To Quit Internet Explorer**

1 **Point to the Close button on the Exhibitions - Microsoft Internet Explorer title bar (Figure 1-66).**

2 **Click the Close button.**

The Exhibitions - Microsoft Internet Explorer window closes and the Windows desktop displays.

3 **Remove the floppy disk from drive A.**

FIGURE 1-66

Project Summary

Project 1 introduced you to the Internet and World Wide Web. You launched Internet Explorer and used the History list, Favorites list, buttons on the Standard Buttons toolbar, and a URL to browse the World Wide Web. You added and removed Web pages on the Favorites list, copied and pasted text from a Web page into a WordPad document, saved and printed the document, and saved text, a picture, and an entire Web page on disk. In addition, you used the Index sheet in Internet Explorer Help to obtain help about Internet Explorer.

What You Should Know

Having completed the project, you now should be able to complete the following tasks:

▶ Access Internet Explorer Help *(IE 1.47)*

▶ Add a Web Page to the Favorites List *(IE 1.26)*

▶ Browse the World Wide Web by Entering a URL *(IE 1.14)*

▶ Close the Microsoft Internet Explorer Help Window *(IE 1.50)*

▶ Copy and Paste a Picture from a Web Page into a WordPad Document *(IE 1.42)*

▶ Copy and Paste Text from a Web Page into a WordPad Document *(IE 1.39)*

▶ Display a Web Page Using the Favorites List *(IE 1.28)*

▶ Display a Web Page Using the History List *(IE 1.24)*

▶ Display the Exhibitions Web Page *(IE 1.37)*

▶ Display the Home Page Using the Home Button *(IE 1.27)*

▶ Launch Internet Explorer *(IE 1.10)*

▶ Launch WordPad *(IE 1.36)*

▶ Move Back and Forward in the History List *(IE 1.21)*

▶ Print a Web Page *(IE 1.45)*

▶ Quit Internet Explorer *(IE 1.50)*

▶ Refresh a Web Page *(IE 1.20)*

▶ Remove a Web Page from the Favorites List *(IE 1.30)*

▶ Save a Picture on a Web Page *(IE 1.34)*

▶ Save a Web Page *(IE 1.32)*

▶ Save the WordPad Document and Quit WordPad *(IE 1.43)*

▶ Stop the Transfer of a Web Page *(IE 1.19)*

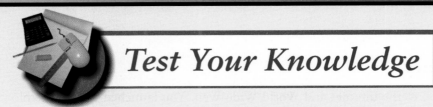

Test Your Knowledge

1 True/False

Instructions: Circle T if the statement is true or F if the statement is false.

T F   1. A link is one or more computer systems connected together for the purpose of resource and data sharing.

T F   2. Browsers simplify using the World Wide Web by removing the complexity of having to remember the syntax of commands to reference pages at Web sites.

T F   3. A typical URL (Uniform Resource Locator) is composed of only two parts: protocol and file specification.

T F   4. The domain name is the Internet address of a computer on the Internet.

T F   5. The title of the Web page that displays on the screen is listed in the Address box.

T F   6. Links you find one day on the Best of the Web and Internet Explorer News Web pages may be gone the next day.

T F   7. When you point to a text hyperlink, the mouse pointer changes to a pointing hand and the hyperlink changes color.

T F   8. The History list is a permanent record of the Web pages you visit.

T F   9. You can save the text on a Web page, but you cannot save the pictures.

T F   10. The Clipboard is a temporary storage area in main memory used for copy and paste procedures when placing portions of a Web page in other Windows documents.

2 Multiple Choice

Instructions: Circle the correct response.

1. The collection of hyperlinks throughout the Internet create an interconnected network of links called the _____.
   a. Favorites list
   b. Internet files
   c. World Wide Web
   d. History list

2. The starting point for browsing a Web site is called a _____.
   a. browser
   b. URL
   c. display area
   d. home page

3. You can customize the Standard Buttons toolbar by _____.
   a. clicking Customize on the Edit menu
   b. clicking the Customize button on the toolbar
   c. right-clicking the toolbar
   d. double-clicking the status bar

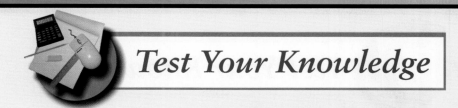

Test Your Knowledge

4. The unique address of a Web page is called a(n) _____.
   a. Uniform Resource Locator
   b. Internet address
   c. domain name
   d. path

5. When you point to a text hyperlink, the _____.
   a. hyperlink displays in reverse video
   b. computer beeps
   c. color of the link changes
   d. hyperlink flashes

6. To reload the Web page in the display area, click the _____ on the Standard Buttons toolbar.
   a. Stop button
   b. Refresh button
   c. Back button
   d. Internet Explorer icon

7. The _____ on the Microsoft Internet Explorer menu bar allows you to retrieve stored URLs.
   a. Favorites menu
   b. Go button
   c. View menu
   d. File menu

8. When you print a Web page, the Web page title and _____ appear on the printout.
   a. heading
   b. HTML (hypertext markup language)
   c. URL (Uniform Resource Locator)
   d. HTTP (hypertext transport protocol)

9. To copy a picture from a Web page to the Clipboard, right-click the _____ and then click Copy.
   a. navigation pane
   b. Web page
   c. Address bar
   d. picture

10. The _____ in the Internet Explorer Help window contains topics organized into categories.
    a. Contents sheet
    b. Index sheet
    c. Help menu
    d. Search sheet

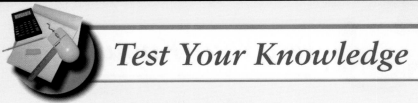

Test Your Knowledge

3 Understanding the Internet Explorer Window

Instructions: In Figure 1-67, the major components of the Microsoft Internet Explorer window are numbered from 1 to 10. Identify the various window components in the spaces provided.

FIGURE 1-67

1. _____
2. _____
3. _____
4. _____
5. _____
6. _____
7. _____
8. _____
9. _____
10. _____

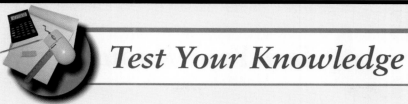

Test Your Knowledge

4 Identifying the Buttons on the Standard Buttons Toolbar and Links Toolbar

Instructions: In Figure 1-68, several buttons on the Standard Buttons toolbar are numbered from 1 to 8. In the spaces provided, briefly explain the purpose of each button.

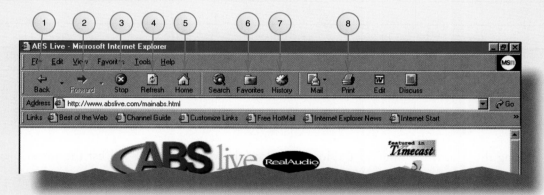

FIGURE 1-68

1. _____

2. _____

3. _____

4. _____

5. _____

6. _____

7. _____

8. _____

Instructions: In Figure 1-69, several buttons on the Links Bar are numbered from 9 to 13. In the spaces provided on the next page, briefly explain the purpose of each button.

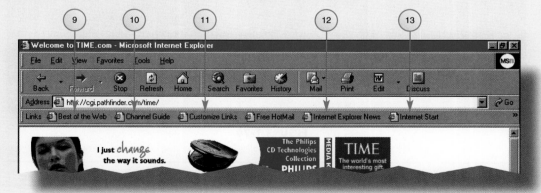

FIGURE 1-69

(continued)

Test Your Knowledge

Identifying the Buttons on the Standard Buttons Toolbar and Links Toolbar (continued)

9. _____
10. _____
11. _____
12. _____
13. _____

5 Understanding Favorites

Instructions: Using the Microsoft Internet Explorer window shown in Figure 1-70, list the steps to create a favorite for the American Ballet Theatre Web page.

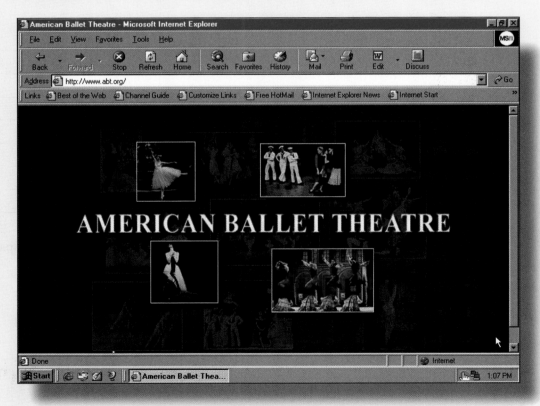

FIGURE 1-70

1. _____
2. _____
3. _____

Use Help

1 Using Internet Explorer Help

Instructions: Use Internet Explorer Help and a computer to perform the following tasks.

1. If necessary, connect to the Internet and launch Internet Explorer.
2. Click Help on the menu bar and then click Contents and Index.
3. If the Contents sheet does not display, click the Contents tab. Help topics in the Contents sheet are organized into the categories shown in Figure 1-71.

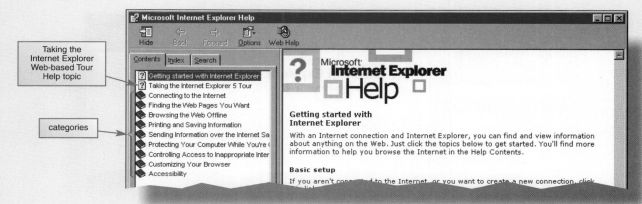

FIGURE 1-71

4. Click the Taking the Internet Explorer 5 Tour Help topic in the Contents sheet.
5. Click the start the Tour hyperlink in the display pane.
6. Maximize the Welcome to the Internet Explorer 5 Tour - Microsoft Internet Explorer window.
7. Click The basics hyperlink and click the Basics of Internet Explorer hyperlink. Answer the following question.
   a. What is the purpose of the Search button on the Standard Buttons toolbar? _____
   _____

8. Click the Getting your work done hyperlink. Click the Setting up your home page hyperlink. Answer the following question.
   a. How do you change the home page?_____
   _____

9. Click the Shopping online hyperlink and then answer the following question.
   a. If you give your credit card number to a Web site, how do you know the site is secure? _____
   _____

10. Click the What's new hyperlink and then answer the following question.
    a. List three features that are new to Internet Explorer. _____
    _____

11. Click the Next steps hyperlink and then answer the following question.
    a. List three things you might do after completing the tour. _____
    _____

12. Click the Close button in the Internet Explorers Tour 5 - Next step - Microsoft Internet Explorer window.
13. Click the Close button in the Microsoft Internet Explorer Help window.
14. Hand in the answers to the questions to your instructor.
15. Click the Close button in the Microsoft Internet Explorer window.

Use Help

2 Using the Internet Explorer Help Tutorial

Instructions: Use Internet Explorer Help and a computer to perform the following tasks.

1. If necessary, connect to the Internet and launch Internet Explorer.
2. Click Help on the menu bar and then click Contents and Index.
3. If the Index sheet does not display, click the Index tab. The Index sheet contains an extensive index to Internet Explorer Help topics (see Figure 1-72).

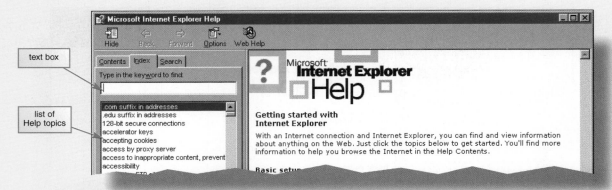

FIGURE 1-72

4. Type cookies in the text box, click the Display button in the Index sheet, and then answer the following questions.
   a. What is a cookie? _____
   b. What does a cookie contain? _____
5. Double-click the text box, type autocomplete in the box, click the how to use Help topic, click the Display button, and then answer the following questions.
   a. What does the AutoComplete feature save?
   b. What does AutoComplete do?
6. Select the text in the text box, type certificates in the box, click the protecting your identity Help topic, click the Display button, and then answer the following questions.
   a. List two types of certificates. _____
   b. What is a digital ID? _____
7. Select the text in the text box, type content advisor in the box, click the controlling access to the Internet Help topic, click the Display button, and then answer the following question.
   a. What is the purpose of Content Advisor? _____
8. Select the text in the text box, type shortcut keys in the box, click the Display button, and then answer the following questions.
   a. What is the shortcut key to go to the next Web page? _____
   b. What is the shortcut key to refresh the current Web page? _____
   c. What is the shortcut key to go stop downloading a Web page? _____
9. Click the Close button in the Microsoft Internet Explorer Help window.
10. Click the Close button in the Microsoft Internet Explorer window.
11. Hand in the answers to the questions to your instructor.

In the Lab

1 Browsing the World Wide Web Using URLs and Hyperlinks

Instructions: Use a computer to perform the following tasks. (If, while entering a URL in this exercise, a 404 error message or the message, The page cannot be displayed, displays, type `www.scsite.com/ie5/exercises.html` in the Address box and then click the exercise number corresponding to this exercise.)

1. If necessary, connect to the Internet and launch Internet Explorer.
2. Click the Address box, type `www.fbi.gov` in the box and then click the Go button to display the Federal Bureau of Investigation's home page (Figure 1-73).

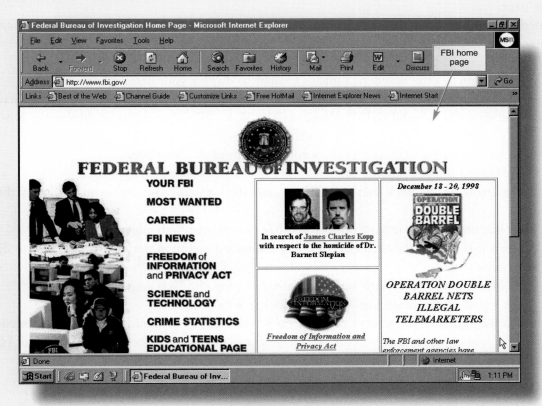

FIGURE 1-73

3. Using hyperlinks in the FBI Web site, find the Web page that contains the list of the ten most wanted fugitives.
4. Click the Print button on the Standard Buttons toolbar to print the Web page.
5. Use the Back button on the Standard Buttons toolbar to display the FBI home page.
6. Click the Print button on the Standard Buttons toolbar to print the Web page.
7. Click the Address box, type `www.nbc.com` in the box, and then click the Go button to display the NBC home page.
8. Using hyperlinks in the NBC Web site, find the Web page that lists the guest stars on the Tonight Show.

(continued)

In the Lab

Browsing the World Wide Web Using URLs and Hyperlinks *(continued)*

9. Click the Print button on the Standard Buttons toolbar to print the Web page.
10. Click the Address box, type www.usatoday.com in the box, and then click the Go button to display the USA Today home page.
11. Using hyperlinks in the USA TODAY Web site, find the Web page that contains the United States weather map.
12. Click the Print button on the Standard Buttons toolbar to print the Web page.
13. Click the Address box, type www.cbs.com in the Address box, and then click the Go button to display the CBS home page.
14. Using hyperlinks in the CBS Web site, find the Web page that contains David Letterman's Top Ten List. If asked, enter your zip code.
15. Click the Print button on the Standard Buttons toolbar to print the Web page.
16. Click the Home button on the Standard Buttons toolbar to display your default home page.
17. Click the History button on the Standard Buttons toolbar, click the nbc (www.nbc.com) folder name in the History list, and then click the NBC TV's Home on The Web - NBC.com entry to display the NBC home page.
18. Click the Print button on the Standard Buttons toolbar to print the Web page.
19. Click the Close button in the Explorer bar.
20. Click the down arrow on the Back button and then click the CBS entry on the menu to display the CBS home page.
21. Click the Print button on the Standard Buttons toolbar to print the Web page.
22. Click the Address box arrow and then click http://www.usatoday.com in the Address list box to display the USA TODAY home page.
23. Click the Print button on the Standard Buttons toolbar to print the Web page.
24. Click the Close button in the Microsoft Internet Explorer window.
25. Discard the second page and subsequent pages of each Web site you printed. Organize the printed Web pages so that the home page is first and the Web page associated with the home page is second. Hand in the eight printed pages to your instructor.

2 Working With the History List

Instructions: Use a computer to perform the following tasks. (If, while entering a URL in this exercise, a 404 error message or the message, The page cannot be displayed, displays, type www.scsite.com/ie5/exercises.html in the Address box, and then click the exercise number corresponding to this exercise.)

Part 1: *Clearing the History List*

1. If necessary, connect to the Internet and launch Internet Explorer.
2. Click Tools on the menu bar and then click Internet Options to display the Internet Options dialog box (Figure 1-74).

In the Lab

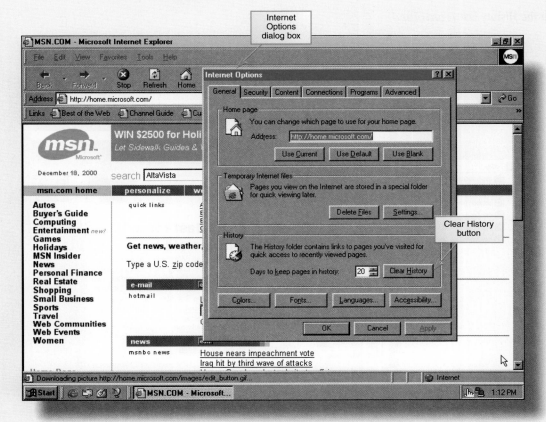

FIGURE 1-74

3. Click the Clear History button and then click the OK button in the Internet Options dialog box.
4. Click the OK button in the Internet Options dialog box.

Part 2: *Browsing the World Wide Web*

1. Click the Address box, type `www.mtv.com` in the Address box, and then click the Go button to display the MTV Online home page.
2. Click the Address box, type `www.cnn.com` in the Address box, and then click the Go button to display the CNN home page.
3. Click the Address box, type `www.amazon.com` in the Address box, and then click the Go button to display the Amazon.com home page.
4. Click the Address box, type `www.espn.com` in the Address box, and then click the Go button to display the ESPN.com home page.
5. Print the Web page.

Part 3: *Using the History List to Print a Web Page*

1. Click the History button on the Standard Buttons toolbar to display the History list (Figure 1-75 on the next page).

(continued)

In the Lab

Working With the History List *(continued)*

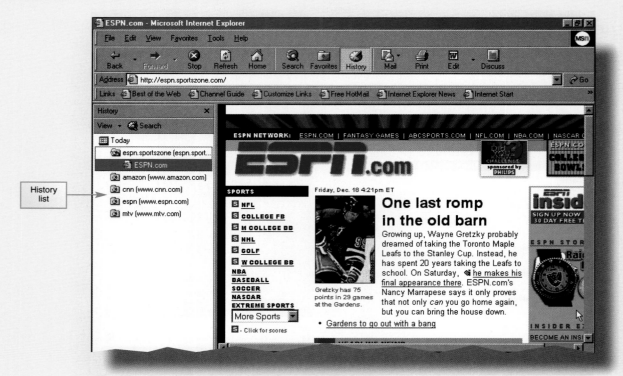

FIGURE 1-75

2. Click the cnn (`www.cnn.com`) folder in the History list and then click the CNN Interactive hyperlink. Print the Web page.

3. Click the mtv (`www.mtv.com`) folder in the History list and then click the MTV Online Home hyperlink. Print the Web page.

4. Click the espn (`www.espn.com`) folder in the History list and then click the ESPN.com hyperlink. Print the Web page.

5. Delete the amazon (www.amazon.com) folder by right-clicking the folder, clicking Delete on the shortcut menu, and then clicking the Yes button in the WARNING dialog box.

6. Click the Close button in the Explorer bar.

Part 4: *Clearing the History List*

1. Click Tools on the menu bar and then click Internet Options to display the Internet Options dialog box.

2. Click the Clear History button and then click the Yes button in the Internet Options dialog box.

3. Click the OK button in the Internet Options dialog box.

4. Click the Close button in the espn.go.com - Microsoft Internet Explorer window.

5. Hand in the printed Web pages to your instructor.

3 Working With the Favorites List

Instructions: Use a computer to perform the following tasks.

Part 1: *Creating a Folder in the Favorites List*

1. If necessary, connect to the Internet and launch Internet Explorer.
2. Click Favorites on the menu bar and then click Organize Favorites to display the Organize Favorites dialog box (Figure 1-76).

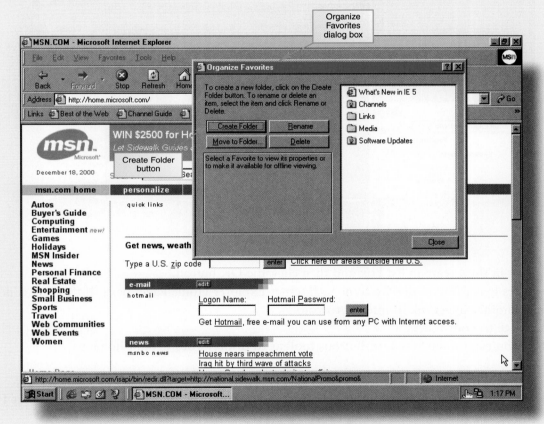

FIGURE 1-76

3. Click the Create Folder button in the Organize Favorites dialog box to create a folder titled New Folder.
4. Click New Folder, click the Rename button, type your first and last name as the folder name, and then press the ENTER key.
5. Click the Close button to close the Organize Favorites dialog box.

Part 2: *Adding Favorites to Your Folder*

1. Click the Internet Explorer News button on the Links bar to display the Welcome to Internet Explorer Home Page! page.

(continued)

In the Lab

Working With the Favorites List *(continued)*

2. Add the Welcome to Internet Explorer Home Page! favorite to the your folder by clicking Favorites on the menu bar, clicking Add to Favorites, and then clicking the Create in button in the Add Favorites dialog box (Figure 1-77).

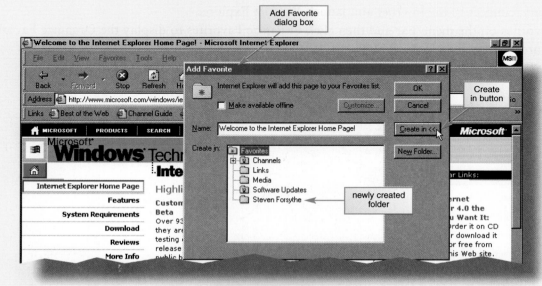

FIGURE 1-77

3. Click your folder in the Create in list box and then click the OK button.
4. Click the Features hyperlink on the Welcome to Internet Explorer Home Page! page. If this link is not available, click another hyperlink of interest to you.
5. Add this Web page to your folder.
6. Click the Home button on the Standard Buttons toolbar to display your default home page.

Part 3: *Displaying and Printing a Favorite From Your Folder*

1. Click Favorites on the menu bar, point to your folder, and then click Welcome to Internet Explorer Home Page!
2. Print the Web page.
3. Click Favorites on the menu bar, point to your folder, and then click Features.
4. Print the Web page.

Part 4: *Deleting a Folder on the Favorites List*

1. Click Favorites on the menu bar and then click Organize Favorites.
2. Click your folder name, click the Delete button, and then click the Yes button in the Confirm Folder Delete dialog box.
3. Click the Close button in the Organize Favorites dialog box.
4. Verify you have deleted your folder.
5. Click the Close button in the Microsoft Internet Explorer window.
6. Hand in the two printed pages to your instructor.

In the Lab

4 Saving a Web Page on a Floppy Disk

Instructions: Use a computer to perform the following tasks. (If, while entering a URL in this exercise, a 404 error message or the message, The page cannot be displayed, displays, type `www.scsite.com/ie5/ exercises.html` in the Address box, and then click the exercise number corresponding to this exercise.)

1. If necessary, connect to the Internet and launch Internet Explorer.
2. Click the Address box, type `http://finance.yahoo.com/?u` in the Address box and then click the Get Quotes button to display the YAHOO! FINANCE Web page (Figure 1-78).

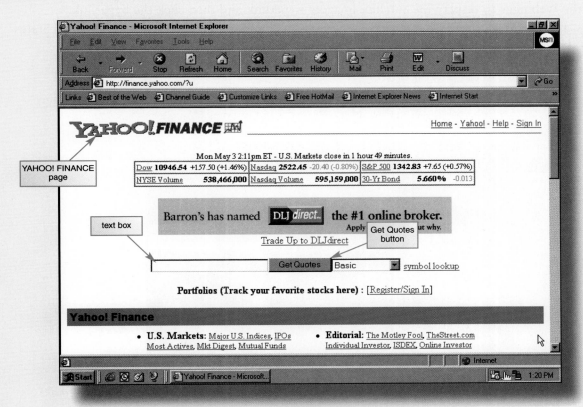

FIGURE 1-78

3. Enter the IBM stock symbol in the text box on the Web page and then click the Get Quotes button to retrieve the current IBM stock price. Print the Web page that displays and then save the Web page on a floppy disk. Click the Back button to display the YAHOO! FINANCE Web page.
4. Repeat Step 3 above using the following stock symbols: INTC, MSFT, TE, TOY, WEN, and WY.
5. Click the Close button in the Microsoft Internet Explorer window.
6. Hand in the printed Web pages to your instructor.

In the Lab

5 Printing Pictures

Instructions: Use a computer to perform the following tasks. (If, while entering a URL in this exercise, a 404 error message or the message, The page cannot be displayed, displays, type `www.scsite.com/ie5/ exercises.html` in the Address box and then click the exercise number corresponding to this exercise.)

1. If necessary, connect to the Internet and launch Internet Explorer.
2. Type `http://covis1.atmos.uiuc.edu/covis/visualizer` in the Address box and then click the Go button to display the Weather Visualizer Web page.
3. Scroll the Web page to display the Satellite Imagery hyperlink and then click the hyperlink.
4. Display a color-enhanced infrared image, without radar summary, for the Continental United States (Figure 1-79).

FIGURE 1-79

5. Print the weather map by right-clicking the map and then clicking Print Target.
6. Display a visible image for the Northwestern States. Print the weather map.
7. Display an infrared image for the Southwestern States. Print the weather map.
8. Display a water vapor image for Hawaii. Print the weather map.
9. Click the Close button to close the Microsoft Internet Explorer window.
10. Hand in the printed weather maps to your instructor.

In the Lab

6 Copying and Pasting a Picture and Text

Instructions: Use a computer to perform the following tasks. (If, while entering a URL in this exercise, a 404 error message or the message, The page cannot be displayed, displays, type `www.scsite.com/ie5/exercises.html` in the Address box, and then click the exercise number corresponding to this exercise.)

Part 1: Retrieving a Web Page

1. If necessary, connect to the Internet and launch Internet Explorer.
2. Type `www.historychannel.com` in the Address box and then click the Go button to retrieve the History Channel Web page (Figure 1-80). The page contains the This Day in History picture.

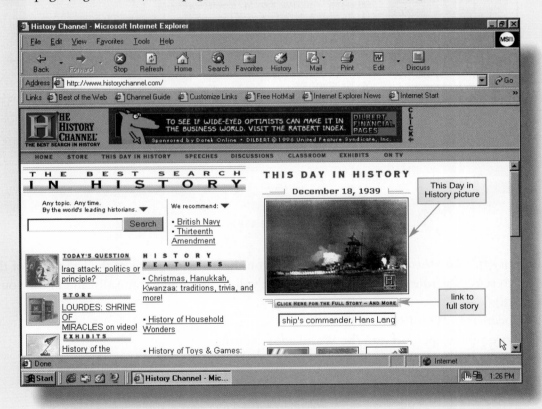

FIGURE 1-80

Part 2: Copying a Picture and Text to Microsoft WordPad

1. Copy the This Day in History picture to the Clipboard.
2. Launch Microsoft WordPad.
3. Paste the picture on the Clipboard into the WordPad document, click anywhere off the picture, and then press the ENTER key.
4. Click the History Channel - Microsoft Internet Explorer button on the taskbar.

(continued)

In the Lab

Copying and Pasting a Picture and Text *(continued)*

5. Click the link that contains the full story associated with The Day in History picture (Figure 1-81).

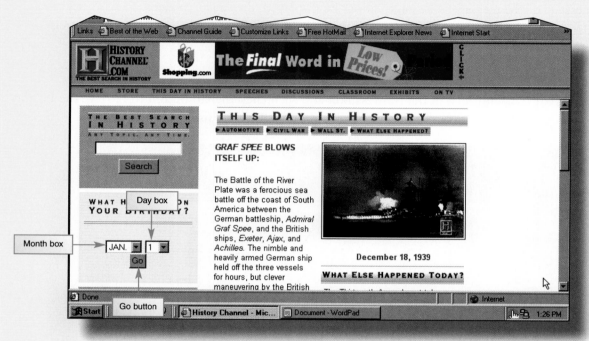

FIGURE 1-81

6. Copy the story title and text to the Clipboard (Position the insertion point at the beginning of the title and drag down to select the title and text. The document will scroll up automatically and allow you to continue selecting text.)
7. Click the Document - WordPad button on the taskbar.
8. Paste the text on the Clipboard into the WordPad document.
9. Save the WordPad document on a floppy disk using the file name, This Day in History.
10. Print the WordPad document.
11. Click the Close button to close the This Day in History - WordPad window.

Part 3: *Displaying Information About Your Birthday*

1. Scroll to the top of the History Channel - Microsoft Internet Explorer window.
2. Use the Month and Day boxes in the Web page (see Figure 1-81) to select your birth month and birthday and then click the Go button to learn what happened on your birthday. Several news stories display about events that occurred in the past on your birthday.
3. Copy and paste two stories from the Web page into a blank WordPad document, save the document on a floppy disk using an appropriate file name, and print the document.
4. Click the Close button to close the WordPad and Microsoft Internet Explorer windows.
5. Hand in both WordPad documents to your instructor.

In the Lab

7 Copying, Pasting, and Saving a Picture

Instructions: Use a computer to perform the following tasks. (If, while entering a URL in this exercise, a 404 error message or the message, The page cannot be displayed, displays, type www.scsite.com/ie5/ exercises.html in the Address box, and then click the exercise number corresponding to this exercise.)

1. If necessary, connect to the Internet and launch Internet Explorer.
2. Click the Address box, type www.senate.gov in the Address box, and then click the Go button to display The United States Senate Web page (Figure 1-82).

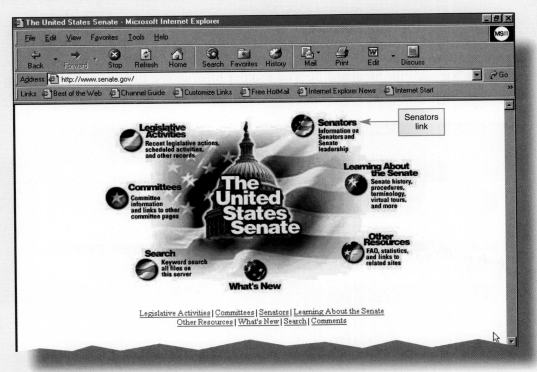

FIGURE 1-82

3. Using the Senators hyperlink on the Web page, find a picture of one of the two senators who represent the state in which you live.
4. Start Microsoft WordPad.
5. Copy and paste the picture from the Web page into a blank WordPad document, click anywhere off the picture, and then press the ENTER key.
6. Find a picture of the other senator who represents the state in which you live.
7. Copy and paste the picture from the Web page into the WordPad document, click anywhere off the picture, and then press the ENTER key.
8. Save the document on a floppy disk using an appropriate file name.
9. Print the document.
10. Click the Close button on the WordPad window.
11. Click the Close button on the Microsoft Internet Explorer window.
12. Hand in the document to your instructor.

In the Lab

8 Working with Toolbars

Instructions: Use a computer to perform the following tasks.

Part 1: *Hiding a Toolbar*

1. If necessary, connect to the Internet and launch Internet Explorer.
2. Right-click a blank area on the Standard Buttons toolbar to display a shortcut menu.
3. Click Links on the shortcut menu to remove the Links toolbar from the Microsoft Internet Explorer window.

Part 2: *Moving and Resizing a Toolbar*

1. Point to the Address title at the left end of the Address bar.
2. Move the Address bar onto the Standard Buttons toolbar by dragging the Address bar toward the Standard Buttons toolbar (Figure 1-83).

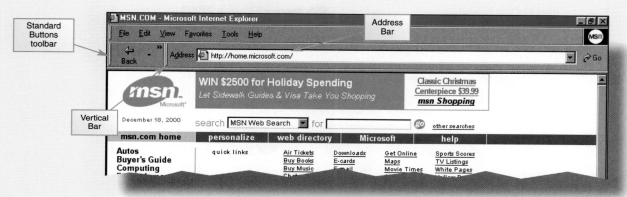

FIGURE 1-83

3. Point to the small vertical bar at the left end of the Address bar.
4. Resize the Address bar by dragging the small vertical bar on the Address bar to the right until only the Address title and Go button display on the Address bar.
5. Point to the Address title at the left end of the Address bar.
6. Move the Address bar back to its original position below the Standard Buttons toolbar by dragging the Address bar toward the bottom of the window.

Part 3: *Displaying the Contents of a Folder Using the Address Bar*

1. Click the Address box and type C:\My Documents in the Address box.
2. Click the Go button to display the contents of the My Documents folder in the display area.

Part 4: *Search for Information on the Internet Using the Address Bar*

1. Type "national weather" in the Address box.
2. Click the Go button to display a list of national weather related hyperlinks in the display area.
3. Click any hyperlink to display its Web page.

In the Lab

Part 5: *Customizing the Standard Buttons Toolbar*

1. Right-click a blank area of the Standard Buttons Toolbar and then click Customize on the shortcut menu to display the Customize Toolbar dialog box (Figure 1-84).

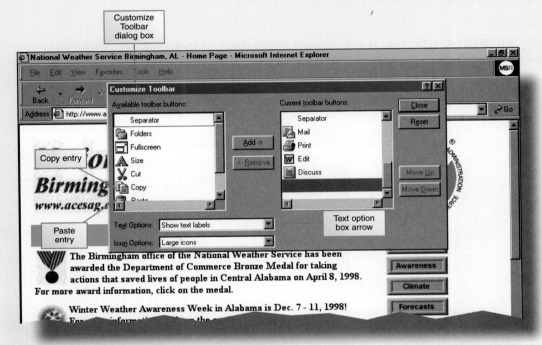

FIGURE 1-84

2. Click Copy in the Available toolbar buttons list box.
3. Click the Add button to add the Copy entry to the Current toolbar buttons list box and display the Copy button on the Standard Buttons toolbar.
4. Click Paste in the Available toolbar buttons list box.
5. Click the Add button to add the Paste entry to the Current toolbar buttons list box and display the Paste button on the Standard Buttons toolbar.
6. Click the Text Options box arrow and then click No text labels in the list box.
7. Click the Close button in the Customize Toolbar dialog box. The Copy and Paste buttons display without text labels on the Standard Buttons toolbar.

Part 6: *Returning the Toolbar to Its Original Configuration*

1. Right-click a blank area of the Standard Buttons Toolbar, click Customize, and then click the Reset button.
2. Click the Text Options box arrow and then click Show text labels in the list box.
3. Click the Close button in the Customize Toolbars dialog box.
4. Right-click a blank area of the Standard Buttons Toolbar and then click Links.
5. Move the Links bar below the Address bar by pointing to the Links title at the left end of the Links bar and dragging the Links bar toward the bottom of the window.
6. Click the Close button in the Microsoft Internet Explorer window.

In the Lab

9 Connecting to the Shelly Cashman Series Web Site

Instructions: Use a computer to perform the following tasks.

Part 1: *Retrieving the Shelly Cashman Series Student Center Web Site*

1. If necessary, connect to the Internet and launch Internet Explorer.
2. Click the Address box, type www.scseries.com in the Address box, and then click the Go button.
3. Click the Student Center link (Figure 1-85).

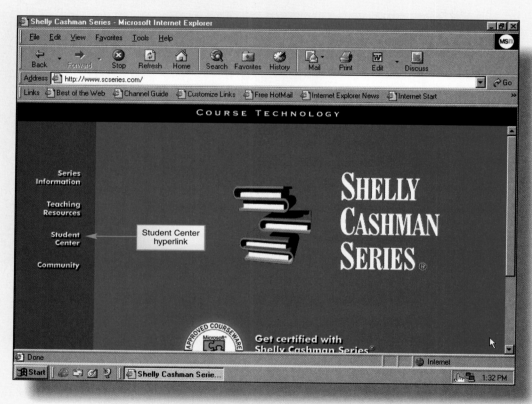

FIGURE 1-85

4. Scroll down and then click Microsoft Internet Explorer 5: An Introduction.
5. Click Project 1 in the left frame of the Microsoft Internet Explorer 5 - Microsoft Internet Explorer window.
6. Complete the activities listed.

Part 2: *Retrieving the Shelly Cashman Series Guide to the World Wide Web*

1. Type www.scsite.com/ie5/app.html in the Address box and then click the Go button.
2. When the Shelly Cashman Series Guide to the World Wide Web page displays, click a category of your choice. Visit and print the information contained at each site in the selected category.
3. Click the Close button to close the Microsoft Internet Explorer window.
4. Hand in the printed Web pages to your instructor.

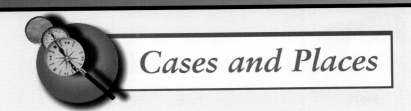

Cases and Places

The difficulty of these case studies varies:
▶ are the least difficult; ▶▶ are more difficult; and ▶▶▶ are the most difficult.

If, while entering a URL in one of the following exercises, you get a 404 error message or the message, The page cannot be displayed, type `www.scsite.com/ie5/exercises.html` in the Address box and then click the exercise number corresponding to this exercise.

1 ▶ While performing research to obtain information about the computer industry, you decide to look for news stories in the *PC Week Online* magazine (`www.pcweek.com`). Find an interesting news story accompanied by a picture and then copy and paste the story and picture into a WordPad document. Print the document and then hand it in to your instructor.

2 ▶ You want to replace your older 4-door car with a newer 2-door model. Before buying, you would like to research the price of a Pontiac Grand Am 2-door coupe GL and a Ford Mustang 2-door coupe GT using Dealernet (`www.dealernet.com`). Find and print the Web page containing the manufacturers suggested retail price and destination charges for each model. Check the availability of each car. Summarize your findings in a brief report.

3 ▶▶ Your uncle would like to invest in the stock market. He has asked you to find fundamental stock information about Bethlehem Steel (BS), Microsoft Corporation (MSFT), and Piedmont Natural Gas (PNY). Use the Data Broadcasting Company Web site (`www.dbc.com`) to obtain today's stock price, dividend rate, daily volume, 52-week high, 52-week low, and price/earnings ratio (p/e ratio) for each stock. Print the Web page containing the information about each stock and summarize the information for your uncle in a brief report. Hand in the printed Web pages and the report to your instructor.

4 ▶▶ Your family is planning a vacation to Cancun, Mexico. Check with Northwest Airlines (`www.nwa.com`), Continental Airlines (`www.flycontinental.com`), and Delta Airlines (`www.deltaairlines.com`) for travel specials to Cancun. Print any Web pages containing travel specials and then summarize the information you find in a brief report.

5 ▶▶▶ Your parents want to purchase a reasonably priced ($2000 or less) multimedia computer. They ask you to check with Gateway (`www.gateway.com`), Dell (`www.dell.com`), Compaq (`www.compaq.com`), International Business Machines (`www.ibm.com`), and Packard Bell (`www.packardbell.com`) to find the best deal on a computer. Before starting, determine the system requirements of the computer you want to purchase (microprocessor speed, amount of RAM, hard drive size, modem speed, monitor size, and so on). Check each Web site, print all the Web pages you find in your search for the computer that is the best bargain, and then summarize your results in a brief report.

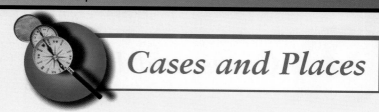

Cases and Places

6 ▶▶▶ Although Internet Explorer may be the most widely used browser program, it is not the only browser program in use today. Using the Internet, computer magazines and newspapers, or other resources, prepare a brief report about three other Web browsers in use today. Describe their features, differences, and similarities.

7 ▶▶▶ Almost every computer magazine has an online version. Visit the Web sites for *PC Magazine* (www.zdnet.com/pcmag/), *PC Computing* (www.zdnet.com/pccomp/), *PC World* (www.pcworld.com), and *Windows Magazine* (www.windowsmagazine.com). Explore each Web site and print the Web pages that are of interest to you. How are the online magazines similar and dissimilar? What do you like or dislike about each magazine? Is it easy to find the information you need? In a brief report, answer these and any other questions that may occur to you.

Internet Explorer 5

PROJECT

2

Web Research Techniques and Search Engines

OBJECTIVES

You will have mastered the material in this project when you can:

- Describe the five general categories of Web pages
- List the criteria for evaluating a Web resource
- Describe the two general types of search engines
- Search the Web using either a directory or keywords
- Search the Web using the Search Assistant
- Customize and refine a search
- Describe the techniques used for successful keyword searches
- Describe how to create a working bibliography
- Compile a list of works cited for Web resources
- Search the Web for maps, encyclopedia articles, and e-mail addresses
- Use the Address bar to search the Web

Go Get It!

Successful Searching on the Web

Millions of pages of information are at your fingertips as you search the largest and, arguably, the most diverse and complete library in the universe. Eager to begin your quest for knowledge, you scan your surroundings, vainly searching for the card catalog that will lead you to your first topic of interest. But none is to be found. With mounting trepidation, you look for librarians, a help desk, or clerks. Your search is futile. A quick perusal of the shelves confirms your fear: the items are in no particular order. Nothing is arranged alphabetically, chronologically, or in any fashion you can fathom. How can you escape this nightmare?

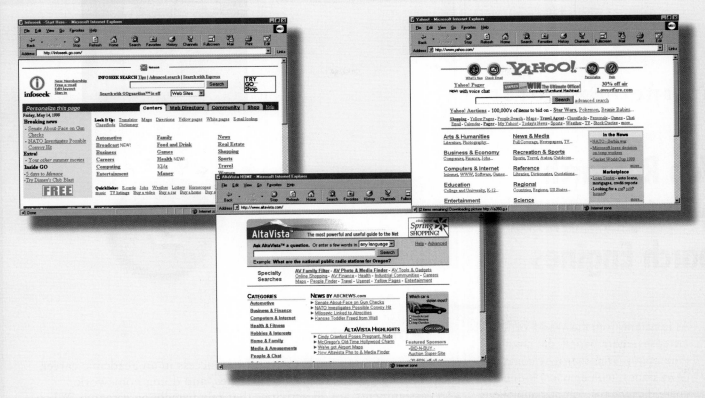

This scenario is similar to what you encounter looking through the estimated 22 million pages (and growing) of information on the World Wide Web. Fortunately, the computer industry is innovative and quick to respond.

To assist users in their searches of the Web, utile devices known as search engines were developed. They bring order to the chaos of the Web by indexing the vast amount of information.

Search engines are to the World Wide Web what a card catalog is to a library. They allow the user quickly to search and locate specific topics on the Web, much as a library card catalog guides patrons to the correct location of printed information. Most search engines share a common method of locating information: the keyword. A user types a word or phrase, such as aviation or global warming, and the search engine scans the sites on the Web to find matches, or hits.

While many search engines exist and are readily available to Web users, several are well known and widely used. One of the more popular is Yahoo! Yahoo! is praised as being the fastest and most current because it is updated daily.

Another favorite search engine is AltaVista, developed by Digital Equipment Corporation. Containing what Digital claims is the largest Web index, AltaVista can perform detailed searches for any type of information.

One search engine differs in its approach to finding information on the Web. Excite uses concept-based navigation on the Web. This unique approach, though slower and more likely to return irrelevant information, can perform more abstract searches. Rather than using Civil War as a keyword, for example, you could type, What caused the Civil War?

This project offers techniques for performing successful research of the vast amount of materials available on the Web. In addition to using the popular Yahoo! and AltaVista search engines, you will learn about the types of Web resources and how to evaluate a Web resource. Searching using a directory and the Search Assistant are two means available that will enable you to perform the online research required for your classroom assignments and distant learning courses. Finally, you will learn methods to record and save relevant information about a research source for future reference and possible course work.

With research being an important tool for success in your academic career, learning the capabilities of Web search engines and successful searching techniques are requisite skills. Currently, search engines are being heralded as the saviors of searching the World Wide Web.

Internet Explorer 5

Web Research Techniques and Search Engines

P R O J E C T

2

CASE PERSPECTIVE

As familiarity with the World Wide Web increases, more people are creating Web pages. Web sites may contain news stories, mathematical formulas, entire dictionaries, famous quotations, or current research findings, all of which make the World Wide Web a powerful research tool.

Finding information on a specific topic is difficult at times because the Web is very large and changes every day. To resolve this problem, search engines index the pages on the Web and list them by topic. While this solution makes it easier to find information on the Web, it does not address another challenge faced by Web users: information may not be correct.

Using evaluation criteria and published style guides, you can supplement your research with materials you obtain from the Web and evaluate, and be relatively certain of its accuracy.

You have been hired as a research assistant to an instructor. Your job is to become proficient with Web search engines and Web resource evaluation techniques so that you can assist the instructor with her research and compile a list of authoritative Web sites.

Introduction

Research is an important tool for success in an academic career. Writing papers, preparing speeches, and doing homework assignments are all activities that rely heavily on research. When researching, you are trying to find information to support an idea or position, to prove a point, or to learn about a topic or concept. Traditionally, research was accomplished using books, papers, periodicals, and other materials found in libraries. The World Wide Web provides a new and useful resource for supplementing the traditional print materials found in the library.

While the Web is a valuable resource, you should not rely solely on the Web for research information. The Web changes quite frequently, which means Web pages may become unavailable. In addition, the information found on Web pages is not always up to date or accurate, or it cannot be verified. Project 2 demonstrates successful techniques for locating information on the Web and then evaluating the information for its usefulness as a source.

Types of Web Resources

Web pages are organized by content into five categories: advocacy, business/marketing, informational, news, and personal. In addition, the Web provides other resources whereby you can access useful information when doing research. The next six sections describe the types of Web pages and other resources.

Advocacy Web Pages

An **advocacy Web page** contains content that describes a cause, opinion, or idea. The purpose of the advocacy Web page is to convince the reader of the validity of an opinion or idea. Some organizations that sponsor advocacy Web pages are the American Association of Retired Persons (AARP), the Democratic Party, and the Greenpeace organization. The URLs of advocacy Web pages usually end with the .org extension. Figure 2-1 shows an advocacy Web page of the Greenpeace organization.

FIGURE 2-1

Business/Marketing Web Pages

A **business/marketing Web page** contains content that tries to promote or sell products or services. The URLs of business/marketing Web pages usually end with the .com extension. Some businesses that maintain business/marketing Web pages are AT&T, Gateway 2000, CDnow, and Amazon.com. Figure 2-2 on the next page shows a business/marketing Web page of Dell Computer Corporation.

More About

Research Materials

Reference materials, such as dictionaries, thesauruses, and collections of quotations, as well as entire literary works are available on the Web. Search for the word, ameliorate, using the Merriam-Webster dictionary Web site (www.m-w.com), and then find a synonym for the word, exciting.

More About

Advocacy Web Pages

Other advocacy Web pages include the American Association of Retired Persons (www.aarp.org), Southern Carolina Democratic Party (www.scdp.org), Maine Democratic Party (www.mainedems.org), Kentucky Republican Party (www.rpk.org), California Republican Party (www.cagop.org), and National Rifle Association (www.nra.org).

More About

Business/ Marketing Web Pages

Other business/marketing pages include Coca-Cola (www.thecoca-colacompany. com), Chevron (www.chevron. com), Disney (www.disney. com), McDonald's (www.mcdonalds.com), DuPont (www.dupont.com), and General Motors (www.gm.com).

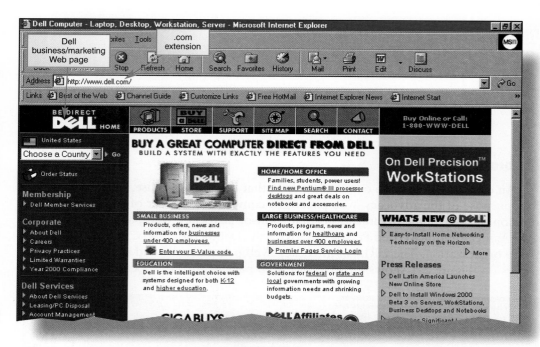

FIGURE 2-2

Informational Web Pages

An **informational Web page** contains factual information, such as public transportation schedules, library holdings, published research findings, or quarterly fiscal results for a corporation. The URLs of informational Web pages usually end in the .gov or .com extension. Some organizations that maintain informational Web pages are the U.S. Government (U.S. census data, tax codes, congressional budget, and so on) and airlines (flight information and schedules). Figure 2-3 shows an informational Web page of the Federal Bureau of Investigation.

FIGURE 2-3

News Web Pages

A **news Web page** contains newsworthy material: stories and articles that contain information about current events, life, money, sports, and the weather. Many magazines and newspapers sponsor Web sites that provide summaries of printed articles, as well as articles not included in the printed versions. Newspapers and television and radio stations are some of the media that maintain news Web pages. The URLs of news Web pages usually end with the .com extension. Figure 2-4 shows a sample news Web page of the USA Today newspaper.

More About

News Web Pages

Other news Web pages include the CNN (www.cnn.com), ESPN (www.espn.com), National Broadcasting Company (www.nbc.com), House of Blues (www.hob.com), L.A. Times (www.losangelestimes. com), and Detroit Free Press (www.freepress.com).

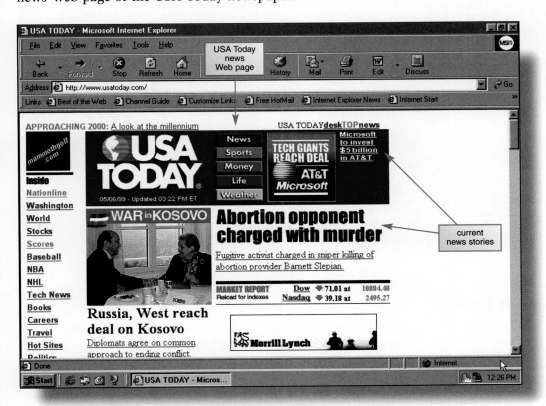

FIGURE 2-4

Personal Web Pages

A **personal Web page** is maintained by an individual and normally is not associated with any organization. People publish personal Web pages for a variety of reasons, and the pages can contain content on just about anything imaginable. The URLs of personal Web pages may end with the .com, .gov, or .edu extension, depending on where the individual is maintaining his or her site. Figure 2-5 on the next page shows a sample personal Web page for Gary's Web.

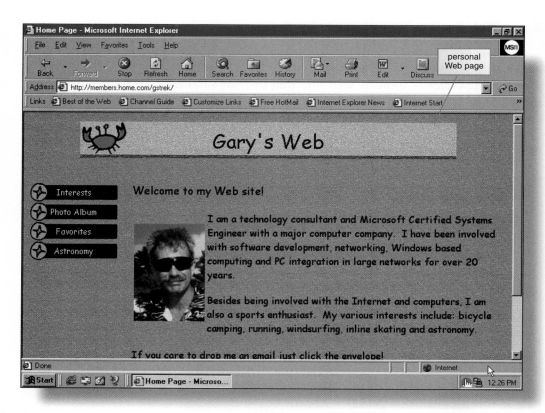

FIGURE 2-5

Other Resources

In addition to the five types of Web pages, a number of other resources where you will find useful information are available on the Internet. File transfer protocol (FTC) and gopher sites, Usenet newsgroups, and for-profit database services all contain information and files that you can use for research purposes.

Papers, documents, manuals, and complete ready-to-execute programs are available using FTP. **File transfer protocol (FTP)** is a method of transferring files over the Internet.

Another file retrieval method available on the Internet is gopher. **Gopher** started out as a document retrieval system to assist people in getting help for computing problems. It since has become a user-friendly, menu-driven method of retrieving files. Many government agencies have organized gopher sites to provide information and distribute documents and forms.

Newsgroups are online discussion groups. Individuals can send messages to a newsgroup, receive replies, and read what others have to say about a topic. Discussion on current events, ongoing research, and other topics that have not yet found their way into print often occur in newsgroup discussions. Newsgroups will be discussed in detail in Project 3.

A number of **database services**, such as Lexis/Nexis and Dow Jones, have been developed that, for a small fee, allow you to perform searches for information. Some schools subscribe to these database services and make the searching services available to the faculty, staff, and students. Ask a librarian how to access these database services.

Determining the exact category into which a Web resource falls is sometimes difficult because of the overlap of information on the page. You will find advertising on news Web pages. Personal Web pages may be advocating some cause or opinion. A business/marketing Web page may contain factual information that is verifiable from other sources. In spite of this overlapping, identifying the general category in which the Web page falls can help you evaluate the usefulness of the Web page as a source of information for a research paper.

Evaluating a Web Resource

Once a promising Web page is found, you should evaluate it for its reliability, significance, and content. Remember, anyone can put a page on the Web, and Web pages do not have to be reviewed for accuracy or verified by editors. You have an obligation to ensure the information and other materials you use are accurate, attributable, and verifiable.

Just as there are criteria for evaluating printed materials, there are criteria for evaluating Web pages. These criteria include: authorship, accuracy of information, currency of information, and topic and scope of coverage. Table 2-1 shows the information you should look for within each criterion when evaluating Web resources.

More About

Evaluating Resources

Although a single evaluating tool does not exist, several colleges/universities have Web sites that contain information about evaluating Web sites. These sites include Cornell University (http://www.library.cornell.edu/okuref/research/skill26.htm), Southern California College (http://www.sccu.edu/faculty/R_Harris/evalu8it.htm), and Purdue University (http://owl.english.purdue.edu/Files/131/d-internet.html).

Table 2-1

CRITERION	INFORMATION TO EVALUATE
Authorship	▶ Is the name of the person or organization publishing the page legitimate? ▶ Is there a link to a page that describes the goals of the organization? ▶ Does the page include a statement of official approval from the parent organization? ▶ Does a copyright notice appear? ▶ What are the author's qualifications? ▶ Are any opinions and biases clearly stated? ▶ Does the page contain advertising? If so, is it differentiated from content? ▶ Is the information provided as a public service?
Accuracy of Information	▶ Are any sources used and are they listed on the page? ▶ Does the page contain links to other Web sites that verify the information on the page? ▶ Are data and statistics clearly displayed and easy to read? ▶ Is the page grammatically correct?
Currency of Information	▶ When was the page written? ▶ When was the page placed on the Web? ▶ When was the page last updated? ▶ Does the page include dates associated with the information on the Web page?
Topic and Scope of Coverage	▶ What is the purpose of the Web page? ▶ Does the page declare a topic? ▶ Does the page succeed in describing or discussing the declared topic? ▶ Are points clear, well stated, and supported? ▶ Does the page contain links to related resources? ▶ Is the page under construction?

You may wish to create an evaluation worksheet to use as an aid in consistently evaluating the Web pages you find as potential resources. Figure 2-6 shows a sample evaluation worksheet template created from the criteria listed in Table 2-1. You can make copies of this worksheet, or create a new worksheet to use each time you find a possible research source.

Finding a valuable resource among the millions of Web pages available on the World Wide Web, however, can be quite a challenge. The most efficient way to find a probable resource from among all those pages is to use the special search tools created specifically for use on the Web. They will guide you to the information you are seeking.

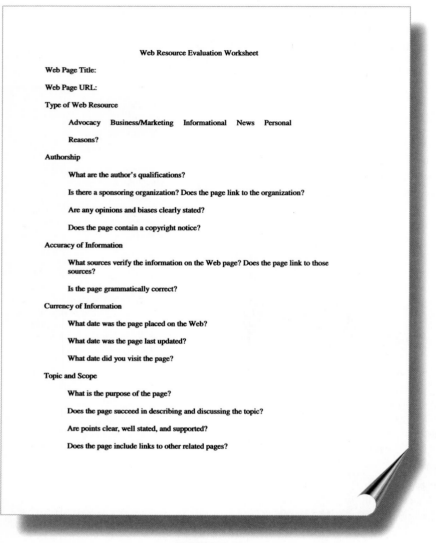

FIGURE 2-6

Web Search Engines

With the advent of the World Wide Web, user-friendly search tools were developed. These tools, called **search engines** or **search services**, fall into two general categories. The first type of search engine organizes related Web resources together by topic. This type of search engine uses a **directory**. A second type of search engine allows you to search the Web and display links to Web pages without having to maneuver through any intermediate pages by using one or more relevant **keywords** (a word or phrase) about the topic in which you are interested.

Figure 2-7 shows a directory that is organized into broad categories. You must decide into which category the search topic falls and then click the corresponding link. When you click the link, another page of links displays with more specific categories from which to choose.

Search Engines

Search engines can provide access to more than just Web pages. Some search engines allow you to search a newsgroup, periodical or newspaper, business directory, and personal directory.

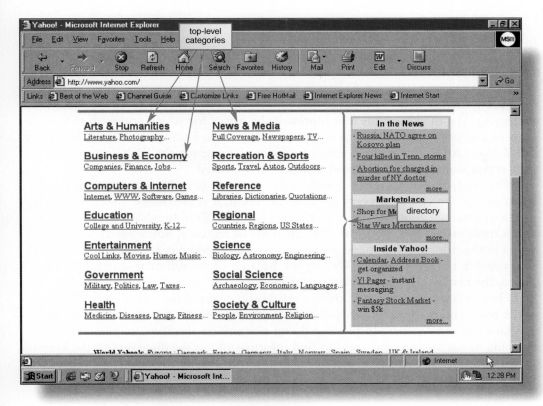

FIGURE 2-7

You continue following the links until you find the information you are seeking. Because directories allow you to choose from a list of categories, you do not have to provide any keywords to find information. You may have to spend considerable time traveling through several levels of categories, however, only to discover that no pages on the topic are available.

Figure 2-8 shows a typical **keyword search form** used to enter keywords to search the Web. You provide one or more relevant keywords about the topic, and the search engine will return links that point directly to Web pages that contain those keywords.

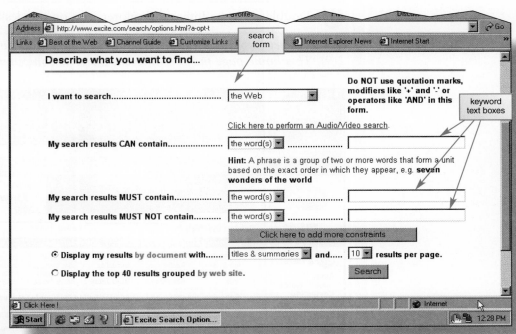

FIGURE 2-8

The search engine uses the keywords to search an index of Web resources. The index is created using several techniques. Automated programs, called **robots** or **spiders**, travel around the Web, automatically following links and adding entries to the index. Individuals also can request that their Web pages be added to a directory or index.

Today, most search tools are made available as Web pages with an input form on which you type the keywords that represent the topics for which you wish to search. Some of the more popular search engines are AltaVista, Excite, HotBot, WebCrawler, and Yahoo!. All of these search engines allow you to search the Web using the information you want to locate, instead of where it is located.

Why study several different search tools? Just as it is impossible for a card catalog to contain an entry for every book in the world, it is impossible for each search engine to catalog every Web page on the World Wide Web. In addition, different search tools on the Web perform different types of searches. Some search for keywords in the title of a Web page, while others scan hyperlinks for the keywords. Still others search the entire text of Web pages. Because of the different searching techniques, the results of a search vary surprisingly.

When developing Internet Explorer, Microsoft realized the importance of using search tools and made several search tools accessible via the Search button on the Standard Buttons toolbar. To practice doing research on the Web, assume you are majoring in Astronomy and want to find information on the discovery of the Perseid meteor shower. The following sections show how to launch Internet Explorer and begin searching the Web for information on the discovery of the Perseid meteor shower.

Launching Internet Explorer

Launch Internet Explorer following the procedure you used at the beginning of Project 1 on pages IE 1.12 and IE 1.13. This step is summarized below.

TO LAUNCH INTERNET EXPLORER

 Double-click the Internet Explorer icon on the desktop.

The Internet Explorer window with the MSN.COM home page displays (Figure 2-9). This home page may be different on your computer.

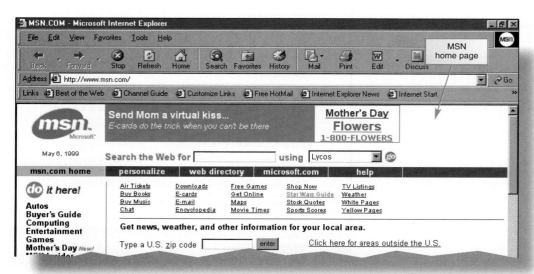

FIGURE 2-9

Searching the Web Using a Directory

Yahoo! is famous for its Internet directory. Starting with general categories and becoming increasingly more specific as links are selected, the Yahoo! directory provides a menu-like interface for searching the Web. Because the Yahoo! directory uses a series of menus to organize links to Web pages, you can perform searches without entering keywords. Perform the following step to display the Yahoo! directory.

 Steps To Display the Yahoo! Directory

1 **Click the Address box, type** www.yahoo.com **as the URL, and then press the** ENTER **key.**

The URL for the Yahoo! Directory (http://www.yahoo.com/) displays in the Address box and the Yahoo! home page displays (Figure 2-10).

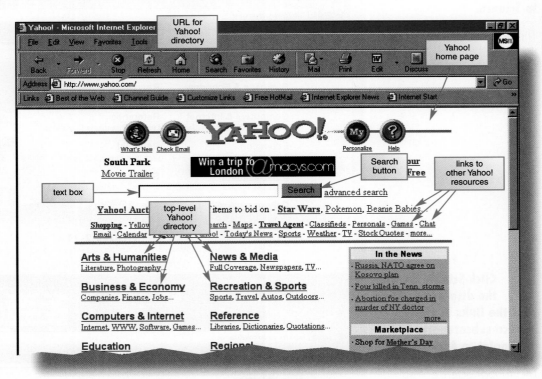

FIGURE 2-10

When you type a URL in the Address box and press the ENTER key, **AutoComplete** remembers the URL you typed. As a result, when you type the URL for the Yahoo! directory in the Address box in Figure 2-10, AutoComplete may display a list of previously entered URLs in a box below the Address box. If this happens, you can select a URL from the list in the Address box by clicking the URL, or you can continue to type the URL from the keyboard.

The text box and Search button below the Yahoo! title allow you to perform a keyword search. The links below the text box allow you to display telephone directories, online maps, Web pages about current events, and more. Below these links is the top-level Yahoo! directory. Web pages in the Yahoo! directory are organized into the broad categories illustrated in Figure 2-10. You must decide into which category the search topic falls and then select the corresponding link. When you select a general link, another page of links displays with more specific topics from which to choose. You continue following the links until you find the information you are seeking.

More About

Directory and Keyword Search Engines

Today, most search engines provide both a directory and the capability of performing keyword searches.

More About

Yahoo!

Two graduate students at Standard University accumulated lists of their favorite Web sites and started Yahoo!. Yahoo!, which became a corporation in 1996, is a household name among Web users.

Because astronomy is part of the major category, Science, this category is appropriate to start the search. The following steps show how to navigate through the Yahoo! directory to retrieve information about the discovery of the Perseid meteor shower.

 Steps To Search the Web Using the Yahoo! Directory

1 **Scroll the display area to display the Science link and then point to Science.**

The Science link displays in the Yahoo! directory (Figure 2-11).

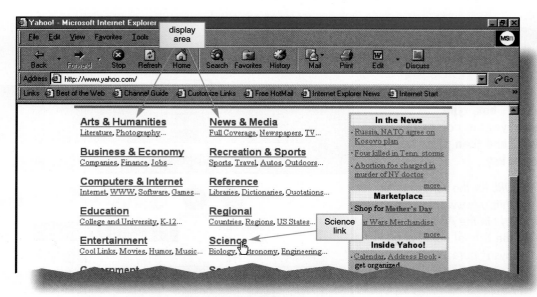

FIGURE 2-11

2 **Click Science, scroll the display area to view the links in the Science subcategory, and then point to Astronomy.**

The Yahoo! Science Web page displays (Figure 2-12). The number in parentheses next to a subcategory indicates how many Web page listings you will find if you click the subcategory. For example, the Astronomy subcategory contains 2235 listings. The word, NEW!, to the right of a link indicates the link recently has been updated with new Web pages.

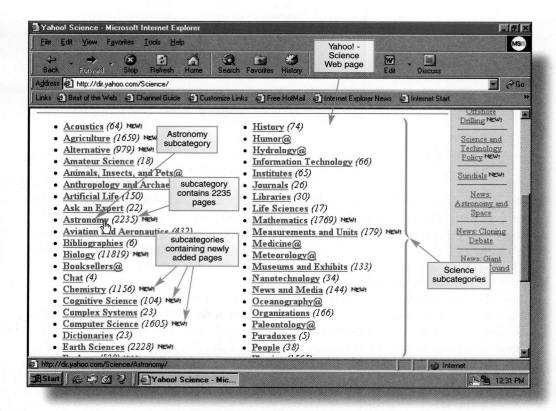

FIGURE 2-12

3 Click Astronomy, scroll the display area to view the links in the Astronomy subcategory, and then point to Solar System.

The Yahoo! Science: Astronomy Web page displays (Figure 2-13). The Solar System subcategory contains 618 listings. An @ symbol next to a link indicates a link to another Yahoo! subcategory.

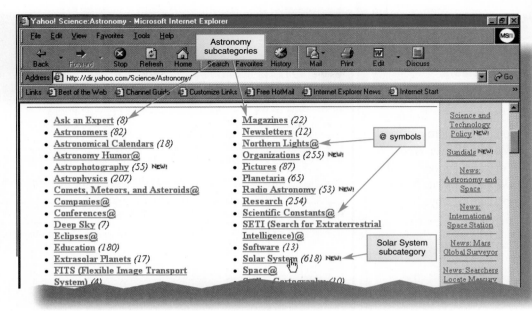

FIGURE 2-13

4 Click Solar System, scroll the display area to view the links in the Solar System subcategory, and then point to Comets, Meteors, and Asteroids.

The Yahoo! Science: Astronomy: Solar System Web page displays (Figure 2-14). The Comets, Meteors, and Asteroids subcategory contains 164 listings.

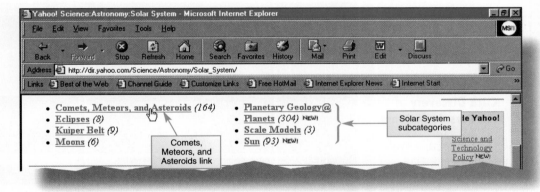

FIGURE 2-14

5 Click Comets, Meteors, and Asteroids, scroll the display area to view links in the Comets, Meteors, and Asteroids subcategory, and then point to Perseid Meteor Shower.

The Yahoo! Science: Astronomy: Solar System: Comets, Meteors, and Asteroids Web page displays (Figure 2-15). The Perseid Meteor Shower subcategory contains 5 listings.

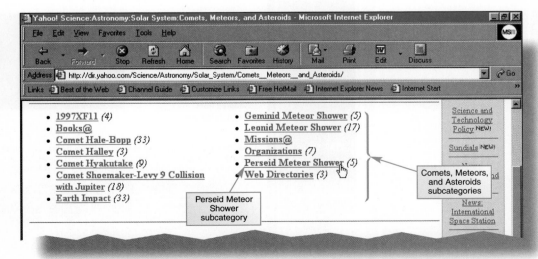

FIGURE 2-15

6 Click Perseid Meteor Shower and then point to Discovery of Perseid Meteors.

The Yahoo Science: Astronomy: Solar System: Comets, Meteors, and Asteroids: Perseid Meteor Shower Web page displays (Figure 2-16). The Discovery of the Perseid Meteors link displays.

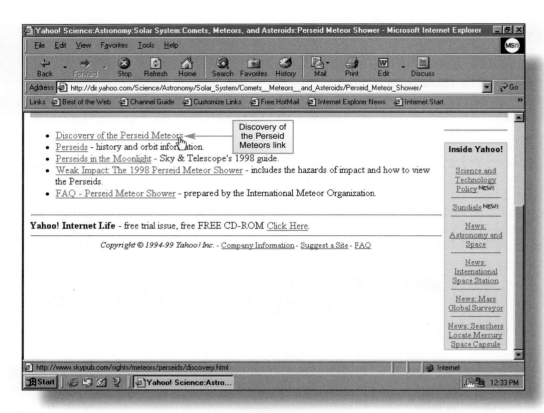

FIGURE 2-16

7 Click Discovery of the Perseid Meteors.

The Sky and Telescope Web page containing the Discovery of the Perseid Meteors article displays (Figure 2-17).

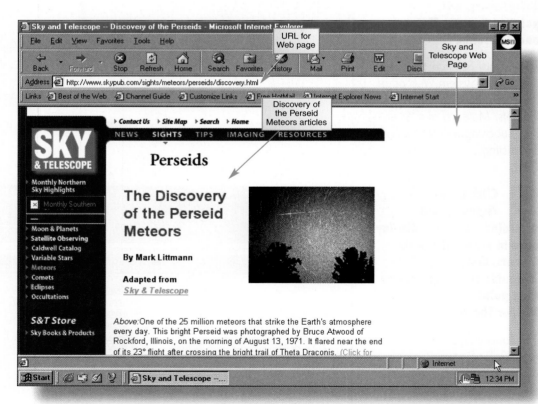

FIGURE 2-17

8 Scroll the display area to view the image and text associated with Edward C. Herrick.

An image and description of Edward C. Herrick displays (Figure 2-18).

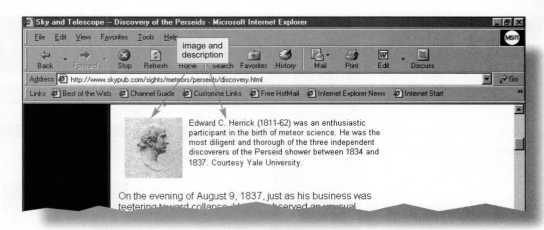

FIGURE 2-18

The description of Edward C. Herrick in Figure 2-18 contains information about the discovery of the Perseid meteor shower. Other areas of the Web page may contain additional information.

Evaluating Web Resources

Now that you have a potentially useful Web page, you should apply the criteria discussed earlier on page IE 2.9 to evaluate the Web page to see if it can be used as a source for research. The following steps illustrate how to use the sample worksheet template shown in Figure 2-6 on page IE 2.10 to evaluate the Sky and Telescope page.

More About

Evaluating a Web Resource

Many Web pages do not have the necessary criteria for being a research source. You will find that you discard many promising Web pages simply because you cannot find the necessary evaluation criteria.

Steps To Evaluate a Web Resource

1 Scroll the display area to display the bottom of the Web page.

The bottom of the Web page is visible (Figure 2-19). The bottom of the page contains the author name, author acknowledgements, sponsoring organization, and copyright notice.

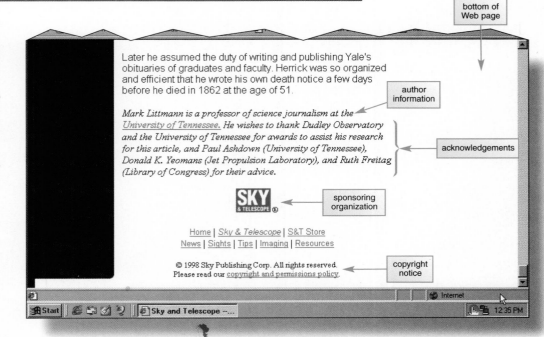

FIGURE 2-19

2 **Scroll the display area to display the top of the Web page.**

The top of the Web page is visible (Figure 2-20). The top of the page contains the Web page URL, link to sponsoring organization, Web page title, and author name.

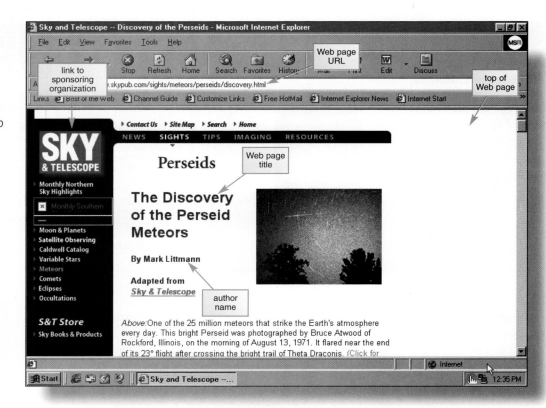

FIGURE 2-20

The information gathered so far is summarized on the worksheet illustrated in Figure 2-21. Based on the current worksheet criteria, the Discovery of the Perseid Meteors page is an exceptionally strong resource.

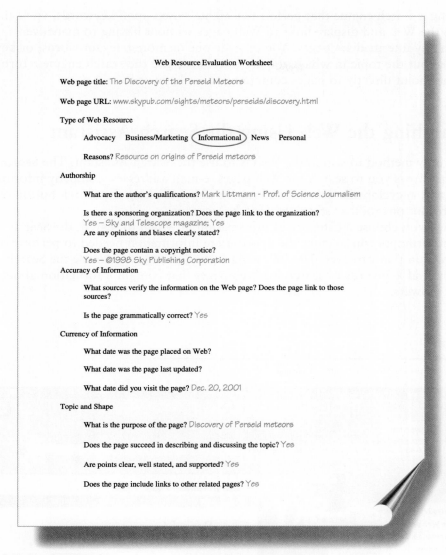

Web Resource Evaluation Worksheet

Web page title: The Discovery of the Perseid Meteors

Web page URL: www.skypub.com/sights/meteors/perseids/discovery.html

Type of Web Resource

    Advocacy   Business/Marketing   (Informational)   News   Personal

    Reasons? Resource on origins of Perseid meteors

Authorship

    What are the author's qualifications? Mark Littmann - Prof. of Science Journalism

    Is there a sponsoring organization? Does the page link to the organization?
    Yes – Sky and Telescope magazine; Yes
    Are any opinions and biases clearly stated?

    Does the page contain a copyright notice?
    Yes – ©1998 Sky Publishing Corporation

Accuracy of Information

    What sources verify the information on the Web page? Does the page link to those sources?

    Is the page grammatically correct? Yes

Currency of Information

    What date was the page placed on Web?

    What date was the page last updated?

    What date did you visit the page? Dec. 20, 2001

Topic and Shape

    What is the purpose of the page? Discovery of Perseid meteors

    Does the page succeed in describing and discussing the topic? Yes

    Are points clear, well stated, and supported? Yes

    Does the page include links to other related pages? Yes

FIGURE 2-21

Instead of manually recording evaluation information on a printed copy of the worksheet, you can create an electronic version of the worksheet using a word processor. Then, for each Web resource you select, you can open a new copy of the worksheet document, record the entries, and save the document using a document name that reflects the Web resource being evaluated. Use one worksheet document per Web resource.

By completing the previous steps, you learned to search the World Wide Web using a menu-driven directory (in this case, Yahoo!). By allowing you to select from a list of categories, such directories eliminate the need for keywords. You may have to spend considerable time, however, traveling through several levels of menus, only to discover that no information on the topic is available.

Using a search engine that performs searches based upon keywords, you can explore the Web and display links to Web pages without having to maneuver through any intermediate pages. You provide one or more relevant words, or keywords, about the topic in which you are interested, and the search engine returns links that point directly to pages containing those keywords.

Searching the Web Using the Search Assistant

An easy method to search the Web is to use the Search Assistant. The **Search Assistant** allows you to search for Web pages, e-mail addresses, company information, maps, encyclopedia articles, and newsgroups. Clicking the Search button on the Standard Buttons toolbar starts the Search Assistant.

When you choose a category of information in which to search, the Search Assistant prompts you to enter the appropriate information needed to perform a search within that category. The following section shows how to use the Search Assistant and keywords to search for Web pages that contain information about meteor showers.

 To Start the Search Assistant

1 **Click the Search button on the Standard Buttons toolbar.**

The Search bar displays (Figure 2-22). The Search bar contains a toolbar, five option buttons, and a rectangular box. Currently, the selected Find a Web page category displays in the Search bar. A text box, a message, Brought to you by InfoSeek, and a Search button display in the rectangular box. The search engine name (InfoSeek) on your computer may be different.

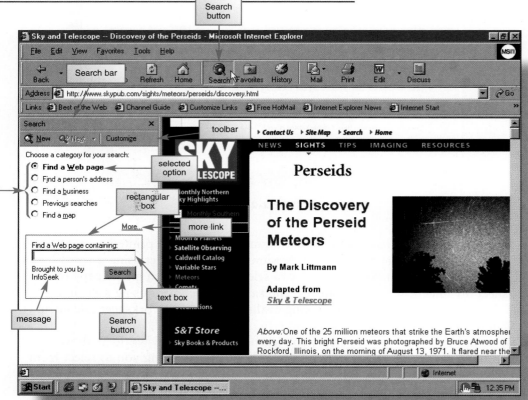

FIGURE 2-22

Other **Ways**

1. Click View on the menu bar, point to Explorer Bar, click Search
2. Press CTRL+E

Each category listed in the Search bar allows you to search for different information. Selecting the Find a person's address category allows you to search for a mailing address or e-mail address. Selecting the Find a business category allows you to search for company or organization information. Selecting the Previous searches category allows you to display previously performed searches. Selecting the Find a map category allows you to search for addresses, company information, and places or landmarks. Two additional categories (Find in encyclopedia and Find in Newsgroups) display when you click the More link in the Search bar.

Typing a keyword in the text box in the Search bar and clicking the Search button will cause the Infoseek search engine, or the default search engine on your computer, to search for the keyword and display a list of links to Web pages that contain the keyword. In this case, the default search engine is the InfoSeek search engine. The default search engine may be different on your computer.

Searching the Web Using Keywords

The Infoseek search engine name displays below the text box in the Search bar (see Figure 2-22). **Infoseek** is one of the many search engines that allow you to search for Web pages based upon a keyword. Perform the following steps to use the Infoseek search engine to search for Web pages that contain the keywords, meteor shower.

 To Search the Web Using the Default Search Engine (Infoseek)

1 **Type** meteor shower **in the text box in the Search bar and then point to the Search button.**

The keywords, meteor shower, are entered in the text box (Figure 2-23).

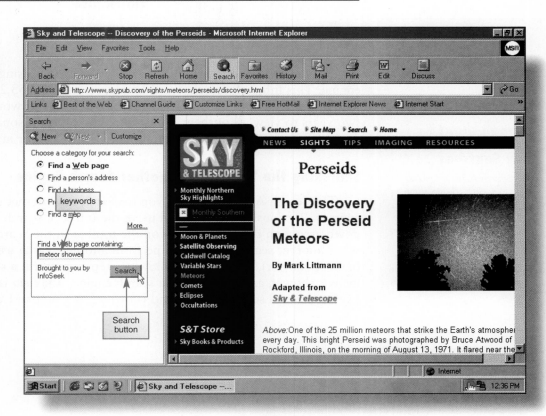

FIGURE 2-23

Click the Search button.

Internet Explorer displays the Infoseek search form in the Search bar and Infoseek performs the search (Figure 2-24). The search results in more than one million links and the first link is partially visible in the Search bar. The link on your computer may be different. To view additional links, scroll the Search bar.

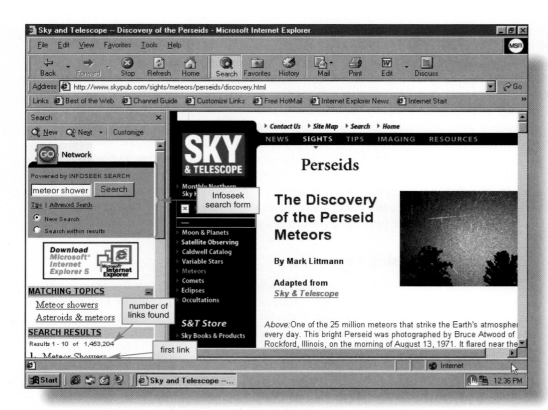

FIGURE 2-24

About

Key Searches

The Search Assistant makes it easy to search for the same keyword using several different search engines. Use the keywords, meteor shower, and the Search Assistant to search each search engine available in Search Assistant. Record the number of hits for each search engine.

**About**

Web Search Engines

Fierce competition exists among search engines. Each search engine claims to have the largest index of Web resources. This competition is healthy and, ensure that there are large, up-to-date indexes of Web resources.

As you can see, it is easy to find many Web pages using a keyword-based search engine. This Infoseek search, for example, returned 1,453,204 links (Figure 2-24). If you spent just one minute looking at each Web page, it would take you more than two years to view all of them. You can obtain more reasonable results by refining the search. Techniques to refine a search will be shown later in this project.

Searching the Web Using Another Search Engine

The Search Assistant allows you to search the Internet using any of nine search engines. Previously, you searched using the Infoseek search engine. Clicking the down arrow on the Next button on the toolbar in the Search bar allows you to select another search engine and perform another search using the same keywords (meteor shower). Perform the following step to perform a search using the keywords, meteor shower, and the AltaVista search engine. **AltaVista** is one of the more popular keyword-based search engines and is owned by Compaq Corporation.

Steps | **To Search the Web Using AltaVista**

1 **Click the down arrow on the Next button on the toolbar in the Search bar and then point to AltaVista on the menu.**

A menu displays below the Next button and the highlighted AltaVista name displays on the menu (Figure 2-25).

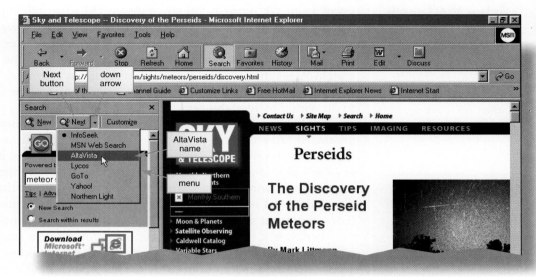

FIGURE 2-25

2 **Click AltaVista.**

The AltaVista simple search form displays in the Search bar, the keywords, meteor shower, display in the text box, and AltaVista performs the search (Figure 2-26). The search results in 222,240 links, and the first ten links display in the Search bar. The links on your computer may be different.

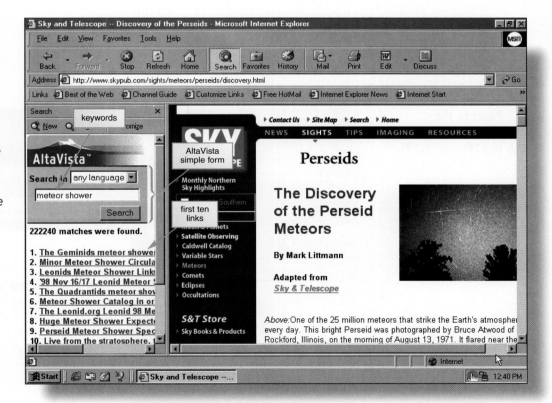

FIGURE 2-26

Refining the Search

You can instruct a search engine to search for two or more words that are physically close to each other by using the NEAR operator. If the keywords are within ten words of each other, the search engine will find the words.

Advanced Search Options

You can design an advanced search that will find Web pages that do not contain the keyword you specify using the NOT operator.

Refining a Web Search

You **refine** the search by providing more information the search engine can use to select a smaller, more useful set of results. Most search engines will perform a search for multiple keywords as if each word carries the same weight. This means Web pages containing any one of a set of multiple keywords or any combination of a set of multiple keywords will satisfy the search engine and be returned as a successful match. Pages that contain the word, meteor, for example, are included in the 222,240 pages returned by the search, even though some of those pages have nothing to do with a meteor shower.

To eliminate these pages, the keywords need to be more selective and better organized. You also can use features such as compound search criteria, in which the words, AND, OR, NOT, and NEAR, are used to control how individual words in a keyword phrase are used. You also may be able to arrange the links in order according to which word in a keyword phrase appears first in the Web page. You can use these advanced search capabilities to tell the search engine which of the keywords is more important and to cause multiple keywords to be considered as one search item.

Fortunately, most search engines help you refine a search by providing advanced searching capabilities. Search engines often have a link on their search pages to access advanced search options. AltaVista's link to advanced search options, labeled Advanced, displays in the expanded simple search form when you click the AltaVista logo in the Search bar. The following steps show how to refine the search using AltaVista's advanced search capability.

 ## To Display AltaVista's Advanced Search Form

1 **Point to the AltaVista logo in the Search bar (Figure 2-27).**

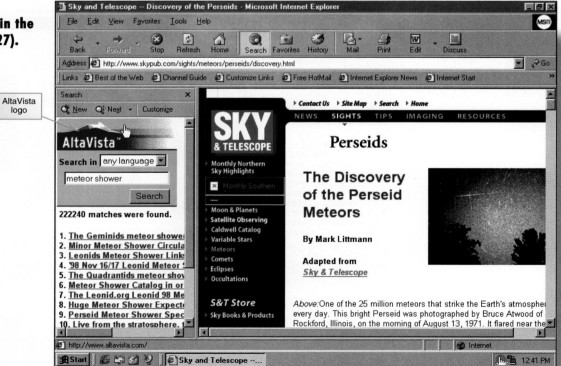

FIGURE 2-27

2 Click the AltaVista logo and then point to the Close button in the Search bar.

The AltaVista home page containing the expanded AltaVista simple search form displays on the screen (Figure 2-28).

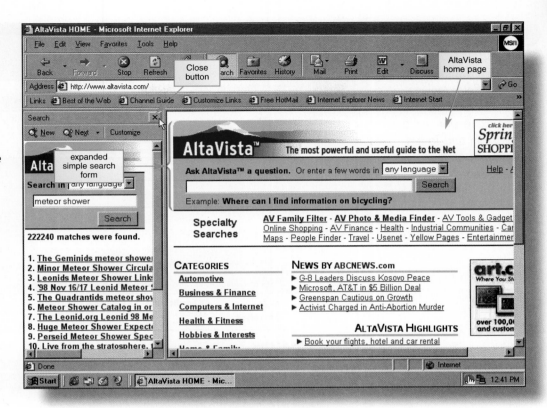

FIGURE 2-28

3 Click the Close button and then point to the Advanced link.

The Search bar closes, the AltaVista home page fills the display area, and the Advanced link displays in the AltaVista expanded simple search form (Figure 2-29). The expanded search form contains a box in which to select the language to use and a text box in which to enter keywords. Scrolling the display area reveals a list of categories, similar to Yahoo!'s directory, to use to search the Web.

FIGURE 2-29

Click Advanced.

The AltaVista advanced search form displays (Figure 2-30). The Enter ranking keywords in text box, Enter boolean expression text box, and the From and To text boxes display on the advanced search form.

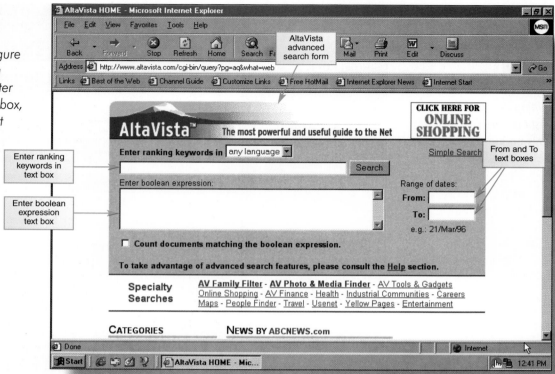

FIGURE 2-30

The Enter boolean expression text box is used to enter one or more keywords, separated by an appropriate **Boolean operator**, such as AND, OR, NOT, or NEAR. The **AND operator** and **OR operator** allow you to create keyword searches containing compound conditions. The **NOT operator** is used to find pages that do not contain certain keywords.

The **NEAR operator** is used to find pages in which two keywords are within ten words of each other. By using these operators, you can exercise greater control over the searching process and obtain a manageable number of links with a high probability they will contain useful information. Table 2-2 describes the operators and gives an example of each one.

Table 2-2	
OPERATOR	*EXAMPLE*
AND	Finds only documents containing all of the specified words or phrases. Mary AND lamb finds documents with both the word, Mary, and the word, lamb.
OR	Finds documents containing at least one of the specified words or phrases. Mary OR lamb finds documents containing either Mary or lamb. The documents found also can contain both words, but do not have to.
NOT	Excludes documents containing the specified word or phrase. Mary AND NOT lamb finds documents with Mary but not containing lamb. NOT cannot stand alone. You must use it with another operator, such as AND. For example, AltaVista does not accept Mary NOT lamb, but does accept Mary AND NOT lamb.
NEAR	Finds documents containing both specified words or phrases within ten words of each other. Mary NEAR lamb would find the nursery rhyme, but probably not religious or Christmas-related documents.

The Enter ranking keywords in text box influences the order in which AltaVista displays the links that are found as a result of performing a search. Links associated with Web pages containing search words entered in the Enter ranking keywords in text box will appear first in the list of links. The following steps show how to use AltaVista's advanced search form to refine the search.

Steps | **To Perform an Advanced Search Using AltaVista**

1 **Click the Enter ranking keywords in text box and then type** Perseid **in the box. Click the Enter boolean expression text box and then type** meteor shower and Perseid **in the box. Point to the Search button.**

The advanced search form displays with the keyword, Perseid, in the Enter ranking keywords in text box and "meteor shower" and Perseid in the Enter boolean expression text box (Figure 2-31).

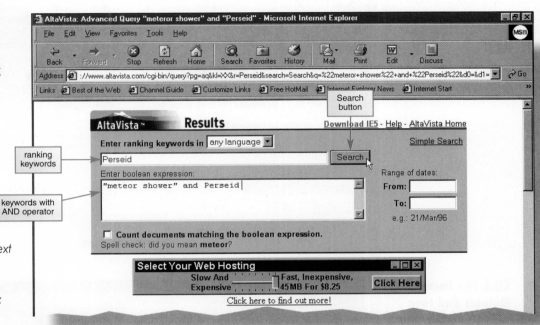

FIGURE 2-31

2 **Click the Search button.**

AltaVista performs the search and finds 1,141 Web pages (Figure 2-32). This search returned a much more manageable number of links.

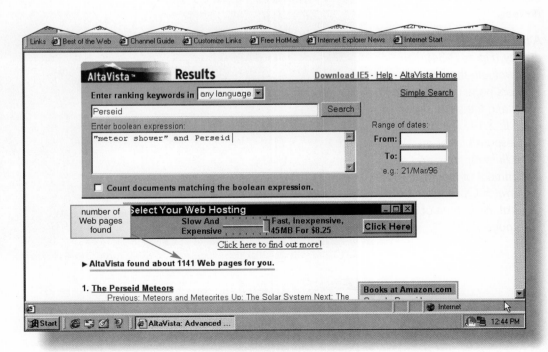

FIGURE 2-32

3 **Scroll to display the first link (The Perseid Meteors) and then point to the link.**

The link contains the title of the Web page (The Perseid Meteors), a few lines of text from the Web page, the URL of the Web page, the date of last modification, the size of the Web page, and the language in which the Web page displays (Figure 2-33).

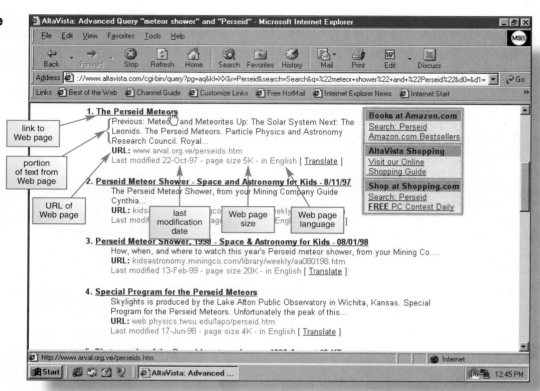

FIGURE 2-33

4 **Click The Perseid Meteors and then scroll down to display the section (The Perseids) that describes the Perseid Meteor.**

A title and three paragraphs display (Figure 2-34). You can evaluate the Perseid Meteors page using the worksheet and the steps shown on page IE 2.10. The organization responsible for the Web page (Information Services Department of the Royal Greenwich Observatory) displays at the bottom of the Web page.

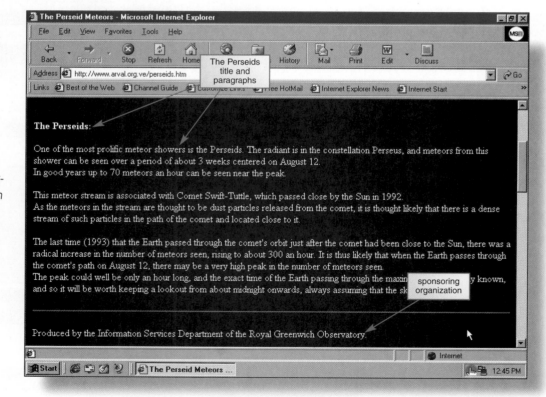

FIGURE 2-34

The AND operator in the keywords creates a compound condition meaning both "meteor shower" and Perseid must be in the Web page for it to be considered a successful match. In addition, because the words, meteor and shower, are enclosed in quotation marks, the two words must appear next to each other on the Web page for the page to be considered a successful match. Finally, placing Perseid in the Enter ranking keywords in text box instructs the search engine to place Web pages containing the keyword first when placing the search results in order. Using keywords and advanced searching techniques, you have refined a search to locate many useful Web resources successfully.

Successful Searching Techniques

Recall that the initial search for meteor showers using the AltaVista simple search form returned 222,240 links (see Figure 2-26 on page IE 2.23). The second attempt using the AltaVista advanced search form returned 1,141 links, and the pages were more useful. This illustrates the first successful searching technique: **be as specific as possible with keywords**. Put some thought into what small group of words most represents the topic or is used frequently with it. Choose the best from this group of words to use with the search engine.

If you receive only a few or no useful links, make the keywords slightly more general and try again. For example, assume you want to find information about tax-exempt municipal bonds. A specific-to-very-general list of keywords might be: "tax-exempt bonds", "municipal bonds", "tax-free bonds", "tax-free investments", bonds, or investments.

Try to match as many relevant words as possible. This returns more links with better odds that something useful will be among them, although you may have to spend some time looking through all of them. Most search engines support the use of Boolean operators, such as AND, OR, NOT, and NEAR, and parenthesis for grouping. Use the operators to specify complex phrases and conditions. For example, you might use the keywords, (rocket OR shuttle) AND experiment, to search for experiments that were performed in outer space. Use the search engine's Help feature to learn which Boolean operators are available and how to use them.

Another useful technique offered by some search engines is to indicate that certain keywords must appear on the Web page, or that certain keywords cannot appear on the Web page. A plus sign (+) indicates inclusion and a minus sign (–) indicates exclusion. You place the + or – immediately before a particular keyword. You can use the **inclusion or exclusion capability** to help narrow the search. For example, searching for the keywords, *gold –motorcycle*, will return links containing the keyword gold, but not those containing the keyword motorcycle, thus eliminating any Goldwing motorcycle pages.

Another useful feature is the **wildcard character**. Several search engines allow you to use the asterisk (*) to indicate zero, one, or more characters in a word. For example, searching for immun* will return hits for immune, immunology, immunologist, and any other word beginning with the letters, i-m-m-u-n. Use wildcards if the spelling of a keyword is unknown or may be incorrectly specified on the Web page. Table 2-3 on the next page provides a guide for useful search tips, including the use of wildcard characters.

More About

Choosing Search Engines

With the Web growing and changing every day, it is impossible for one search engine to catalog all the available Web pages. Many people choose one favorite search engine, however, and use it exclusively. This makes it easier to search because they are familiar with the search engine's search form.

Table 2-3

TIP OR WILDCARD	DESCRIPTION
Use parentheses to group items	Use parentheses ( ) to specify precedence in a search. For example, to search for documents that contain information about both President Clinton and President Bush try this advanced query: president AND ((George NEAR Bush) AND ((Bill OR William) NEAR Clinton)).
Use wildcard character	Use an asterisk (*) to broaden a search. To find any words that start with gold, use gold* to find matches for gold, goldfinch, goldfinger, golden, and so on. Use this character if the word you are searching for could have different endings (for example, do not search for dog, search for dog* if it may be plural).
Use quotes to surround a phrase	If you know a certain phrase will appear on the page you are looking for, put the phrase in quotes (for example, try entering song lyrics such as "you ain't nothin' but a hound dog").
Use either specific or general keywords	Carry out searches using specific keywords to obtain fewer, more precise links, or general keywords to obtain numerous, less precise links.

More About

Citing Web Sources

All of the style guides mentioned in the text differ slightly from one another on the format of the citation used to cite a Web source. Check with your instructor for the accepted format your school uses. Check out the two most widely used style guides - Modern Language Association (www.mla.org) and American Psychological Association (www.apa.org).

Creating a Working Bibliography

Once you find a good Web source, how do you record it? A **working bibliography** will help you organize and compile the resources you find, so that you can cite them as sources in the list of works cited. For Web resources, you should note the author or authors, title of the page, URL, date of publication, date of the last revision, date you accessed the resource, heading of any part or section where the relevant information is located, navigation instructions necessary to find the resource, and other pertinent information.

When you are compiling your information, you often will need to look for an e-mail address on the Web page to find the author. You may have to write to the person responsible for the Web site, or **Webmaster**, and ask for the author's name. First, display the home page of the Web site to see if a directory or contact section is listed, as you did for the Discovery of the Perseid Meteors Web page. If you do not find a directory or contact section, display the bottom of the Web page. Many Web pages include the e-mail address of the Webmaster at the bottom of the page.

Traditionally, index cards have been used to record relevant information about a work, and you still can use index cards to record Web research. However, several electronic means are now available for keeping track of the Web sites you visit and the information you find.

- You can e-mail pertinent information to yourself and store the messages in separate folders. Use one folder for each point or category you are researching.
- You can store the pertinent information in separate document files using copy and paste techniques. Use a separate file for each point or category you research.
- You can create a folder in the Favorites list and then place related favorites you find on the Web in that folder.
- You can print the promising Web page.

To demonstrate how to record relevant information about a Web resource, the following steps show how to copy information from The Perseid Meteors Web page and paste it into a WordPad document. The copy and paste technique you will use was illustrated in Project 1 on page IE 1.41.

To Record Relevant Information About a Research Source Using WordPad

1 **Click the Start button on the taskbar, point to Programs, point to Accessories, and then click WordPad. Point to The Perseid Meteors button on the taskbar.**

Windows launches the WordPad application and the WordPad window displays (Figure 2-35). A Document - WordPad button displays on the taskbar.

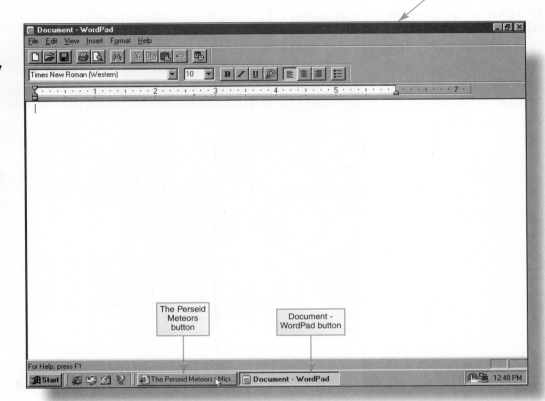

FIGURE 2-35

2 **Click The Perseid Meteors button to display the Microsoft Internet Explorer window and then point to the beginning of the title above the three paragraphs.**

The Microsoft Internet Explorer window, containing The Perseid Meteors Web page, displays (Figure 2-36). The mouse pointer displays to the left of the title.

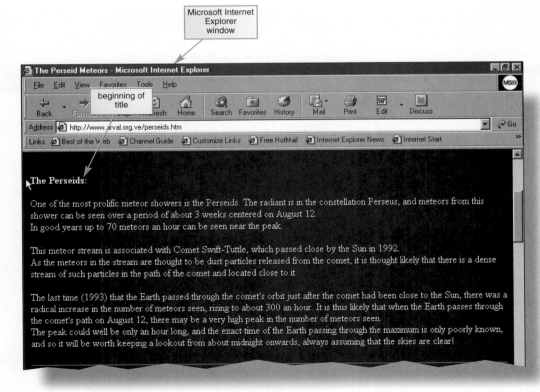

FIGURE 2-36

3 **Drag to select the title and three paragraphs, right-click the selected text, and then point to Copy on the shortcut menu.**

The text is selected and a shortcut menu displays (Figure 2-37).

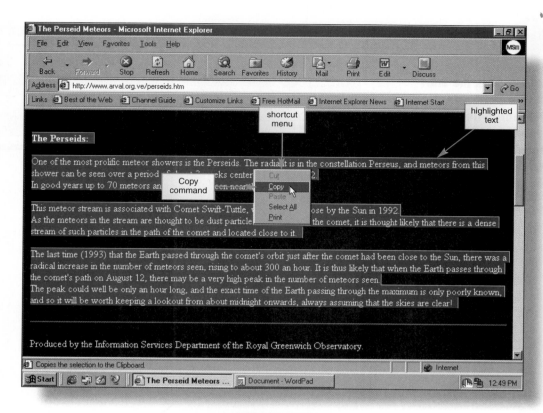

FIGURE 2-37

4 **Click Copy and then click the Document - WordPad button on the taskbar.**

Windows copies the high-lighted text to the clipboard and the Document - WordPad window displays (Figure 2-38).

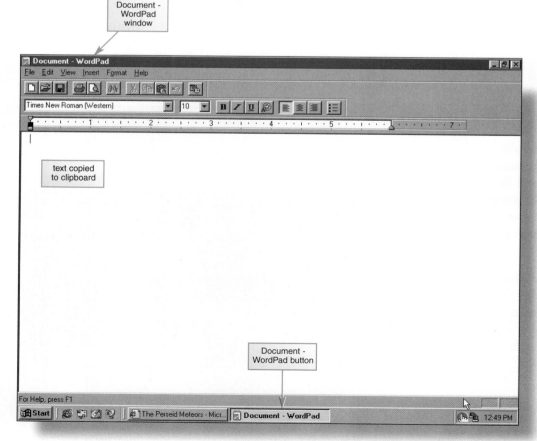

FIGURE 2-38

5 Type www.arval.
org.ue/perseids.
htm **in the WordPad document, press the ENTER key,
type** Royal Greenwich
Observatory **in the
WordPad document, press
the ENTER key, type today's
date in the WordPad
document, and then press
the ENTER key twice.**

*The URL, organization name,
and today's date display in
the WordPad window (Figure
2-39). These are some of the
pieces of information needed
when citing the work in a
research paper.*

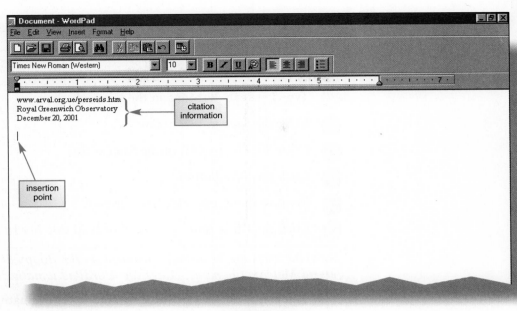

FIGURE 2-39

6 **Right-click the
blank document,
click Paste on the shortcut
menu, and then scroll to
view the top of the Web
page.**

*Windows pastes the contents
of the clipboard in the
WordPad window at the location of the insertion point
(Figure 2-40).*

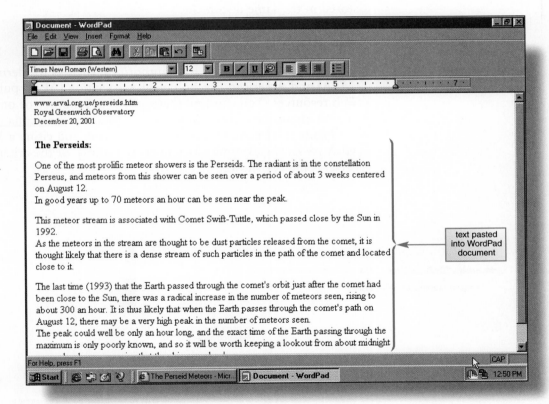

FIGURE 2-40

Saving a WordPad Document

To prevent the accidental loss of the WordPad document, you should formulate
an appropriate file name, such as Perseid Meteors, for the document and save the
document on a 3½-inch floppy disk in drive A. After saving the file, quit WordPad.
Perform the steps on the next page to save the WordPad document on the floppy
disk in drive A using the file name, Perseid Meteors, and quit WordPad.

TO SAVE A WORDPAD DOCUMENT AND QUIT WORDPAD

1 Insert a formatted floppy disk in drive A.

2 Click the Save button on the toolbar.

3 Type Perseid Meteors in the File name box.

4 Click the Save in box arrow.

5 Click 3½ Floppy (A:) in the Save in list.

6 Click the Save button.

7 Remove the floppy disk from drive A.

8 Click the Close button in the WordPad title bar to quit WordPad.

WordPad saves the WordPad document on the floppy disk in drive A using the Perseid Meteors file name, closes the WordPad window, and quits WordPad.

If you are using the electronic technique for evaluating a Web source, you can save the research information at the bottom of the worksheet document. Then, both the evaluation criteria and the research information for a particular Web page are stored in the same document.

Citing Web Sources

Most of the preferred style authorities, such as Modern Language Association (MLA) and American Psychological Association (APA), publish standards for citing Web resources. You can find these guides at a library or on the Web. Online information about these style guides can be found at www.mla.org and www.apa.org.

Figure 2-41 contains an example of using and citing a Web resource using the MLA style. The example documents the source of the criteria for the activity of the Perseids meteor shower.

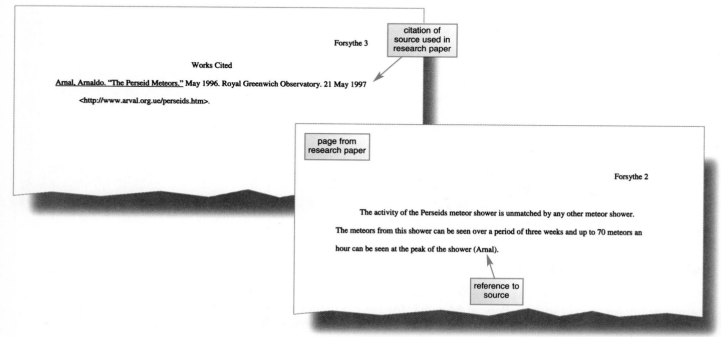

FIGURE 2-41

As you have learned in this project, the World Wide Web can be an informative and valuable source of information. By using proper searching and note-taking techniques, and asking the right questions about the usefulness of a Web resource, you can add to the information base you use to write a paper or speech. Always remember, however, that Web sources should complement, not replace, printed sources for locating information.

Other Ways to Use Search Assistant

In this project, you first searched for Web pages using the Yahoo! directory and then searched for Web pages using the Search Assistant and the keyword-based Infoseek and AltaVista search engines. You also can use the Search Assistant to search for e-mail addresses, company information, maps, encyclopedia articles, and newsgroups. The following sections illustrate how to search for an e-mail address, a landmark, and an encyclopedia article.

Searching the Web for an E-Mail Address

When you select the Find a person's address category in the Search bar, the Search Assistant prompts you to search for a mailing address or an e-mail address by entering the first and last name, city, and state/province. Clicking the Search button searches the BigFoot or InfoSpace Web site for the mailing address or e-mail address. Perform the following steps to search for the e-mail address of one of the authors of this book when you know only the author's first and last name.

Steps To Search the Web for an E-Mail Address

1 **Click the Search button on the Standard Buttons toolbar and then point to the New button on the toolbar in the Search bar.**

The Search bar displays in the Microsoft Internet Explorer window (Figure 2-42).

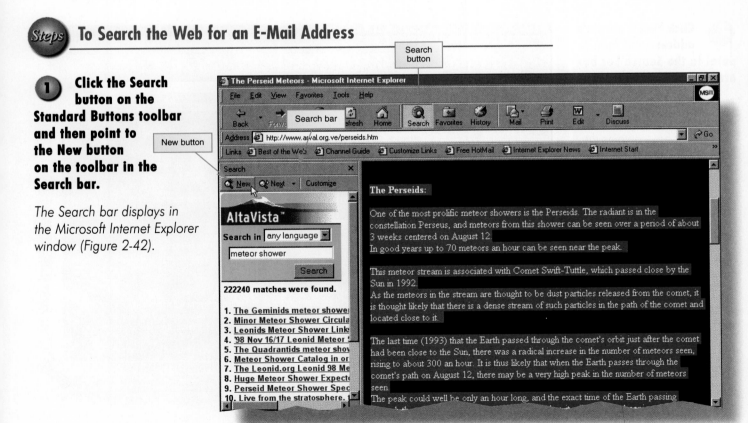

FIGURE 2-42

2 **Click the New button and then point to Find a person's address in the Search bar.**

Internet Explorer begins a new search, the Find a Web page category remains selected, and the insertion point displays in the text box (Figure 2-43).

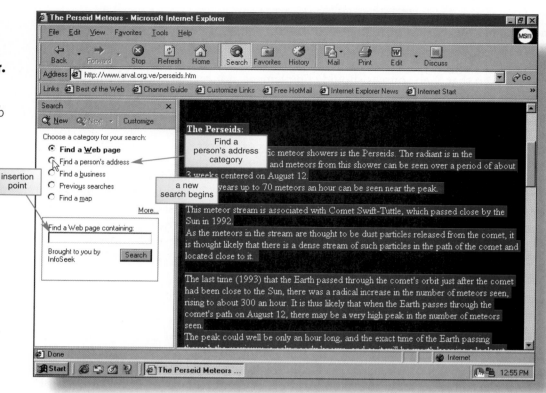

FIGURE 2-43

3 **Click Find a person's address and then point to the Search For box arrow.**

The Find a person's address category is selected and the rectangular box contains the Search For box, First Name text box, Last Name text box, City text box, and State/ Province text box (Figure 2-44). The Search For box contains the mailing address entry and the rectangular box contains the Bigfoot entry. The Bigfoot entry may be different on your computer.

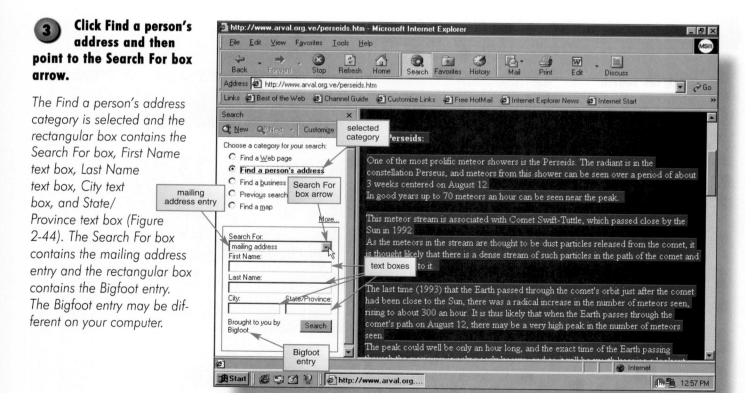

FIGURE 2-44

4 Click the Search For box arrow, click e-mail address, type Steven in the First Name text box, type Forsythe in the Last Name text box, and then point to the Search button.

The words, e-mail address, display in the Search For box, the author's first name (Steven) displays in the First Name text box, and the author's last name (Forsythe) displays in the Last Name text box (Figure 2-45).

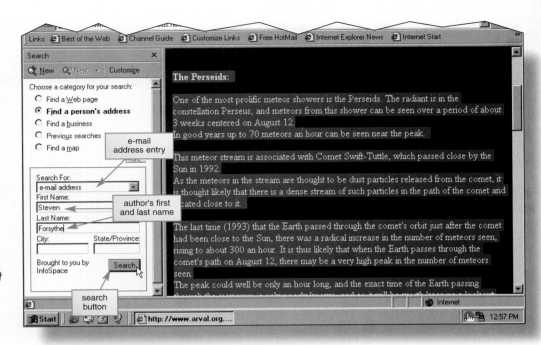

FIGURE 2-45

5 Click the Search button and scroll the Search bar to display the results of the search.

Internet Explorer searches the Bigfoot database for the e-mail address of the author and displays in the Search bar three links found during the search (Figure 2-46). The links on your computer may be different.

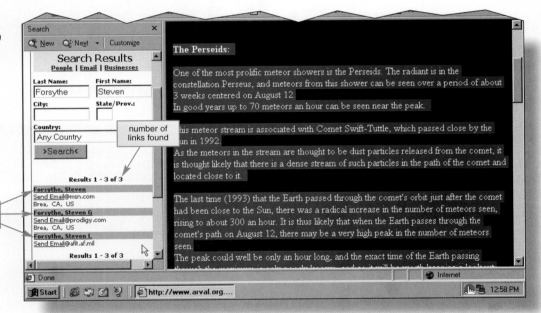

FIGURE 2-46

Searching the Web for a Map

When you select the Find a map category in the Search bar, the Search Assistant prompts you to search for an address, company information, or place or landmark, and then enter the appropriate information to perform the search. When you enter a place or landmark and click the Search button, the Expedia Maps Web site is searched for the appropriate map. Perform the steps on the next page to search for the Cobo Hall landmark in Detroit, Michigan.

Other Ways

1. Type www.bigfoot.com in Address box, click Go button, type first and last name in Search text box, press ENTER key

2. Type www.infospace.com in Address box, click Go button, click White Pages, type last name, type first name, click Search button

To Search for a Place or Landmark

1 **Click the New button on the toolbar on the Search bar and then click the Find a map category.**

The selected Find a map category displays in the Search bar, the word, Address, displays in the Search For box, and the Expedia Maps search engine name displays (Figure 2-47). Unless you decide to use another search engine, Expedia will search for an address.

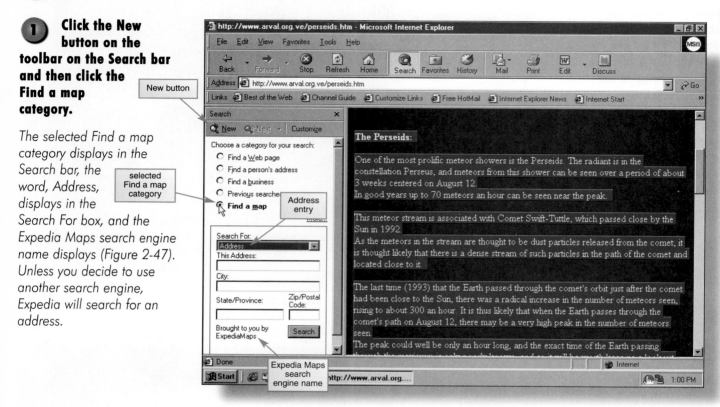

FIGURE 2-47

2 **Click the Search For box arrow and then click Place or landmark. Type** Cobo Hall **in the This place or landmark text box, and then point to the Search button.**

The words, Place or land-mark, display in the Search For box and the landmark name, Cobo Hall, displays in the This place or landmark text box (Figure 2-48).

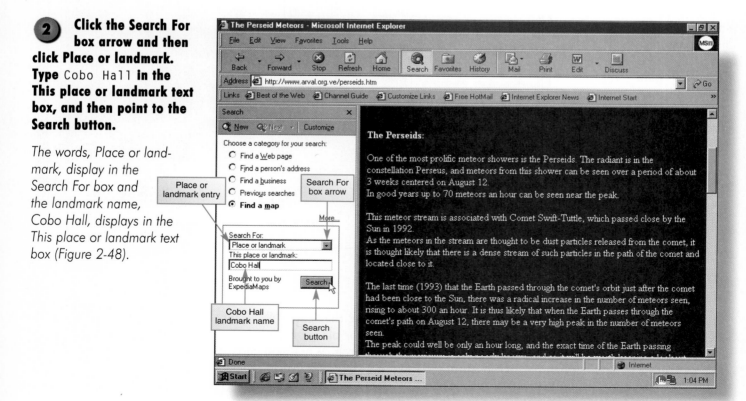

FIGURE 2-48

3 **Click the Search button and then point to the Cobo Hall, point of interest, Michigan, United States link.**

A list of possible locations meeting the search criteria displays in the Search bar (Figure 2-49).

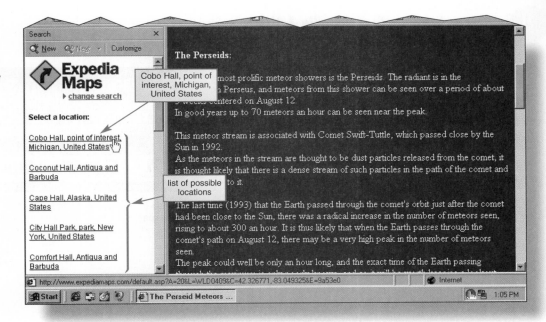

FIGURE 2-49

4 **Click Cobo Hall, point of interest, Michigan, United States.**

Expedia searches the Microsoft Expedia Maps database and displays the Expedia Maps home page in the display area (Figure 2-50). The home page contains a list of links, the Detroit area map (including the location of the Cobo Hall) associated with the first link in the list, and the local highlights for the area. The search results, local highlights, and map shown on your computer may be different.

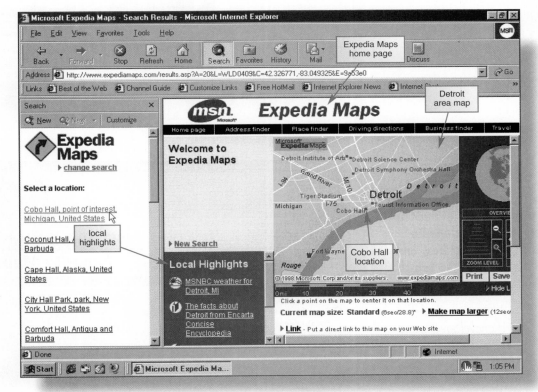

FIGURE 2-50

Searching the Web for an Encyclopedia Article

When you select the Find in encyclopedia category in the Search bar, the Search Assistant prompts you to enter a subject. Clicking the Search button performs a search of the Encarta encyclopedia and returns a list of links to articles in the encyclopedia. Perform the steps on the next two pages to search for articles on the greenhouse effect.

Other **Ways**

1. Type www.expediamap.com in Address box, click Go button, click Place finder, type landmark name in Geographic name or point of interest text box, click Go button

Steps **To Search for an Encyclopedia Article**

1 **Click the New button on the toolbar of the Search bar and then point to the more link in the Search bar.**

A new search begins and the contents of the Search bar change (Figure 2-51).

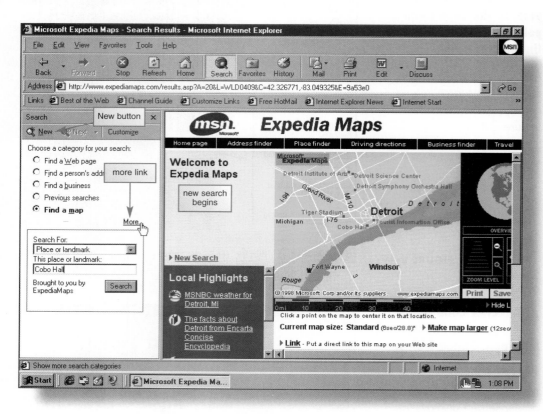

FIGURE 2-51

2 **Click more, click Find in encyclopedia, type** greenhouse effect **in the Find encyclopedia articles on text box, and then point to the Search button.**

Two additional categories (Find in encyclopedia and Find in Newsgroups) and the Find encyclopedia articles on text box display in the Search bar (Figure 2-52). The Find in encyclopedia category is selected, and the words, greenhouse effect, display in the Find encyclopedia articles on text box (Figure 2-52).

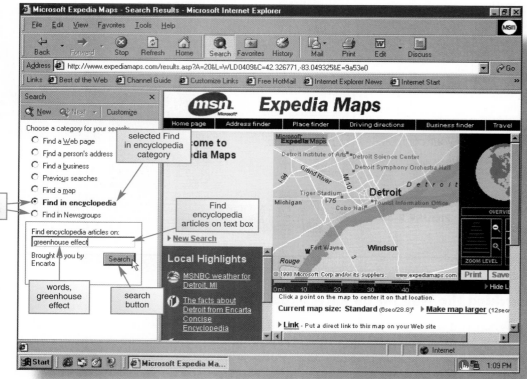

FIGURE 2-52

3 **Click the Search button and then point to Greenhouse Effect in the Search bar.**

Expedia searches the Microsoft Encarta encyclopedia and then displays a list of links (Figure 2-53). The search results displayed on your computer may be different.

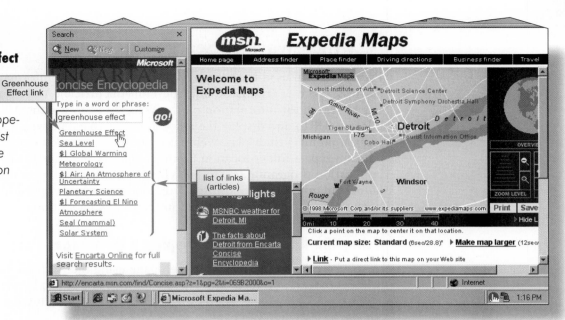

FIGURE 2-53

4 **Click Greenhouse Effect.**

Internet Explorer displays the Encarta home page, search form, various links, and the definition for Greenhouse Effect (Figure 2-54).

5 **Scroll the display area to read about the greenhouse effect.**

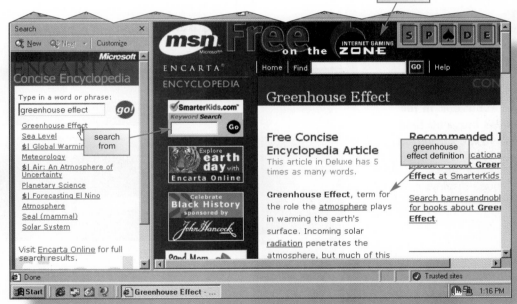

FIGURE 2-54

Closing the Search Bar

After you have finished searching, close the Search bar. Perform the following step to close the Search bar.

TO CLOSE THE SEARCH BAR

1 Click the Close button on the Search bar.

The Search bar closes.

Other Ways

1. Type www.encarta.com in Address box, click Go button, type word or phrase in find in text box, click GO button, click word or phrase link

Other Ways to Search the Web

Previously you used the Search Assistant to search for information (Web page, e-mail address, place or landmark, and encyclopedia article). You also can use the Address bar to search for information on the Web. You can use the Address bar to type an address (URL) and display the associated Web page or type a keyword or phrase (search inquiry) to display Web pages containing the keyword or phrase. In addition, you can type a folder location (path) to display the contents of the folder, type an application program name to launch a program, and type a document name to launch an application and display the document in the application window. Three of these operations are illustrated in the following sections.

Using the Address Bar to Display a Web Page

To search for and display a Web page using the Address bar, you must type an address (URL), and then click the Go button. For example, the URL for the ESPN.com Web page is www.espn.com. Perform the following steps to type the URL for the ESPN.com Web page in the Address box and display the ESPN.com Web page in the browser window.

To Display a Web Page Using the Address Bar

1 **Click the Address box, type** www.espn.com **in the Address box, and then point to the Go button.**

The URL for the ESPN.com Web page displays in the Address box (Figure 2-55).

FIGURE 2-55

2 **Click the Go button.**

The URL for the ESPN.com Web page displays in the Address box and the ESPN.com Web page displays in the ESPN.com - Microsoft Internet Explorer window (Figure 2-56).

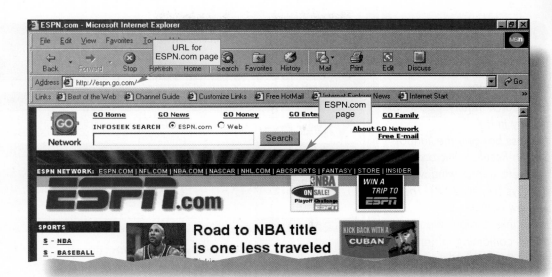

FIGURE 2-56

Using the Address Bar to Search for Information on the Internet

To search for information on the Web using the Address bar, you must type a keyword or phrase and then click the Go button. For example, you might enter the phrase, national weather, enclosed in quotation marks, to search for and display the hyperlinks of all Web pages that contain the phrase, national weather. Entering the phrase without quotation marks will result in displaying Web pages that contain either the word (national or weather) instead of the phrase, national weather.

Perform the steps below to type the phrase "national weather" in the Address box and display all Web pages containing the phrase.

 To Search for Information on the Web Using the Address Bar

1 **Click the Address box, type** "national weather" **in the Address box, and then point to the Go button.**

The phrase "national weather" displays in the Address box (Figure 2-57)

FIGURE 2-57

2 Click the Go button.

The Internet Explorer icon, Web page URL, and search inquiry display in the Address box and the Yahoo! Search Results - Microsoft Internet Explorer window displays (Figure 2-58). The window contains several hyperlinks to other Web pages containing information about the national weather.

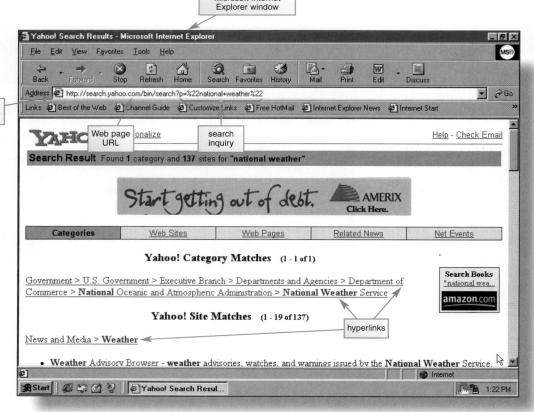

FIGURE 2-58

Using the Address Bar to Display the Contents of a Folder

To display the contents of a folder using the Address bar, you must type the path of the folder and then click the Go button. A **path** is the means of navigating to a specific location on a computer or network. To specify a path, you must type the driver letter, followed by a colon (:), a backslash (\), and the folder name. For example, the path for the Windows folder on drive C is C:\WINDOWS.

Perform the following steps to type the path of the Windows folder and display the contents of the Windows folder.

 To Display the Contents of a Folder Using the Address Bar

1 Click the Address box, type
c:\windows **in the Address box, and then point to the Go button.**

The path of the Windows folder displays in the Address box (Figure 2-59).

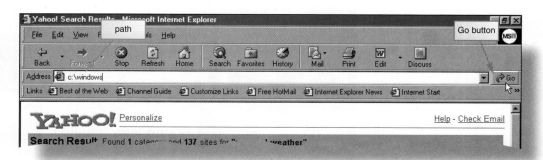

FIGURE 2-59

2 **Click the Go button.**

A folder icon and the Windows path display in the Address box and the Windows - Microsoft Internet Explorer window containing the contents of the Windows folder opens on the desktop (Figure 2-60).

3 **Click the Close button in the Windows window.**

The Windows window closes.

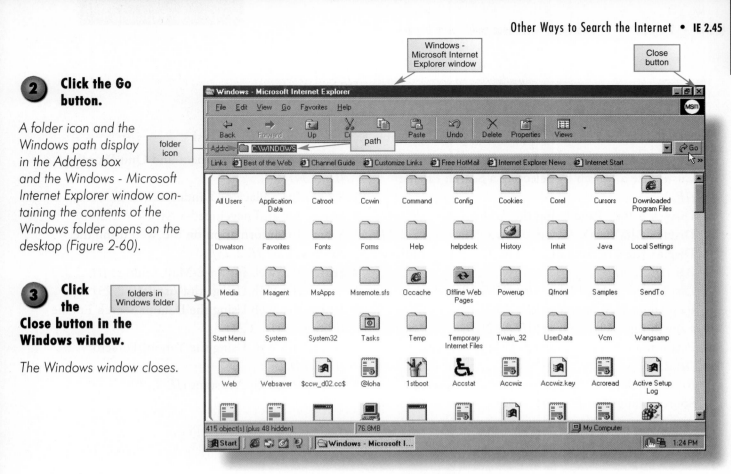

FIGURE 2-60

In addition to using the Address bar to display a Web page, search for information on the Web, and display the contents of a folder, you also can use the Address bar to launch a program and open a document. To launch an application, such as the Notepad application, you type the application name (Notepad) in the Address box and then click the Go button. The Untitled - Notepad window will display on the desktop. To display a document, such as the Tips.txt document, you type the document name (Tips.txt) in the Address box and click the Go button. The Tips document will display in the Tips - Notepad window.

Project Summary

In this project, the five general types of Web pages and the two general types of search engines were described. You learned how to evaluate a Web page as a potential source for research. You learned how to search the Web using the Yahoo! directory. You used the Infoseek and AltaVista search engines to enter keywords and use advanced search techniques. You recorded relevant information about a potential source for future reference and learned how to write a citation for a Web resource. In addition, you searched the Web for an e-mail address, a map, and an encyclopedia article.

What You Should Know

Having completed this project, you now should be able to perform the following tasks:

- Close the Search Bar *(IE 2.41)*
- Customize a Search by Selecting a Search Engine *(IE 2.22)*
- Display a Web Page Using the Address Bar *(IE 2.42)*
- Display AltaVista's Advanced Search Form *(IE 2.24)*
- Display the Contents of a Folder Using the Address Bar *(IE 2.44)*
- Display the Yahoo! Directory *(IE 2.13)*
- Evaluate a Web Resource *(IE 2.17)*
- Launch Internet Explorer *(IE 2.12)*
- Perform an Advanced Search Using AltaVista *(IE 2.27)*
- Record Relevant Information About a Research Source Using WordPad *(IE 2.31)*
- Save a WordPad Document and Quit WordPad *(IE 2.34)*
- Search for a Place or Landmark *(IE 2.38)*
- Search for an Encyclopedia Article *(IE 2.40)*
- Search for Information on the Web using the Address Bar *(IE 2.43)*
- Search the Web for an E-Mail Address *(IE 2.35)*
- Search the Web Using AltaVista *(IE 2.23)*
- Search the Web Using the Default Search Engine (Infoseek) *(IE 2.21)*
- Search the Web Using the Yahoo! Directory *(IE 2.14)*
- Start the Search Assistant *(IE 2.20)*

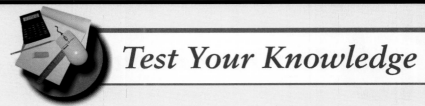

Test Your Knowledge

1 True/False

Instructions: Circle T if the statement is true or F if the statement is false.

T F 1. You can rely solely on the Web for research information because the Web does not change frequently.

T F 2. An advocacy Web page contains content that describes a cause, opinion, or idea.

T F 3. A personal Web page usually is associated with a larger, well-known organization.

T F 4. File transfer protocol is a method for transferring files over the Internet.

T F 5. Once a potential source of information is found, it should be evaluated for its reliability, significance, and content.

T F 6. The criteria for evaluating a Web source are authorship, accuracy, accountability, and topic and scope of coverage.

T F 7. A search engine that organizes Web pages in a hierarchical menu is called a directory.

T F 8. The word or phrase that describes the topic you are searching for is called a searchword.

T F 9. Providing more information for the search engine so it can select a smaller, more useful set of hits is called tunneling.

T F 10. Plus and minus signs are useful with keywords to force inclusion or exclusion of certain words.

2 Multiple Choice

Instructions: Circle the correct response.

1. Web pages can be organized into several categories: news, business/marketing, personal, informational, and
   _____.
   a. advocacy
   b. government
   c. FTP
   d. reference

2. FTP stands for _____.
   a. find the program
   b. file transfer protocol
   c. file transfer program
   d. file text parameters

3. _____ is **not** a Boolean operator.
   a. AND
   b. OR
   c. WITH
   d. NEAR

4. Determining whether a copyright notice appears on a Web page falls under the _____ evaluation criteria.
   a. advocacy
   b. accuracy
   c. copyright
   d. authorship

5. A search engine that does not use keywords to perform a search is called a _____.
   a. directory
   b. gopher
   c. FTP
   d. robot

6. Search engines search indexes that are compiled using special programs called _____.
   a. autosearchers
   b. gophers
   c. directories
   d. spiders

(continued)

Test Your Knowledge

Multiple Choice *(continued)*

7. A word or phrase used by a search engine to carry out a search is called a _____.
   a. directory   b. gopher   c. keyword   d. link
8. A successful match results in a list of _____.
   a. links   b. directories   c. search engines   d. marks
9. To indicate that a certain word should **not** appear in a Web page, place _____ immediately before the word when defining the search criteria.
   a. +   b. –   c. "   d. |
10. You can search for a folder on a hard drive if you know the path and use the _____.
   a. Search bar
   b. AltaVista search engine
   c. Address bar
   d. Yahoo! directory

3 Understanding Web Page Classifications

Instructions: Listed below are the five general categories into which most Web pages fall. In the spaces provided, write a brief description of the indicated category. For each category, include two examples of groups, organizations, or other entities that may publish that type of page on the Web.

1. Advocacy:

_____

_____

_____

2. Business/marketing:

_____

_____

_____

3. Informational:

_____

_____

_____

4. News:

_____

_____

_____

5. Personal:

_____

_____

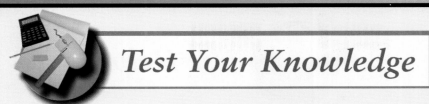

Test Your Knowledge

4 Understanding Web Page Evaluation Criteria

Instructions: Because most Web pages are not reviewed for accuracy, you should evaluate the usefulness of any Web resource you decide to use. Listed below are four criteria used to evaluate Web pages. In the spaces provided, list at least three pieces of information found on a Web page and related to the criterion that can be used to evaluate a Web page.

1. Authorship

_____
_____
_____

2. Accuracy

_____
_____
_____

3. Currency

_____
_____
_____

4. Topic and Scope of Coverage

_____
_____
_____

5 Understanding Internet Explorer Searching Terminology

Instructions: Define the following terms.

TERM   **DEFINITION**

1. search engine   _____
2. directory   _____
3. keyword   _____
4. wildcard character _____
5. spider   _____
6. Boolean operator   _____
7. FTP   _____
8. gopher   _____

Use Help

1 Obtaining Help for Infoseek

Instructions: Use Internet Explorer and a computer to perform the following tasks.

1. If necessary, connect to the Internet and launch Internet Explorer.

2. Click the Address box, type www.infoseek.com in the box, and click the Go button to display the Infoseek home page.

3. Click the How to search link at the top of the home page (Figure 2-61).

4. Print the Web page containing the How to Search information.

5. Click the Help Index link (Figure 2-62).

6. Print the Web page containing the Help index.

7. Write your name on the printouts and hand them in to your instructor.

8. Close all Help windows.

FIGURE 2-61

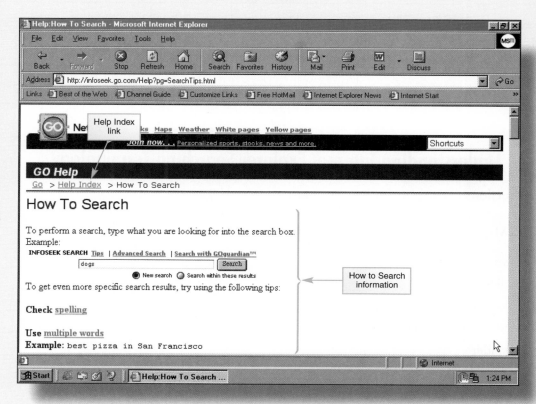

FIGURE 2-62

2 Obtaining Help for AltaVista

Instructions: Use Internet Explorer and a computer to perform the following tasks.

1. If necessary, connect to the Internet and launch Internet Explorer.
2. Click the Address box, type `www.altavista.com` in the box, and click the Go button to display the AltaVista home page (Figure 2-63).

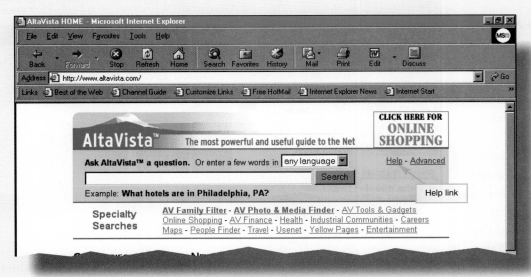

FIGURE 2-63

3. Click the Help link on the AltaVista home page.
4. Click the Basics link and answer the following questions:
   a. What is an index? _____
   b. What does a wildcard allow you to do? _____
   c. Excluding text, what are three other items you can search for on a Web page?
   _____
5. Click the Advanced Help link and answer the following questions:
   a. The Boolean operators are AND, OR, NOT, and NEAR. What symbols can you use in place of these words in a Boolean search? _____
   b. What is Web archeology? Give an example. _____
6. Click the Usenet link and answer the following questions:
   a. What is Usenet? _____
   b. When you choose to search Usenet, how old are the articles you find? _____
7. Click the Frequently Asked Questions link and answer the following questions:
   a. How does AltaVista determine which site comes up first in the search results?
   _____
   b. List two of the top ten frequently asked questions. _____
8. Close all windows.

In the Lab

1 Searching the Web For Web Pages

Instructions: Use Internet Explorer and a computer to perform the following tasks.

1. If necessary, connect to the Internet and launch Internet Explorer.
2. Click the Address box, type www.yahoo.com in the box, and click the Go button to display the Yahoo! directory.
3. Using the Yahoo! directory, find and print one Web page that is representative of each of the five general Web

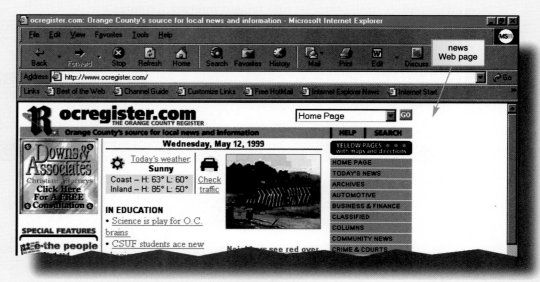

FIGURE 2-64

page types (advocacy, informational, business/marketing, news, and personal). Figure 2-64 shows an example of a news Web page.
4. On each printout, write your name, general type the page represents, and brief explanation supporting your decision as to the type. Hand in the pages to your instructor.
5. Quit Internet Explorer.

2 Searching the Web Using the Yahoo! Directory

Instructions: Use Internet Explorer and a computer to perform the following tasks.

1. If necessary, connect to the Internet and launch Internet Explorer.
2. Click the Address box, type www.yahoo.com in the box, and click the Go button to display the Yahoo! directory.
3. Using the Yahoo! directory, search for and print a Web page containing a graphic image that is representative of each of the following types of artwork: computer generated artwork, graffiti, furniture design, sculpture, and landscape architecture. Figure 2-65 shows a gallery of digital images created by Douglas Armand.
4. On each printout, write your name and the type of artwork the Web page represents. Hand in the pages to your instructor.
5. Quit Internet Explorer.

In the Lab

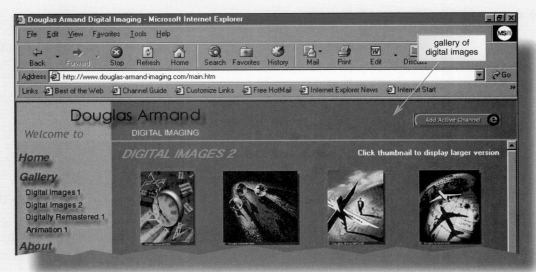

FIGURE 2-65

3 Searching the Web Using the Lycos Directory

Instructions: Use Internet Explorer and a computer to perform the following tasks.

1. If necessary, connect to the Internet and launch Internet Explorer.

2. Click the Address box, type www.lycos.com in the box, and click the Go button to display the Lycos directory.

3. Using the Lycos directory, search for and print a Web page containing a graphic image that is representative of each of the following types of sports: cricket, curling, lacrosse, rugby, and squash. Figure 2-66 shows a Web page dedicated to the sport of bocce.

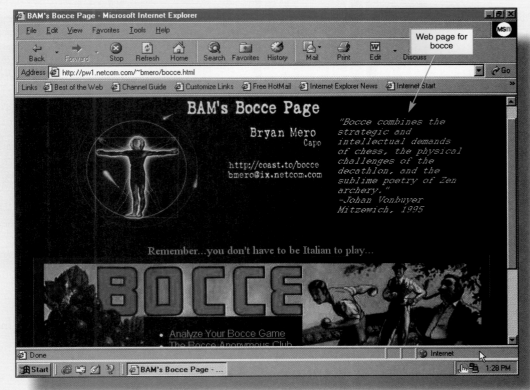

FIGURE 2-66

(continued)

In the Lab

Searching the Web Using the Lycos Directory *(continued)*

4. On each printout, write your name and the type of sport it represents. Hand in the pages to your instructor.
5. Quit Internet Explorer.

4 Searching the Web Using the Infoseek Directory

Instructions: Use Internet Explorer and a computer to perform the following tasks.

1. If necessary, connect to the Internet and launch Internet Explorer.
2. Click the Address box, type www.infoseek.com in the box, and click the Go button to display the InfoSeek window.
3. Using the Infoseek directory, search for and print a Web page containing a photograph of each of the following famous people: Rebecca Lobo (athlete), Charles De Gaulle (politician), David Copperfield (magician), Fabio (model), Mother Teresa (religious leader), and Prince Andrew (royalty). Figure 2-67 shows a Web page dedicated to Winston Churchill, an English politician.

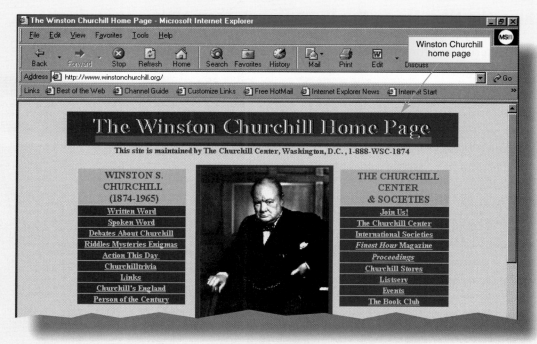

FIGURE 2-67

4. On each printout, write your name and the name of the famous person. Hand in the pages to your instructor.
5. Quit Internet Explorer.

In the Lab

5 Searching the Web Using AltaVista and Keywords

Instructions: Use Internet Explorer and a computer to perform the following tasks.

1. If necessary, connect to the Internet and launch Internet Explorer.
2. Click the Address box, type www.altavista.com in the box, and click the Go button.
3. Perform a search using AltaVista and any ONE of the following topics: virtual reality, computer generated graphics, Java applets, MLA style, APA style, or extreme sports. Figure 2-68 shows a Web page about bungee jumping from the Bridge to Nowhere in Southern California.

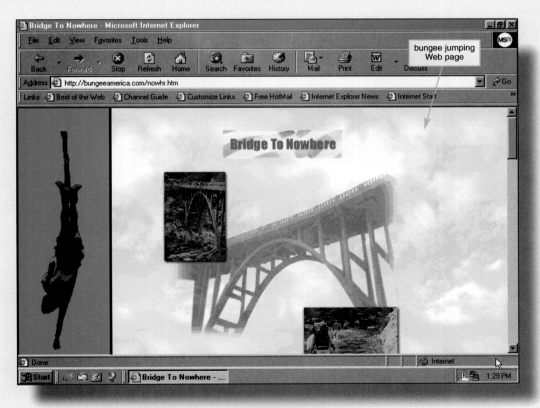

FIGURE 2-68

4. Find one or more informative Web sites about the topic you select. Using WordPad copy information about the topic from the Web sites into a WordPad document and develop a short report about the topic.
5. Add the URLs of the Web sites you used and your name to the end of the report.
6. Print out the WordPad document and hand in the report to your instructor.
7. Quit Internet Explorer.

In the Lab

6 Searching the Web Using Infoseek and Keywords

Instructions: Use Internet Explorer and a computer to perform the following tasks.

1. If necessary, connect to the Internet and launch Internet Explorer.
2. Click the Address box, type `www.infoseek.com` in the box, and click the Go button.
3. Perform a search using Infoseek and any one of the following topics: government spending, a historical event, life of a current political figure, an extreme weather event, asteroid collisions with the earth, an extraterrestrial sighting, biological weapons, or genetic engineering. Figure 2-69 shows a Web page about tornadoes.

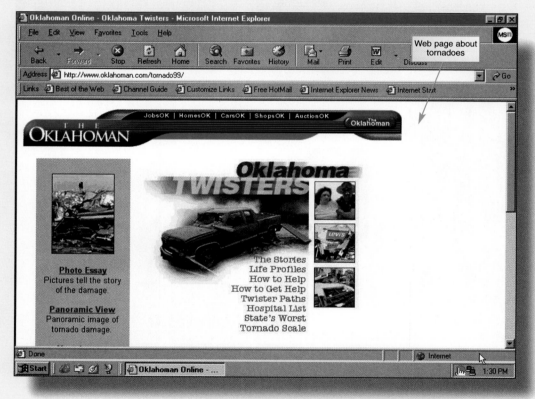

FIGURE 2-69

4. Find one or more informative Web sites about the topic you select. Using WordPad copy information about the topic from the Web sites into a WordPad document and develop a short report about the topic.
5. Add the URLs of the Web sites you used and your name to the end of the report.
6. Print out the WordPad document and hand in the report to your instructor.
7. Quit Internet Explorer.

In the Lab

7 Searching the Web Using the Search Assistant and Address Bar

Instructions: Use Internet Explorer and a computer to perform the following tasks.

1. If necessary, connect to the Internet and launch Internet Explorer.

Part 1: Searching for a Business Address

1. Click the Search button on the Standard Buttons toolbar and click Find a business in the Search bar.
2. Search for the address and telephone number of each of the following businesses: Course Technology (Massachusetts), Microsoft Corporation (Washington), Flagler Museum (Florida), and Recreational Equipment (Seattle, Washington). Click the New button after completing each search.
3. Use WordPad to create a list of business names, addresses, and telephone numbers.
4. Print out the WordPad document and hand in the document to your instructor.

Part 2: Searching for a Map

1. Click the New button and click Find a map in the Search bar.
2. Find a map for each of the following places or landmarks: Salzburg (Austria), Eiffel Tower (France), Statue of Liberty (New York), Key West (Florida), and White House (District of Columbia). Click the New button after completing each search.
3. Use the Print button on the Standard Buttons toolbar to print each map. Circle the place or landmark on the map and write your name on each map. Hand in all maps to your instructor.

Part 3: Searching for an Encyclopedia Article

1. Click the New button, click the More link, and click Find in encyclopedia.
2. Find an encyclopedia article on black widow spiders. Use WordPad to create a report on black widow spiders that consists of the main article from the encyclopedia, the scientific classification, and a picture of the spider.
3. Find an encyclopedia article on blowfish (also called puffer or globefish). Use WordPad to create a report on blowfish that consists of the main article from the encyclopedia, the scientific classification, and a picture of the blowfish.
4. Find an encyclopedia article on the cobra snake. Use WordPad to create a report on cobra snakes that consists of the main article from the encyclopedia, the scientific classification, and a picture of the snake.
5. Find an encyclopedia article on killer bees (also called Africanized honey bees). Use WordPad to create a report on bees that consists of the main article from the encyclopedia, the scientific classification, and a picture of a bee.
6. Print out the WordPad documents, write your name on each report, and hand in the reports to your instructor.
7. Quit Internet Explorer.

In the Lab

8 Connecting to the Shelly Cashman Series Web Site

Instructions: Perform the following steps.

1. Start Internet Explorer and then click the Address box.
2. Type www.scseries.com and then click the Go to button.
3. Click the Student Center link (Figure 2-70).

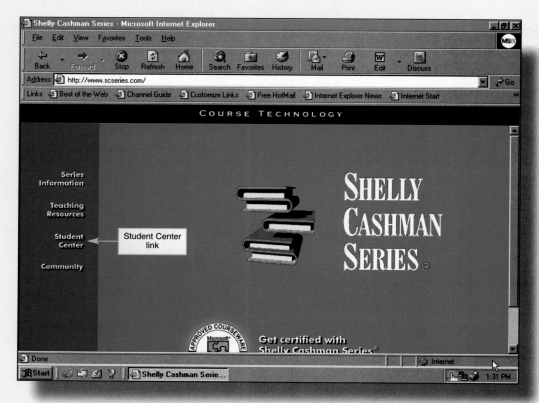

FIGURE 2-70

4. Scroll down and then click Microsoft Internet Explorer 5: An Introduction In the Lab.
5. Click Project 2 in the left frame. Complete the activities listed for Project 2.
6. Close all windows.

Cases and Places

The difficulty of these case studies varies:
▶ are the least difficult; ▶▶ are more difficult; and ▶▶▶ are the most difficult.

1 ▶ Many new bands have their own home pages on the Web. Using the search engine of your choice, find out when and where the Red Elvises will be playing next. Find and print their home page. Next, find out when and where your favorite performer, band, or musical group will be playing next. Find and print their home page. Do these pages qualify as informational Web pages? Write your answer and the reasons supporting your position on one of the printouts and then hand it in to your instructor.

2 ▶ You have been hired by a local bicycle shop to compare their store prices to the prices available on the Internet. Search the Internet for Web pages that sell bicycles and bicycle parts. Find at least ten items being sold by three different online bicycle stores. Develop a price list to compare the prices of the ten items and hand in the price list to your instructor.

3 ▶ You recently graduated from college and took a job at a small investment firm. Your first job is to search for and compare the services of the major online brokers. Find five online brokers and compare their services, costs to buy and sell stocks, Web sites, and any other pertinent information. Summarize your findings in a report.

4 ▶▶ Web search engines use different techniques for searching Web resources. If you were designing a search engine, what would you have the engine look for when determining whether a Web page successfully matches the keywords? Visit the Help page of a few search engines to get an idea of what criteria they use, and then write a list containing the criteria you would have your search engine use to determine whether a Web page is a successful match for keywords. Include an explanation for each item, such as the relative importance assigned, and then hand in the list and explanations to your instructor.

5 ▶▶▶ A gopher is a computer system that allows computer users to find files on the Internet. Some federal, state, and local government agencies continue to use a gopher site to provide information and distribute documents and forms. Find one government agency that provides gopher services, learn to use its gopher, and write a brief report about the gopher. Include instructions to follow to use the gopher, documents you found using the gopher, and whether you like or disliked this method of finding information on the Internet.

6 ▶▶▶ Computer security is a major concern for systems administrators. A very important first line of defense is an account name or user name and password. Choosing good passwords is important for security issues. Using the search engine of your choice, find three different Web sources that describe criteria for creating a good password. Record the relevant information necessary for citing the sources using the MLA or APA style. Print the three pages, write the citation on the page using either the MLA or APA style, and then hand in the pages to your instructor.

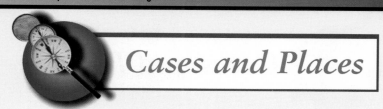

Cases and Places

7 ▶▶▶ The World Wide Web and the Internet provide another source for information in addition to libraries, encyclopedias, and reference materials. Finding useful resources on the Web can be challenging for reasons such as unknown authorship, lack of verification of the materials, and the ever-changing nature of the Web. Choose a topic of interest to you and then narrow down a research topic. Using the Web and Internet resources, find at least five sources of information on the topic. Evaluate the five sources using the evaluation criteria discussed in Project 2. Print the Web resources and then hand them in to your instructor along with your evaluations.

Internet Explorer 5

PROJECT

3

Communicating Over the Internet

You will have mastered the material in this project when you can:

O B J E C T I V E S

- Launch Outlook Express
- Open, read, print, reply to, and delete electronic mail messages
- Compose, format, and send electronic mail messages
- Search for and display newsgroups
- Read, post, and print newsgroup articles
- Expand and collapse a thread
- Subscribe and unsubscribe to a newsgroup
- Launch Microsoft NetMeeting
- Change directory information and ILS server
- Place a call and send a typed message
- Launch Microsoft FrontPage Express
- Create a personal Web page using a wizard
- Edit and save a Web page
- Display the Radio toolbar and radio station guide
- Listen to an Internet radio station

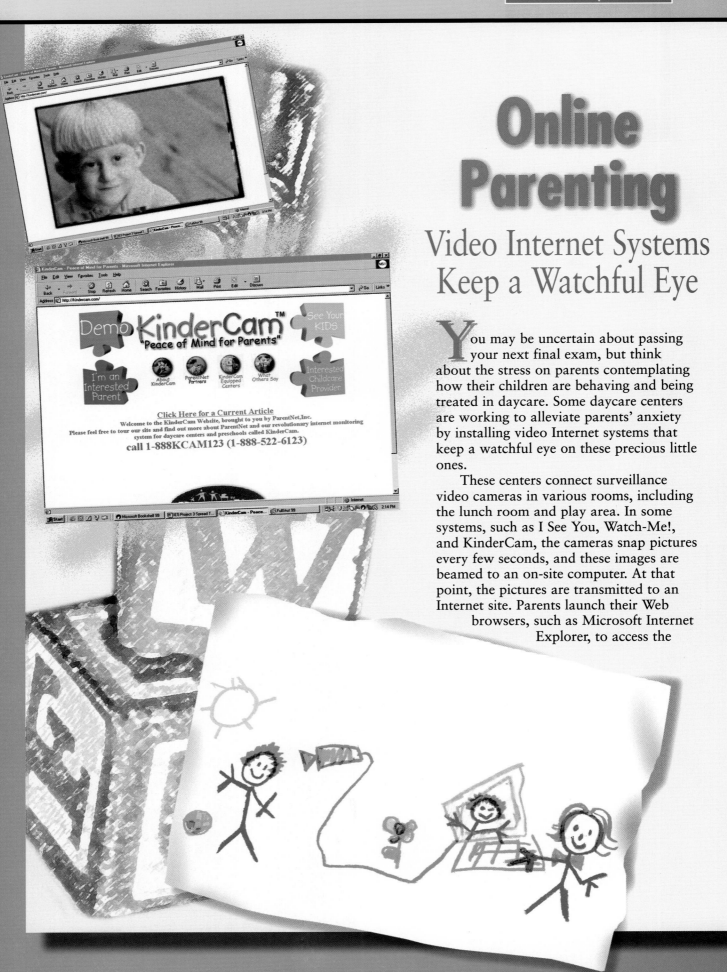

Online Parenting

Video Internet Systems Keep a Watchful Eye

You may be uncertain about passing your next final exam, but think about the stress on parents contemplating how their children are behaving and being treated in daycare. Some daycare centers are working to alleviate parents' anxiety by installing video Internet systems that keep a watchful eye on these precious little ones.

These centers connect surveillance video cameras in various rooms, including the lunch room and play area. In some systems, such as I See You, Watch-Me!, and KinderCam, the cameras snap pictures every few seconds, and these images are beamed to an on-site computer. At that point, the pictures are transmitted to an Internet site. Parents launch their Web browsers, such as Microsoft Internet Explorer, to access the

Web site and then enter their secure passwords to view their children. Teachers and classroom supervisors are not aware of when parents are observing the center's activities.

In this project, you will learn to communicate over the Internet in a number of ways: by sending and receiving electronic mail messages, searching for and displaying newsgroups where you can read, post, and print newsgroup articles, participating in live videoconferencing, and even creating your own personal Web page that will provide a forum for communication.

To participate in live videoconferences, this project presents a section that shows you how to launch Microsoft Net-Meeting and place a call. Likewise, cyberparents can send e-mail to their children's teachers, participate in discussion groups with other day-care center parents, and read information via newsgroups regarding lesson plans, menus, field trips, holidays, and fund-raising activities.

Some systems, such as the Kid Chat Station, expand the traditional Internet conversation norms by allowing parents to interact with their children via teleconferencing, similarly to conversing live with Microsoft NetMeeting as described in this project.

If the parents have a sound card, video camera, speakers, and a microphone, they can place an Internet call to the center and converse with their children. Parents can expect to pay at least $10 per month for the service. The system could cost a center with five rooms a minimum of $10,000 for installation plus a $500 monthly Internet access fee.

Security is an enormous concern, as centers want to keep their sites protected from cyberprowlers. In some sophisticated systems, parents are allowed to peer only into the rooms where their children are playing, eating, or napping. In this manner, parents of an infant do not have access to the toddler room. Some systems record who has visited the site and for how long. Passwords are updated frequently, and the Web page does not identify the childcare center's name or location.

Video cyberparenting is expanding beyond the traditional work or school environment. Some parents find the service useful when they travel. They also can authorize out-of-town grandparents to view grandchildren in action between visits. Some employers have found that permitting workers to view their children via the Internet is a viable alternative to providing expensive on-site daycare. Other companies are considering broadening the scope to include hospitals and homes with nannies.

Daycare centers evaluate the systems as a win-win-win situation: teachers report the children behave better knowing their parents may be watching; children can discuss their daily activities with parents who can reinforce the lessons; and parents are more productive at work and school knowing of their children's well-being.

Internet Explorer 5

Communicating Over the Internet

C A S E   P E R S P E C T I V E

You recently attended a free Microsoft seminar on how to use the Internet to communicate. Before attending the seminar, you were unsure how to use the Internet to communicate. At the seminar, you watched an impressive presentation that included using Microsoft Outlook Express to send and receive e-mail messages and read and post messages to a newsgroup, using Microsoft NetMeeting to conduct live videoconferences, using FrontPage Express to create a Web page, and using Internet Explorer to listen to music from radio stations around the world.

You were careful to make a list of the various ways to communicate over the Internet and the software programs that allow you to communicate. The list also included a reminder to buy a video camera and try the videoconferencing features of Microsoft NetMeeting.

You thought videoconferencing might be a solution to the high cost of using the telephone to communicate with out-of-town business associates, friends, and family. Your goal is to learn more about communicating using the Internet and the Internet Explorer, Outlook Express, NetMeeting, and FrontPage Express software.

Introduction

In Projects 1 and 2, you used Internet Explorer to search for information on the World Wide Web. In addition to searching for information, you also may use the Internet to communicate with other individuals. Web services designed for communicating over the Internet include Microsoft Outlook Express, which allows you to send and receive electronic mail and read and post messages to a newsgroup; and NetMeeting, which permits you to engage in a live videoconference. In addition, FrontPage Express allows you to create Web pages and the Radio toolbar allows you to listen to radio stations throughout the world. Project 3 illustrates the different types of communications available while using Internet Explorer.

Launching Internet Explorer

Before you can send and receive e-mail messages, read and post messages to a newsgroup, engage in a videoconference, create Web pages, and listen to the radio, you must launch Internet Explorer following the procedure you used in Project 1. This procedure is summarized below.

TO LAUNCH MICROSOFT INTERNET EXPLORER

 Double-click the Internet Explorer icon on the desktop.

The Microsoft Internet Explorer window with the MSN.COM home page displays (Figure 3-1). The home page may be different on your computer.

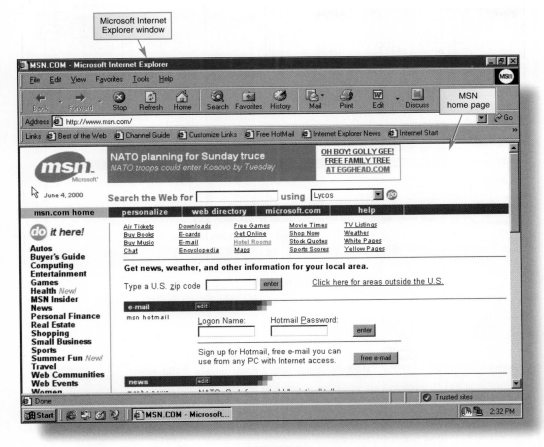

Microsoft Internet
Explorer window

MSN
home page

FIGURE 3-1

Electronic (E-Mail) Messages

Electronic mail (e-mail) has become an important means of exchanging messages and files between business associates and friends. Businesses find that using e-mail to send documents electronically saves both time and money. Parents with students away at college or relatives who are scattered across the country find that exchanging e-mail messages is a cheap and easy way to stay in touch with their children or relatives. In fact, exchanging e-mail messages is one of the more widely used features of the Internet.

Besides exchanging e-mail messages, another popular method of exchanging information among individuals is to use Internet newgroups. An **Internet newsgroup** contains articles and messages about many varied and interesting topics.

Microsoft Outlook Express allows you to receive and store incoming e-mail messages, compose and send e-mail messages, maintain a list of frequently used e-mail addresses, and read and post messages to Internet newsgroups.

Launching Microsoft Outlook Express

After starting Internet Explorer, you can launch Microsoft Outlook Express using the Mail button on the Standard Buttons toolbar in the Microsoft Internet Explorer window. Perform the steps on the next page to launch Outlook Express.

More About

Electronic Mail Addresses

Many search engines contain an electronic mail search feature. For example, AltaVista (www.altavista.com) allows you to search for a person or e-mail address using SwitchBoard (www.switchboard.com). In addition, AltaVista allows you to search for a business using YellowPages (www.yellowpages.com).

More About

Outlook Express

Outlook Express allows you to change the appearance of e-mail by using special fonts, changing the background graphic, attaching files and pictures, and adding a hyperlink to a Web page. Many schools and businesses, however, still use older, less sophisticated mail programs that do not recognize these newer features.

Steps: To Launch Microsoft Outlook Express

1 Click the Mail button on the Standard Buttons toolbar and then point to Read Mail.

The Mail menu displays (Figure 3-2). The menu contains commands to start Outlook Express (Read Mail), compose a new e-mail message (New Message), send an e-mail message containing a hyperlink of the currently displayed Web page (Send a Link), send an e-mail message containing the currently displayed Web page (Send Page), and access a newsgroup (Read News).

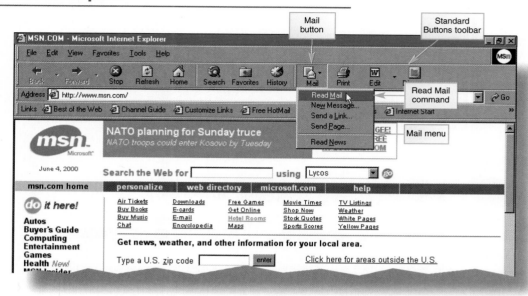

FIGURE 3-2

2 Click Read Mail. If necessary, maximize the Inbox – Outlook Express window.

The Outlook Express introductory screen displays momentarily while Outlook Express launches and then the maximized Inbox - Outlook Express window displays (Figure 3-3). The window contains the folders list, contacts list, message list, and preview pane.

Other Ways

1. Click Tools on menu bar, point to Mail and News, click Read Mail

2. Double-click Outlook Express icon on desktop

3. Click Launch Outlook Express icon on Quick Launch toolbar

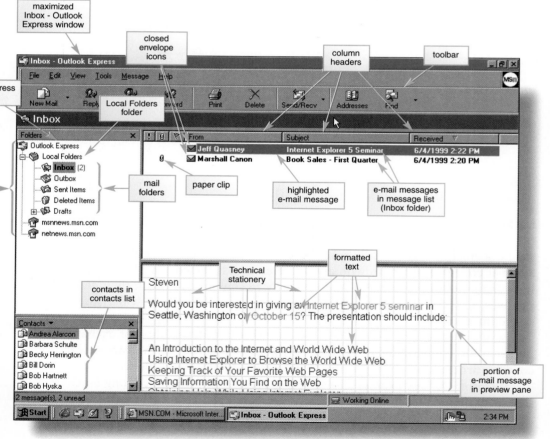

FIGURE 3-3

The Inbox - Outlook Express window shown in Figure 3-3 contains a number of elements. Below the title bar and menu bar is a toolbar containing buttons specific to Outlook Express (New Mail, Reply, Reply All, Forward, and so on). Table 3-1 contains the toolbar buttons and a brief explanation of their functions.

The Inbox - Outlook Express window is divided into four frames. The **folders list** in the upper-left frame contains, in hierarchical structure, the Outlook Express folder, Local Folders folder, and the five mail folders contained in the Local Folders folder. Five standard mail folders (Inbox, Outbox, Sent Items, Deleted Items, and Drafts) display when you first launch Outlook Express. Although you cannot rename or delete these folders, you can create additional folders.

The two highest levels in the hierarchy are Outlook Express and Local Folders. Connected by a dotted vertical line below the Local Folders icon are the five standard mail folders icons. On some computers, the Local Folders folder may not display and the mail folders are connected by a dotted vertical line below the Outlook Express folder.

The **Inbox folder** is the destination for incoming mail. The **Outbox folder** temporarily holds messages you send until Outlook Express delivers the messages. The **Sent Items folder** retains copies of messages that you have sent. The **Deleted Items folder** contains messages that you have deleted. As a safety precaution, you can retrieve deleted messages from the Deleted Items folder if you later decide you wish to keep them. Deleting messages from the Deleted Items folder removes the messages permanently. The **Drafts folder** retains copies of messages that you are not yet ready to send. The last two folders (msnnews.msn.com and netnews.msn.com) contain lists of newsgroups.

Folders can contain e-mail messages, faxes, and files created in other Windows applications. Folders in bold type followed by a number in parentheses (**Inbox** (2)) indicate the number of messages in the folder that are unopened. Other folders may display on your computer instead of or in addition to the folders shown in Figure 3-3.

The **contacts list** in the lower-left frame contains an alphabetical list of the contacts in the Address Book. The **Address Book** is a central location for storing business and personal information (name, address, telephone number, e-mail address, and so on) about those individuals you contact frequently. An entry in the Address book is commonly referred to as a **contact**.

The name or e-mail address of six contacts displays in Figure 3-3. Double-clicking an entry in the contacts list displays the New Message window that allows you to compose and send an e-mail message to the contact. Other contacts may display on your computer instead of or in addition to the contacts shown in Figure 3-3. If the Contacts list does not display, read the More About on this page to learn how to display the Contacts list.

Table 3-1	
BUTTON	**FUNCTION**
New Mail	Displays the New Message window used to compose a new e-mail message.
Reply	Displays a window used to reply to an e-mail message. The e-mail address, original subject of the e-mail message preceded by the Re: entry, and the original e-mail message display in the window.
Reply All	Displays a window used to reply to an e-mail message. The e-mail addresses of all recipients, subject of the e-mail message preceded by the Re: entry, and the original e-mail message display in the window.
Forward	Displays a window used to forward an e-mail message to another recipient. The original subject of the e-mail message preceded by the Fw: entry and the original e-mail message display in the window.
Print	Prints the highlighted e-mail message in the message list.
Delete	Deletes the highlighted e-mail message in the message list by moving the message to the Deleted Items folder.
Send/Recv	Displays the Outlook Express dialog box, contacts the mail server, sends any e-mail messages in the Outbox folder, and places new e-mail messages in the Inbox folder.
Addresses	Displays the Address Book window containing a list of frequently used e-mail addresses.
Find	Displays the Find Message window that allows you to search for an e-mail message in the message list based upon sender name, recipient name, e-mail subject, e-mail message, and date.

More About

Mail Folders

You can create additional folders in the Local Folders folder to save important messages. For example, you may wish to save all messages from Aunt Shirley. Right-click the Local Folders icon, click New Folder, type Aunt Shirley in the Folder name text box, and then click the OK button. To save an e-mail message, drag the message to the Aunt Shirley folder.

More About

The Contacts List

If the Contacts list does not display in the Inbox - Outlook Express window, click View, click Layout, click Contacts to place a check mark in the Contacts box, and then click the OK button.

More About

Message Headings

You can change the column widths of the column headers in the message list by dragging the vertical line between two column headers. To change the size of the two areas, drag the vertical line that separates the folders list and contacts list from the message list and preview pane.

More About

Message List Icons

For a complete list of message list icons, click Help on the menu bar, click Contents and Index, click Index tab, type `mail icons` in the text box, and click the Display button.

The contents of the Inbox folder automatically display in the **message list** at the top of the upper-right frame of the window when Internet Explorer launches Outlook Express. Six column headers display above the message list. An exclamation point icon (High Priority) identifies the first header, a paper clip icon (Attachment) identifies the second header, and flag (Flagged) identifies the third header. An exclamation point icon in the column below the first header indicates the e-mail message has been marked high priority by the sender and you should read it immediately. A paper clip icon in the column below the second header indicates the e-mail message contains an attachment (file or object). The second e-mail message in the message list (Marshall Canon) contains an attachment, as indicated by the paper clip icon. A flag icon in the column below the third header indicates the e-mail message has been flagged by the sender.

Entries in the columns below the fourth header (From), fifth header (Subject), and sixth header (Received) indicate the e-mail author's name or e-mail address, subject of the e-mail message, and date and time the message was received. Collectively, these last three entries are referred to as the **message heading**.

A closed envelope icon in the From column and a message heading that displays in bold type identifies an unread e-mail message. In Figure 3-3 on page IE 3.6, the first e-mail message from Jeff Quasney contains a closed envelope icon and a message heading that displays in bold type. The icon and bold message heading indicate the e-mail message has not been read (opened). In addition, the e-mail message is highlighted because it is the first message in message list. The second e-mail message from Marshall Canon contains a paper clip icon, a closed envelope icon, and a message heading that displays in bold type. The icon and bold message heading indicate the e-mail message has not been read and the paper clip indicates the e-mail message has an attachment. Other e-mail messages may display on your computer instead of these messages.

The closed envelope icon is one of several icons, called **message list icons**, that display in the From column. Different message list icons may display in the From column to indicate the status of the message. The icon may indicate an action that was performed by the sender or one that was performed by the recipient. The actions may include reading, replying to, forwarding, digitally signing, or encrypting a message. Table 3-2 contains a partial list of message list icons and the action performed on the mail message.

The lower-right frame contains a **preview pane** containing a portion of the highlighted e-mail message (Jeff Quasney) in the message list. The e-mail message in the preview pane in Figure 3-3 is formatted.

Formatting is the process of enhancing the appearance of a document by changing the background of the document, and the style, size, and color of the text in the document. Jeff Quasney, the sender of the e-mail message, formatted the e-mail message shown in Figure 3-3 using a colorful background and various text colors. When only a portion of an e-mail message displays in the preview pane, the vertical scroll bar allows you to view the hidden part of the message.

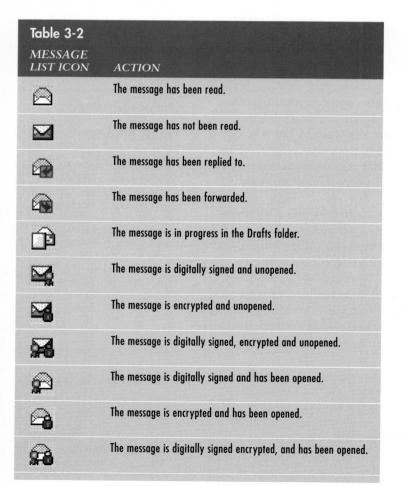

Table 3-2

MESSAGE LIST ICON	ACTION
	The message has been read.
	The message has not been read.
	The message has been replied to.
	The message has been forwarded.
	The message is in progress in the Drafts folder.
	The message is digitally signed and unopened.
	The message is encrypted and unopened.
	The message is digitally signed, encrypted and unopened.
	The message is digitally signed and has been opened.
	The message is encrypted and has been opened.
	The message is digitally signed encrypted, and has been opened.

Opening and Reading E-Mail Messages

In Figure 3-3 on page IE 3.6, the highlighted message heading of the Jeff Quasney message displays in the message list, and a portion of the e-mail message displays in the preview pane. If you wish to view the entire e-mail message in a separate window, you must open the e-mail message. Perform the following steps to open the e-mail message from Jeff Quasney.

More About

Reading E-Mail Messages

Many people minimize the Inbox - Outlook Express window. When they receive a new e-mail message, Outlook displays an envelope icon in the tray status area on the taskbar and plays the sound of a telephone ringing.

 To Open (Read) an E-Mail Message

1 Point to the closed envelope icon to the left of the Jeff Quasney name in the message list (Figure 3-4).

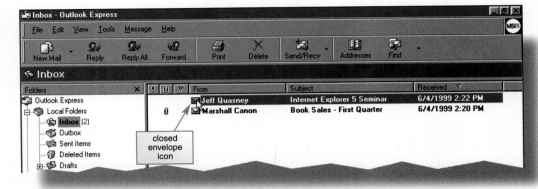

FIGURE 3-4

2 Double-click the closed envelope icon and then maximize the Internet Explorer 5 Seminar window. If the envelope icon does not display in the message list, double-click another closed envelope icon.

The maximized Internet Explorer 5 Seminar window displays (Figure 3-5). The window contains a menu bar, a toolbar, identifying information about the e-mail message, and a message pane. The subject of the e-mail message (Internet Explorer 5 Seminar) becomes the window title.

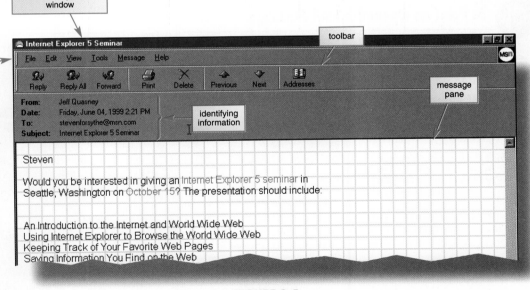

FIGURE 3-5

Other Ways

1. Right-click closed envelope icon, click Open
2. Click closed envelope icon, on File menu click Open
3. Select message heading, press CTRL+O

Table 3-3

BUTTON	FUNCTION
Reply	Displays a window used to reply to an e-mail message. The e-mail address, original subject of the e-mail message preceded by the Re: entry, and original e-mail message display in the window.
Reply All	Displays a window used to reply to an e-mail message. The e-mail addresses of all recipients, subject of the e-mail message preceded by the Re: entry, and original e-mail message display in the window.
Forward	Displays a window used to forward an e-mail message to another recipient. The original subject of the e-mail message preceded by the Fw: entry and the original e-mail message display in the window.
Print	Prints the e-mail message in the window.
Delete	Deletes the e-mail message in the window by moving the message to the Deleted Items folder and displays the next e-mail message in the message list.
Previous	Displays the previous e-mail message in the message list.
Next	Displays the next e-mail message in the message list.
Addresses	Displays the Address Book window containing a list of frequently used e-mail addresses.

When you double-click a closed envelope icon in the message list, Outlook Express displays the message in a separate window, changes the closed envelope icon to an opened envelope icon, and no longer displays the message heading in bold type.

Below the title bar and menu bar shown in Figure 3-5 on the previous page is a toolbar that contains the buttons needed to work with opened e-mail messages (Reply, Reply All, Forward, and so on). Table 3-3 contains the toolbar buttons and a brief explanation of their functions.

Printing an E-Mail Message

You can print the contents of an e-mail message before or after opening the message. The following steps describe how to print an opened e-mail message.

Steps To Print an Opened E-mail Message

1 **Click the Print button on the toolbar and then point to the OK button.**

The Print dialog box displays (Figure 3-6).

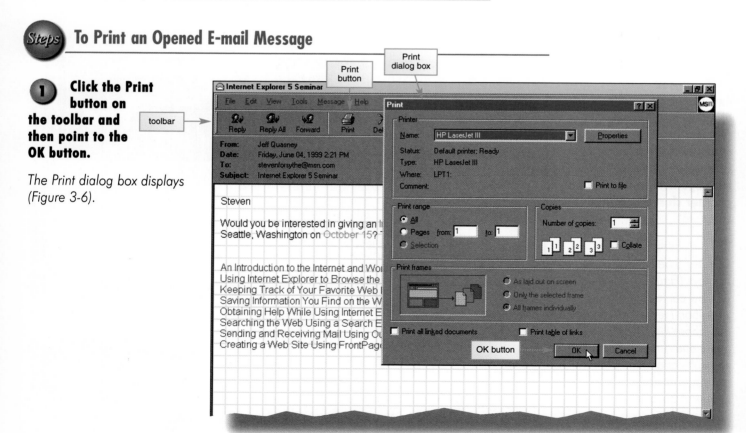

FIGURE 3-6

2 Click the OK button.

The printed message consists of a header at the top of the page containing the page number (Page 1 of 1), the recipient's name (Steven Forsythe), and a horizontal line (Figure 3-7). The line is heavier under the recipient's name. Below the header are the From, To, Sent, and Subject entries, and the e-mail message. A footer at the bottom of the page contains the current date (6/5/2000).

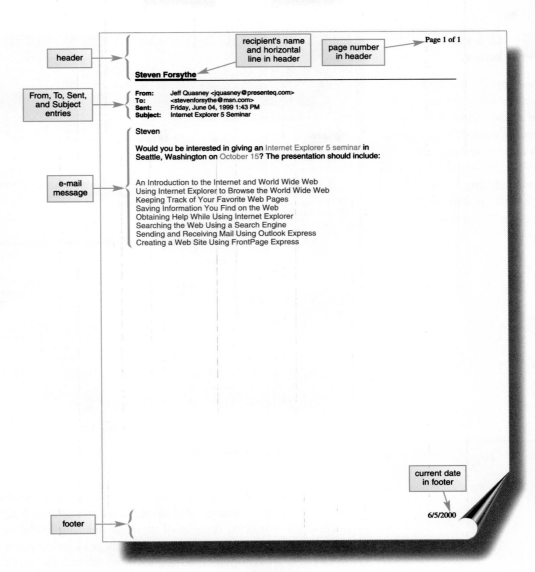

FIGURE 3-7

Closing an E-Mail Message

When you have finished opening and reading an e-mail message, you can close the window containing the e-mail message by performing the following steps.

Other Ways

1. Click Print on File menu, click OK button
2. Press ALT+F, press P, press ENTER
3. Press CTRL+P, press ENTER

Steps To Close an E-Mail Message

1 Point to the Close button on the title bar (Figure 3-8).

FIGURE 3-8

Click the Close button.

The Internet Explorer 5 Seminar window closes and the Inbox - Outlook Express window displays (Figure 3-9). An open envelope icon replaces the closed envelope icon preceding the Jeff Quasney message heading to indicate the e-mail has been opened.

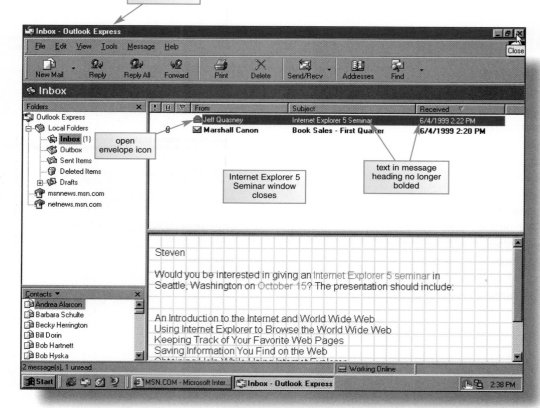

FIGURE 3-9

Other Ways

1. On File menu click Close

When you double-click a closed envelope icon in the message list, Outlook Express opens the message and displays its contents in a separate window. When you close the window, the e-mail message heading in the message list in the Inbox - Outlook Express window no longer displays in bold type and the closed envelope icon changes to an open envelope icon to indicate the e-mail message has been opened.

More About

Replying to an E-Mail Message

Some people who receive reply e-mail messages find it awkward that the original e-mail message displays with the reply message. To remove the original message from all e-mail replies, click Tools on the menu bar, click Options, click Send tab, click Include message in reply check box, and then click the OK button.

Replying to an E-Mail Message

As mentioned previously, the Address Book is a central location for storing business and personal information about individuals you contact frequently. When you reply to an e-mail message, Outlook Express adds the business and personal information about the sender to the Address Book. Once a contact is added to the Address Book, Outlook Express can use the Address Book to find the e-mail address needed to reply to the e-mail message or to use when you compose a new e-mail message.

After closing the e-mail message from Jeff Quasney, you decide to compose and send an e-mail reply to Jeff Quasney. The Reply button on the Standard Buttons toolbar allows you to reply quickly to an e-mail message using the sender's e-mail address. Perform the following steps to reply to Jeff Quasney.

Steps | **To Reply to an E-mail Message**

1 If necessary, click the Jeff Quasney icon in the message list. Point to the Reply button on the Standard Buttons toolbar (Figure 3-10).

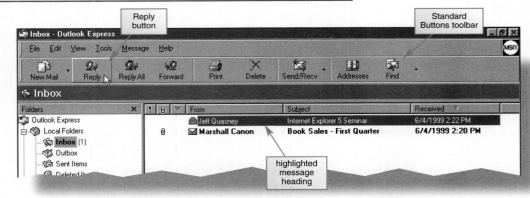

FIGURE 3-10

2 Click the Reply button. Click a blank area above the original e-mail message to display the insertion point. Type the e-mail reply as shown in Figure 3-11 and then point to the Send button.

The Re: Internet Explorer 5 Seminar window displays (Figure 3-11). The Re: entry and subject display in the window title and Subject text box, three text boxes and the Formatting toolbar display, and the e-mail reply and original message display in the message pane.

FIGURE 3-11

3 Click the Send button.

The Re: Internet Explorer 5 Seminar window closes, Outlook Express stores the reply e-mail message in the Outbox folder while it sends the message, and then moves the message to the Sent Items folder. The icon to the left of the Jeff Quasney entry in the message list contains an arrow to indicate you have replied to the e-mail message (see Figure 3-12 on page IE 3.15).

1. On Message menu click Reply to Sender
2. Press CTRL+R

In Figure 3-11, the underlined Jeff Quasney name displays in the To text box and the original e-mail message is identified by the words, Original Message, a vertical line, and the From, To, Sent, and Subject entries in the message pane. In addition, the window contains two toolbars. A toolbar displays below the menu bar and the Formatting toolbar displays below the Subject text box. The buttons on the toolbar below the menu bar are useful when replying to a message (Send, Cut, Paste, Undo, and so on). Table 3-4 shows the buttons on the toolbar below the menu bar and their functions.

Table 3-4	
BUTTON	**FUNCTION**
Send	Places the e-mail message in the Outbox folder temporarily while the message is sent and then moves the message to the Sent Items folder.
Cut	Moves a selected item in an e-mail message to the Clipboard.
Paste	Copies an item from the Clipboard to an e-mail message.
Undo	Undoes the previous operation.
Check	Checks the recipient's name against the Address Book.
Spelling	Spell checks the e-mail message.
Attach	Attaches a file to the e-mail message.
Priority	Sets the priority (high, normal, or low) of an e-mail message.
Sign	Digitally signs an e-mail message, allowing the recipient to verify the sender's identity.
Encrypt	Encrypts, or scrambles, an e-mail message, preventing someone other than the recipient from reading the message.

The Formatting toolbar shown in Figure 3-11 on the previous page displays because the sender of the original e-mail message formatted the e-mail message. The Formatting toolbar allows you to change the appearance, size, and color of text; bold, italicize, or underline text; create a numbered or bulleted list; change paragraph indentation or align text; and create a hyperlink or insert a picture in an e-mail message. You will use the Formatting toolbar later in this project to format a new e-mail message.

As you send and reply to messages, the number of messages in the Sent Items folder increases. To delete an e-mail message from the Sent Items folder, click the Sent Items folder icon in the folders list, highlight the message in the message list, and then click the Delete button in the Outlook Express dialog box.

More About

Mail Folders

You can reduce the hard disk space required by a mail folder by clicking the folder in the folders list, clicking File on the menu bar, pointing to Folder, and then clicking Compact. To compact all folders, click the Compact All command instead of the Compact command. Compacting all folders may take several minutes.

Deleting an E-Mail Message

After reading and replying to an e-mail message, you may wish to delete the original e-mail message from the message list. Deleting a message removes the e-mail message from the Inbox folder. If you do not delete unwanted messages, large numbers of messages in the Inbox folder make it difficult to find and read new messages and wastes disk space. Perform the following steps to delete the e-mail message from Jeff Quasney.

To Delete an E-Mail Message

1 **If necessary, click the Jeff Quasney envelope icon in the message list. Point to the Delete button on the toolbar.**

The highlighted Jeff Quasney message heading displays in the message list and a portion of the e-mail message displays in the preview pane (Figure 3-12). The open envelope icon contains an arrow to indicate you have replied to the message.

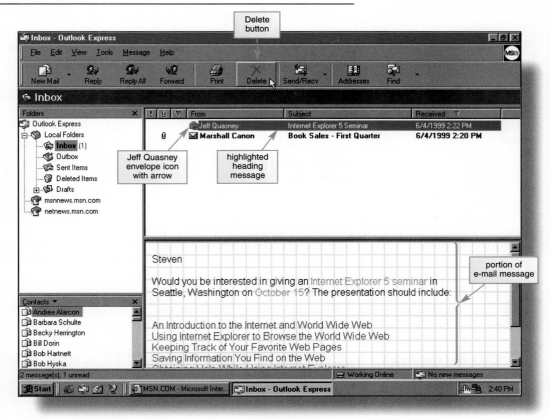

FIGURE 3-12

2 **Click the Delete button.**

Outlook Express moves the Jeff Quasney e-mail message from the Inbox folder to the Deleted Items folder and removes the e-mail entry from the message list (Figure 3-13).

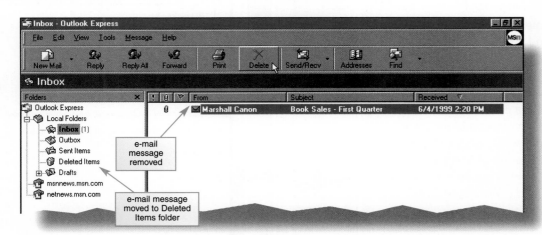

FIGURE 3-13

As you delete messages from the Inbox, the number of messages in the Deleted Items folder increases. To delete an e-mail message from the Deleted Items folder, click the Deleted Items folder icon in the folders list, highlight the message in the message list, click the Delete button, and then click the Yes button in the Outlook Express dialog box.

Other Ways

1. Drag e-mail message to Deleted Items folder in folders list
2. On Edit menu click Delete
3. Right-click e-mail message, click Delete
4. Press ALT+E, press D
5. Press CTRL+D

Mo**re** About

Stationery

To use stationery for all your outgoing messages, click Tools on the menu bar, click Options, click the Compose tab, select the Mail and/or News check box in the Stationery area, and then click Select.

Composing a New Mail Message

In addition to opening and reading, replying to, and deleting e-mail messages, you may wish to compose and send a new e-mail message. When you compose an e-mail message, you must know the e-mail address of the recipient of the message, enter a brief one-line subject that identifies the purpose or contents of the message, and type the message itself.

As mentioned previously, you also can format an e-mail message to enhance the appearance of the message. One method of formatting an e-mail message is to select a stationery. **Stationery** allows you to add a colorful background image, unique text sizes and colors, and custom margins to an e-mail message. In the following steps, selecting the Tiki Lounge stationery causes a custom margin to display and the text of the e-mail message to display using the Comic Sans MS font and gold text. The Comic Sans MS font is one of many fonts, or typefaces, available to format an e-mail message. In addition, any hyperlinks within the e-mail message will be underlined and display in purple text.

Perform the following steps to select the Tiki Lounge stationery and compose an e-mail message to one of the authors (Steven Forsythe) of this book.

 To Compose an E-Mail Message Using Stationery

1 Click the arrow on the New Mail button on the toolbar and then point to Tiki Lounge.

The New Mail menu, containing a list of ten stationeries, displays (Figure 3-14). The Tiki Lounge entry is highlighted and three commands at the bottom of the menu allow you to select from a larger list of stationeries, select to use no stationery, or send a Web page as an e-mail message.

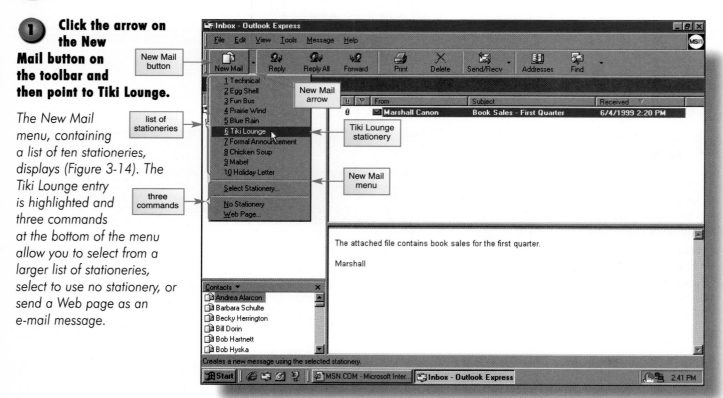

FIGURE 3-14

2 Click Tiki Lounge.

The New Message window displays (Figure 3-15). The window contains a menu bar, toolbar, three text boxes, the dimmed Formatting toolbar, and the message pane. The insertion point is located in the To text box and the Tiki Lounge stationery, containing a custom left margin, displays in the message pane.

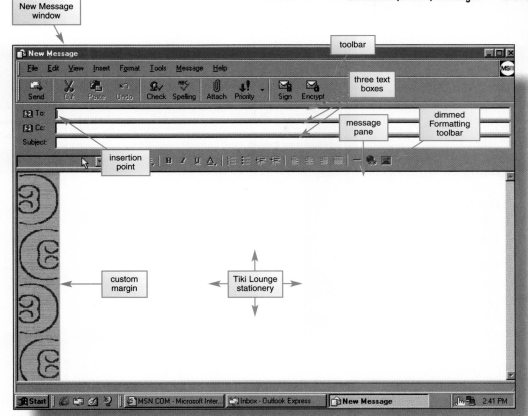

FIGURE 3-15

3 Type stevenforsythe @msn.com **in the To text box, click the Subject text box, and then** type Internet Bookstore **in the Subject text box.**

The destination e-mail address displays in the To text box and the subject of the message displays in the Subject text box (Figure 3-16). The title of the New Message window changes to the subject of the e-mail message.

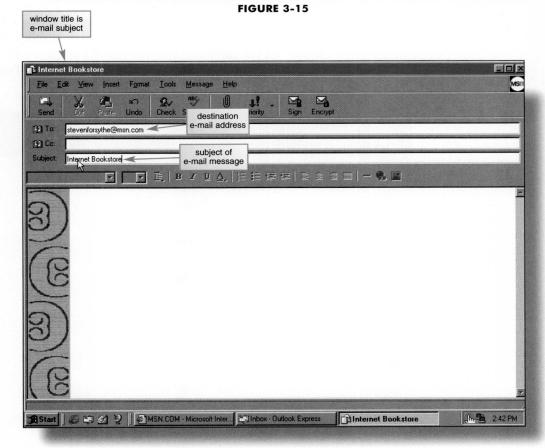

FIGURE 3-16

4 **Press the TAB key.**
Type Great News!!
and press the ENTER key
twice. Type Your books
are being sold on the
Internet. Click this
URL to look
for your
books: www.amazon.com
and press the ENTER key
twice. Type your name and
press the ENTER key.

The formatted e-mail message
displays in the message pane
(Figure 3-17). The message
displays using the Comic Sans
MS font in gold color and the
hyperlink is underlined and
displays in purple text.

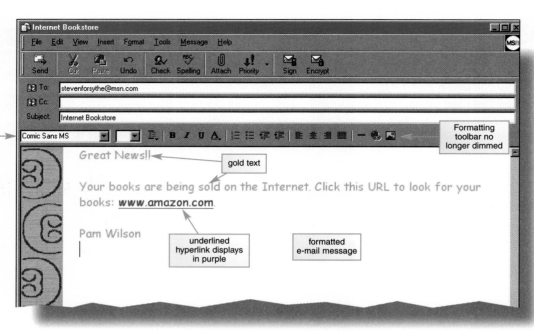

FIGURE 3-17

The New Message window shown in Figure 3-17 contains two toolbars. The toolbar containing buttons specific to composing a new e-mail message displays below the menu bar, and the Formatting toolbar displays below the Subject text box. The buttons on the toolbar below the menu bar are explained in Table 3-4 on page IE 3.14. Table 3-5 shows the buttons and boxes on the Formatting toolbar and their functions.

Table 3-5

BUTTON/BOX	FUNCTION	BUTTON/BOX	FUNCTION
Comic Sans MS	Changes the font of text in the message.		Decreases the indentation of a paragraph.
	Changes the font size of text in the message.		Increases the indentation of a paragraph.
	Changes the paragraph style in the message.		Aligns text with the left margin.
B	Bolds text in the message.		Centers text between the left and right margins.
I	Italicizes text in the message.		Aligns text with the right margin.
U	Underlines text in the message.		Aligns text with the left and right margins.
A	Changes the color of text in the message.	—	Adds a horizontal line to the message.
	Creates a numbered list in the message.		Inserts a hyperlink in the message.
	Creates a bulleted list in the message.		Inserts a picture in the message.

Formatting an E-Mail Message

When you select the Tiki Lounge stationery, the stationery formats the text in the e-mail message to display using the Comic Sans MS font and gold color. In addition to selecting a stationery, the Formatting toolbar allows you to add additional formatting to an e-mail message. Formatting includes changing the appearance, size, and color of text; bolding, italicizing, and underlining text; creating a numbered or bulleted list, changing paragraph indentation or aligning text; and creating a hyperlink and inserting a picture into an e-mail message.

In the following steps you will center and change the size of text (Great News!!) in the e-mail message. You change the size of text by selecting a font size. A **font size** is measured in **points**. One inch contains seventy-two points. Thus, a font size of thirty-six points is approximately one-half inch in height. Perform the following steps to center the text, Great News!!, and display the text using the 36-point font size.

 To Format an E-Mail Message

1 Select the words, Great News!!, in the first line of the e-mail message by pointing to either word (Great or News!!) and triple-clicking the word. Point to the Center button on the Formatting toolbar.

The words, Great News!!, are highlighted (Figure 3-18).

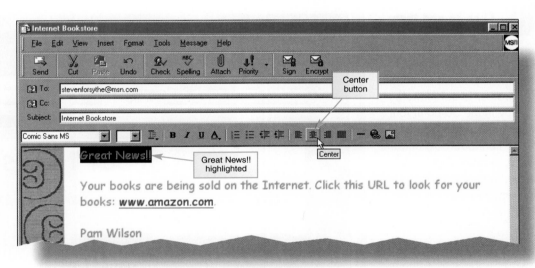

FIGURE 3-18

2 Click the Center button and then point to the Font Size box arrow.

The words, Great News!!, are centered on the first line of the e-mail message and the Center button on the Formatting toolbar is recessed (Figure 3-19).

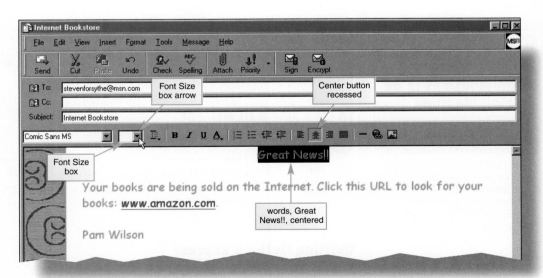

FIGURE 3-19

③ **Click the arrow and then point to 36 in the Font Size list.**

The Font Size list displays and the number 36 is highlighted in the list (Figure 3-20).

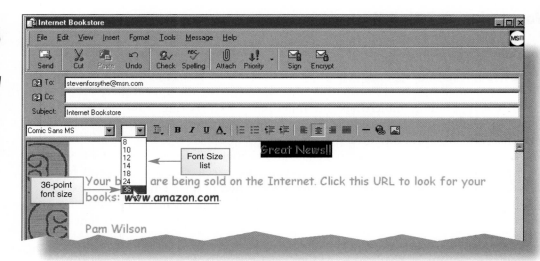

FIGURE 3-20

④ **Click 36 and then click the highlighted text to remove the highlight.**

The words, Great News!!, display in the 36-point font size, the font size 36 displays in the Font Size box, and the insertion point displays between the two words (Figure 3-21).

FIGURE 3-21

 About

Abbreviations in an E-Mail Message

The use of abbreviations has become popular when composing an e-mail message. For example, you can use ASAP for As soon as possible, CU for See you later, NRN for No reply necessary, PLS for Please, and THX for Thank you.

Sending an E-Mail Message

After composing and formatting an e-mail message, send the message by performing the following step.

TO SEND AN E-MAIL MESSAGE

① Click the Send button on the toolbar.

The Internet Bookstore window closes, Outlook Express stores the e-mail message in the Outbox folder temporarily while it sends the message, and then it moves the message to the Sent Items folder.

Quitting Outlook Express

When you have finished reading, replying to, and sending e-mail messages, you should quit Outlook Express by performing the following step.

PROJECT 3

TO QUIT OUTLOOK EXPRESS

1 Click the Close button in the Inbox - Outlook Express window.

The Outlook Express window closes and Outlook Express quits.

Internet Newsgroups

Besides exchanging e-mail messages, another popular method of communicating over the Internet is to read and place messages on a newsgroup. A **newsgroup** is one of a collection of news and discussion groups that you can access via the Internet. Each newsgroup is devoted to a particular subject. A special computer, called a **news server**, contains related groups of newsgroups.

To participate in a newsgroup, you must use a program called a **newsreader**. The newsreader enables you to access a newsgroup to read a previously entered message, called an **article**, or add an article, called **posting**. A newsreader also keeps track of which articles you have and have not read. In this project, you will use Outlook Express, which is a newsreader, to read and post articles.

Newsgroup members often post articles in reply to other articles - either to answer questions or to comment on material in the original articles. These replies often cause the author of the original article, or others, to post additional articles related to the original article. This process can be short-lived or go on indefinitely depending on the nature of the topic and the interest of the participants. The original article and all subsequent related replies are called a **thread**. Figure 3-22 shows some articles and threads from a newsgroup called alt.archery.

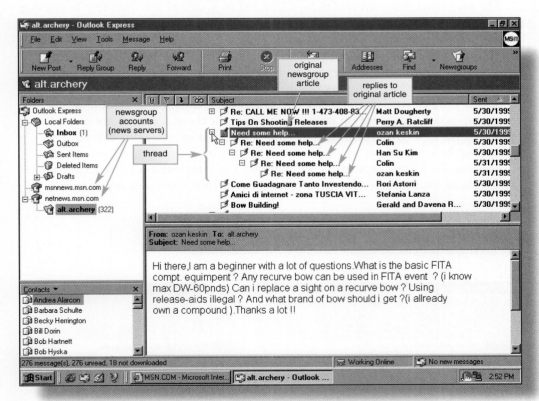

FIGURE 3-22

Newsgroups exist on products from vendors such as Microsoft and IBM; on subjects such as recipes, gardening, and music; or on just about any other topic you can imagine. A **newsgroup name** consists of a prefix and one or more subgroup names. For example, the comp.software newsgroup name consists of a **prefix** (comp), which indicates the subject of the newsgroup is computers, a period (.), and a **subgroup name** (software), which indicates the subject is further narrowed down to a discussion of software. A list of some prefix names and their descriptions are shown in Table 3-6.

The newsgroup prefixes found in Table 3-6 are not the only ones used. Innovative newsgroups are being created every day. Many colleges and universities have their own newsgroups on topics such as administrative information, tutoring, campus organizations, and distance learning.

In addition, some newsgroups are supervised by a **moderator**, who reads each article before it is posted to the newsgroup. If the moderator thinks an article is appropriate for the newsgroup, then the moderator posts the article for all members to read.

Table 3-6	
PREFIX	*DESCRIPTION*
alt	Groups on alternative topics
biz	Business topics
comp	Computer topics
gnu	GNU Software Foundation topics
ieee	Electrical engineering topics
info	Information about various topics
misc	Miscellaneous topics
news	Groups pertaining to newsgroups
rec	Recreational topics
sci	Science topics
talk	Various conversation groups

Accessing Newsgroups Using Internet Explorer

Before accessing the articles in a newsgroup or posting an article to a newsgroup, you must establish a newsgroup account on your computer. A **newsgroup account** allows access to the news server with the same name. Two newsgroup accounts (msnnews.msn.com and netnews.msn.com) display in the folders list in the Outlook Express window shown in Figure 3-22 on the previous page. Thus, for this project, access is available to the msnnews.msn.com and netnews.msn.com news servers.

The msnnews.msn.com and netnews.msn.com accounts are available because The Microsoft Network (MSN) is the Internet service provider used to connect to the Internet and display the window shown in Figure 3-22. The Microsoft Network makes access available to these accounts as part of their Internet services. Other Internet service providers (America Online, Prodigy, CompuServe, and so on) make access to different newsgroups available as part of their Internet services.

In this project, it is assumed that the msnnews.msn.com and netnews.msn.com newsgroup accounts are set up on your computer. If these accounts are not set up, use one of the newsgroup accounts in your folders list or ask your instructor for instructions to set up these accounts.

Perform the following steps to use Internet Explorer and Outlook Express to display the newsgroups on the default news server (msnnews.msn.com).

 To Display the Newsgroups on the Default News Server

1 **Click the Mail button on the Standard Buttons toolbar and then point to Read News.**

The Mail menu displays (Figure 3-23). The highlighted Read News command displays in the Mail menu.

FIGURE 3-23

Click Read News, click the No button in the Outlook Express dialog box, and then point to the Newsgroups button.

The Outlook Express window contains a toolbar, banner, and three frames (Figure 3-24). The default account name displays in the window title, banner, and folders list. A second account name displays in the folders list and the right frame contains a message, three buttons, and a message area. The news accounts on your computer may be different.

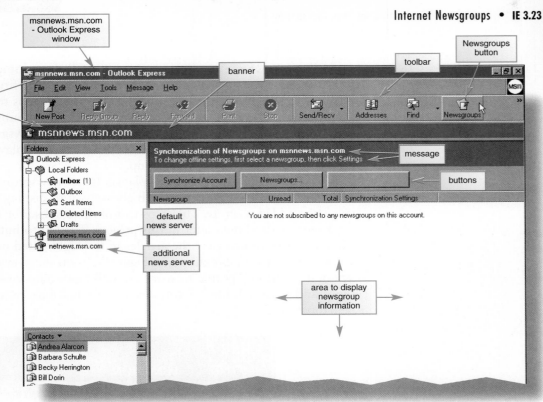

FIGURE 3-24

Click the Newsgroups button. If necessary, click the All tab.

The Newsgroup Subscriptions dialog box displays (Figure 3-25). The highlighted msnnews.msn.com icon and netnews.msn.com icon display in the Account(s) list box and the insertion point displays in the Display newsgroups which contain text box. A partial list of the newsgroups on the msn.news.com news server displays in alphabetical order in the Newsgroup list box. The newsgroups on your computer may be different.

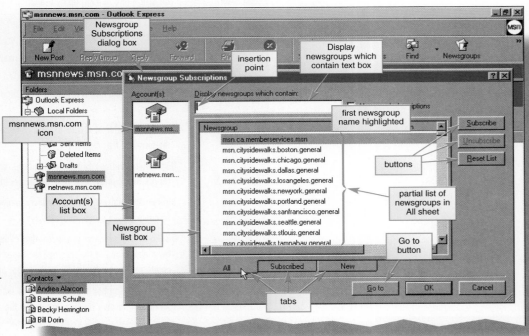

FIGURE 3-25

Other Ways

1. Click Newsgroups button in right frame
2. On Tools menu click Newsgroups
3. Press ALT+T, press W
4. Press CTRL+W

In Figure 3-25 on the previous page, the All sheet contains a partial list of the newsgroups on the msnnews.msn.com news server. The first newsgroup name (msn.ca.memberservices.msn) is highlighted. The buttons to the right of the News-group list box allow you to subscribe to a newsgroup (Subscribe), unsubscribe from a newsgroup (Unsubscribe), and redisplay the list of newsgroups (Reset List). When you **subscribe** to a newsgroup, the newsgroup name displays in the folders list, making it easy to return to the newsgroup.

Clicking the Subscribed tab displays a list of newsgroups to which you have subscribed and clicking the New tab allows you to display new newsgroups that have been added recently. The steps to follow to subscribe to and unsubscribe from a newsgroup are shown later in this project. The Go to button below the Newsgroup list box allows you to view the articles in the highlighted newsgroup.

Below the menu bar shown in Figure 3-24 on the previous page is a toolbar containing buttons specific to working with news messages (New Post, Reply Group, Reply, and so on). Table 3-7 contains the toolbar buttons and a brief explanation of their functions.

Table 3-7	
BUTTON	**FUNCTION**
New Post	Displays a window used to post a reply to a newsgroup article.
Reply Group	Displays a window that allows you to reply to the author of an article in a newsgroup by e-mail.
Reply	Displays a window that allows you to reply to all authors of articles in newsgroup by e-mail.
Forward	Displays a window that allows you to forward an article in a newsgroup by e-mail.
Print	Prints the highlighted article in the message list.
Stop	Stops the transfer of articles from a news server to the the message list.
Send/Recv	Displays the Outlook Express dialog box, contacts the news server, and displays new news messages in the message list.
Addresses	Displays the Address Book window containing a list of frequently used e-mail addresses.
Find	Displays the Find Message window that allows you to search for a newsgroup in the message list based upon sender name, recipient name, subject, message, and date.
Newsgroups	Displays a dialog box that allows you to select a news server and display the newsgroups on the server.

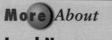

More *About*

Local Newsgroups

Many schools maintain a local newsgroup to disseminate information about school events and answer technical questions asked by students. To locate your local news-group, search for the school's name in the list of newsgroup names.

Searching for a Newsgroup

After displaying a list of the newsgroups on a news server, you should locate an interesting newsgroup and display the articles in the newsgroup. Two methods can be used to locate a newsgroup. The first method is to scroll the Newsgroup list box to locate a newsgroup. The second method is to type a keyword in the Display news-groups which contain text box and let Outlook Express search for and display a list of newsgroup names that contain the keyword.

Perform the following steps to search for and display the newsgroup names that contain a keyword (birds). Select one of the newsgroups found, and then display the articles in the newsgroup.

 To Display the Articles in a Newsgroup

1 **Type** birds **in the Display newsgroups which contain text box and then point to msn.forums.pets.birds.wild.**

When you type the word, birds, a list of three newsgroup names that contain the word, birds, displays (Figure 3-26). The first newsgroup name in the list (msn.expedia.snowbirds) is highlighted, and the msn.forums.pets.birds.wild name displays in the list.

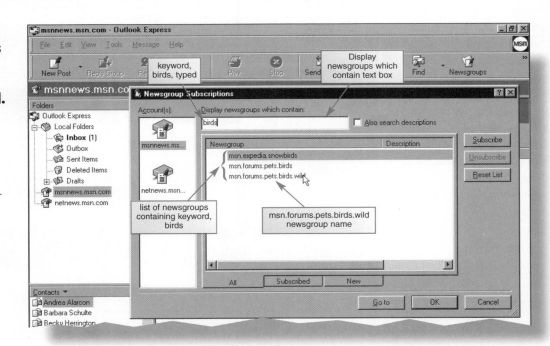

FIGURE 3-26

2 **Click msn.forums. pets.birds.wild and then point to the Go to button.**

The msn.forums.pets. birds.wild name is highlighted (Figure 3-27).

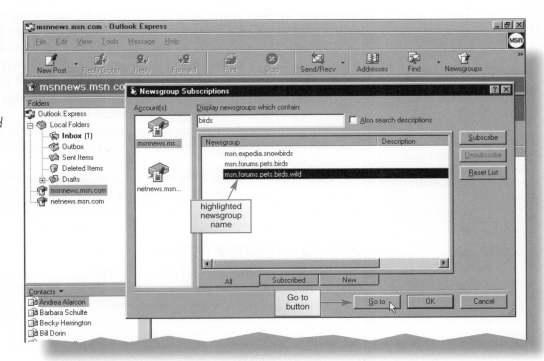

FIGURE 3-27

3 Click the Go to button.

The Newsgroup Subscriptions window closes, the newsgroup name (msn.forums.pets.birds.wild) displays in the window title and banner and indented below the msnnews.msn.com news server name in the folders list (Figure 3-28). The message list and preview pane display on the right side of the Outlook Express window and a list of articles in the newsgroup displays in the message list.

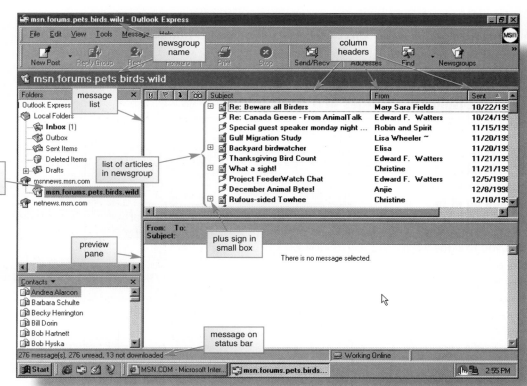

FIGURE 3-28

Other Ways

1. Scroll Newsgroup list box, click newsgroup, click Go to button

Column Headers

You can change the widths of columns in the message list by dragging the vertical line between two column headers. Likewise, you can drag the vertical line that separates the folders list and contacts list from the message list and preview pane to change the size of the two areas.

The upper-right frame (message list) contains column headers and a list of the original articles (postings) in the msn.forums.pets.birds.wild newsgroup. Each original article consists of the subject of the article, author name, date and time article was sent, and file size. The file size is not visible in Figure 3-28.

The plus sign in a small box to the left of some of the articles indicates the article is part of a thread. Clicking the plus sign expands the thread so you can see a list of the replies to the original article. A minus sign in a small box icon to the left of an article indicates the article is expanded. Clicking the minus sign collapses the thread so you cannot see the replies to the original article.

When you select an article in the message list, the text of the article displays in the lower-right frame (preview pane). In Figure 3-28, the preview pane indicates no message is selected.

The status bar at the bottom of the Outlook Express window indicates that 276 articles have been retrieved, 276 articles have not been read, and 13 have not been downloaded.

Reading Newsgroup Articles

The entries in the Subject column in the message list allow you to look at the subject of an article before deciding to read the article. Perform the following steps to read the Cardinal, cardinals everywhere! article.

Steps: To Read a Newsgroup Article

1 Scroll the message list to display **Cardinal, cardinals everywhere!** and then click the entry article.

The contents of the article display in the preview pane (Figure 3-29). A header in the preview pane contains the name of the person who posted the article, newsgroup name, and subject. The contents of the article display below the header.

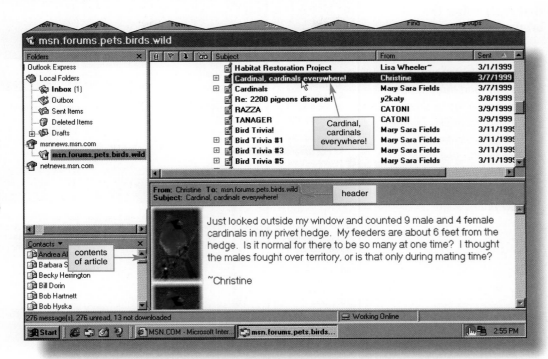

FIGURE 3-29

Expanding a Thread

When a plus sign displays to the left of an article in the message list, the article is part of a thread and can be expanded. **Expanding the thread** displays the replies to the original article indented below the original article and changes the plus sign to a minus sign. To expand the Cardinal, cardinals everywhere! thread and view the replies to the article, complete the following steps.

Other Ways

1. Press CTRL+< to read previous article
2. Press CTRL+> to read next article

Steps: To Expand a Thread

1 Point to the plus sign in the small box to the left of the Cardinal, cardinals everywhere! article (Figure 3-30).

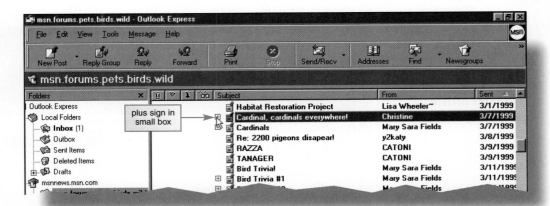

FIGURE 3-30

2 **Click the plus sign and then click the first reply below the original article.**

The plus sign to the left of the original article changes to a minus sign and three replies display below the original article (Figure 3-31). The Re: entry displays to the left of each reply, the first reply is highlighted, and the text of the first reply displays in the preview pane.

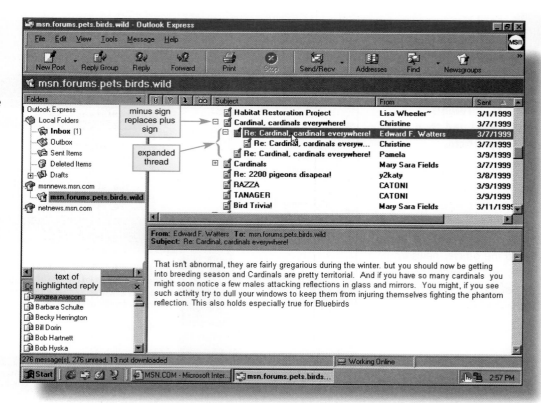

FIGURE 3-31

Other Ways

1. Press CTRL+PLUS on numeric keypad
2. Press CTRL+RIGHT ARROW

Collapsing a Thread

When you expand a thread, a minus sign replaces the plus sign to the left of the original article within the thread. Sometimes, after reading the replies within a thread, you will want to collapse the expansion. **Collapsing the thread** removes the replies from the thread, displays the original article in the preview pane, and changes the minus sign to the left of the original article to a plus sign. To collapse the Cardinal, cardinals everywhere! thread, perform the following steps.

 To Collapse a Thread

1 **Point to the minus sign in the small box to the left of the original Cardinal, cardinals everywhere! article (Figure 3-32).**

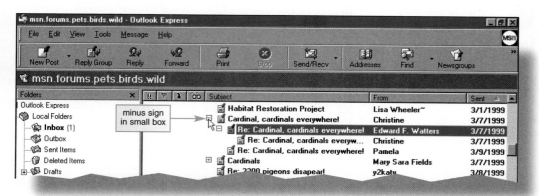

FIGURE 3-32

2 Click the minus sign.

The minus sign to the left of the original article changes to a plus sign and the replies to the original article no longer display (Figure 3-33).

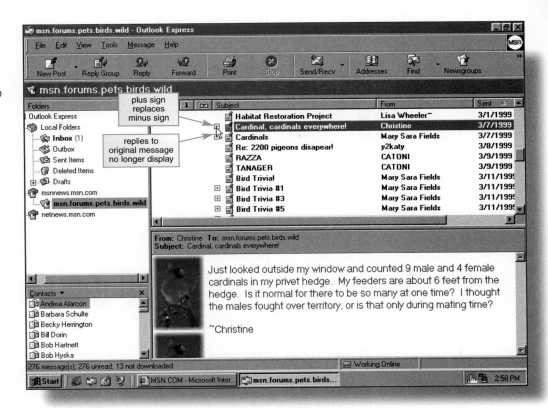

FIGURE 3-33

Printing a Newsgroup Article

After displaying and reading an article, you may wish to print the article. The printout is similar to the printout that results when you print an e-mail message (see Figure 3-7 on page IE 3.11). Perform the following steps to print the contents of the original Cardinal, cardinals everywhere! article.

TO PRINT A NEWSGROUP ARTICLE

 Click the Print button on the toolbar.

 Click the OK button in the Print dialog box.

The printed message consists of a header at the top of the page containing the page number (Page 1 of 1), the user's name (Steven Forsythe), and a horizontal line that is heavier under the user's name (Figure 3-34). Below the header are the From, Newsgroups, Sent, and Subject entries and the body of the newsgroup article. The Newsgroups entry contains the newsgroup name and the Subject entry contains the article name. A footer at the bottom of the page contains the current date (6/5/2000). The pictures in the newsgroup article do not print.

Other Ways

1. Press CTRL+MINUS on numeric keypad
2. Press CTRL+LEFT ARROW

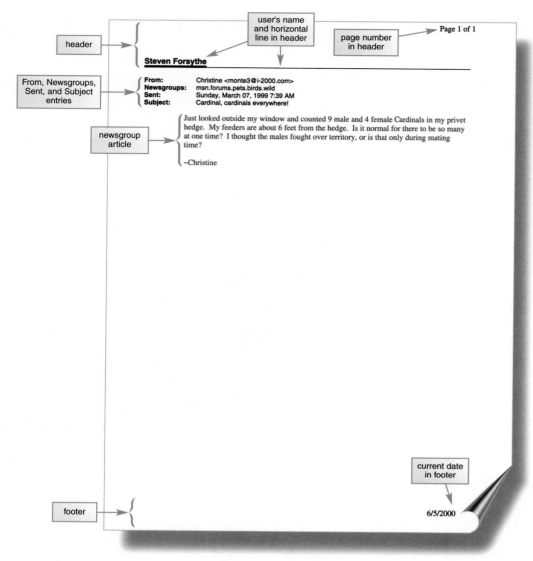

FIGURE 3-34

Subscribing to a Newsgroup

There may be several hundred newsgroups listed in the Newsgroup Subscriptions dialog box. Searching for a previously visited newsgroup or scrolling the newsgroup list to find a previously visited newsgroup can be time consuming. To quickly find a previously visited newsgroup, Outlook Express allows you to subscribe to a newsgroup. **Subscribing to a newsgroup** permanently adds the newsgroup name to the folders list and allows you to quickly return to the newsgroup by clicking the newsgroup name in the folders list instead of searching or scrolling to find the newsgroup name. Perform the following steps to subscribe to the msn.forums.pets.birds.wild newsgroup.

Steps ## To Subscribe to a Newsgroup

1 **Right-click the msn.forums.pets. birds.wild newsgroup name in the folders list and then point to Subscribe on the shortcut menu.**

A shortcut menu, containing the Subscribe command, displays (Figure 3-35).

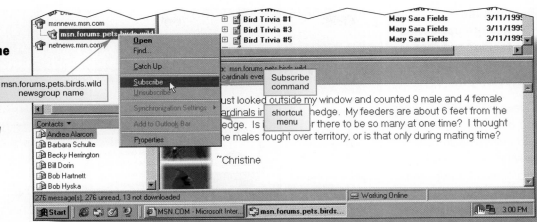

FIGURE 3-35

2 **Click Subscribe.**

The folder and stick pin icon to the left of the newsgroup name in the folders list changes color to indicate a subscription to the newsgroup has been made and the newsgroup name is added to the subscription list (Figure 3-36).

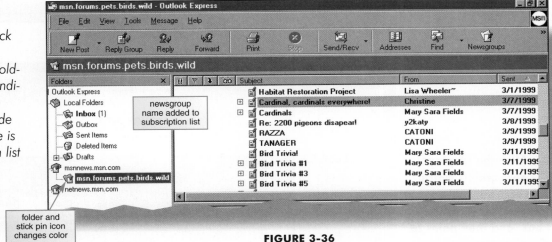

FIGURE 3-36

A subscription to the msn.forums.pets.birds.wild newsgroup has been made.

At some point in time you may wish to **post**, or send, a reply to a newsgroup article. The steps on the following pages show how to submit a newsgroup article for posting to the microsoft.test newsgroup, which is located on the netnews.msn.com server. This is a newsgroup just for miscellaneous purposes. Posting to this newsgroup will not disturb any other newsgroup articles.

Displaying the Newsgroups on Another Server

To display the newsgroups on the netnews.msn.com news server, you must first select the netnews.msn.com news server in the Account(s) list box in the Newsgroup Subscriptions dialog box. Perform the steps on the following pages to select the netnews.msn.com news server and display the newsgroups on the server.

Other **Ways**

1. Select newsgroup name in Newsgroup list box, click Subscribe button

2. Double-click newsgroup name in Newsgroup list box

Steps To Display the Newsgroups on Another News Server

1 **Click the Newsgroups button on the toolbar and then click netnews.msn.com in the Account(s) list box.**

The Newsgroup Subscriptions dialog box displays, the high-lighted netnews.msn.com news server name displays in the Account(s) list box, and a partial list of the newsgroups on the netnews.msn.com server displays in the News-group list box (Figure 3-37). The newsgroups on your computer may be different.

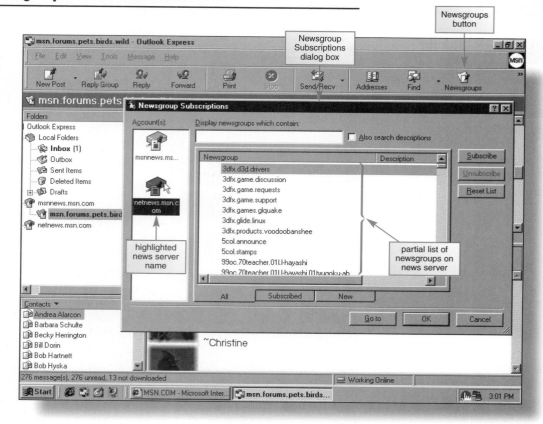

FIGURE 3-37

2 **Click the Display newsgroups which contain text box, type** microsoft.test **in the text box, and then point to the Go to button.**

The keyword, microsoft.test, displays in the Display news-groups which contain text box and one newsgroup name (microsoft.test) displays in the Newsgroup list box (Figure 3-38).

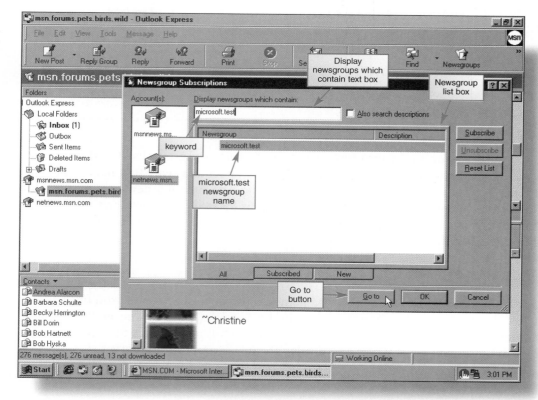

FIGURE 3-38

3 Click the Go to button.

The Newsgroup Subscriptions window closes, the microsoft.test newsgroup name displays indented below the netnews.msn.com entry in the folders list, in the window title, and in the banner (Figure 3-39). A partial list of articles in the microsoft.test newsgroup displays in the message list. Several test articles display in the message list.

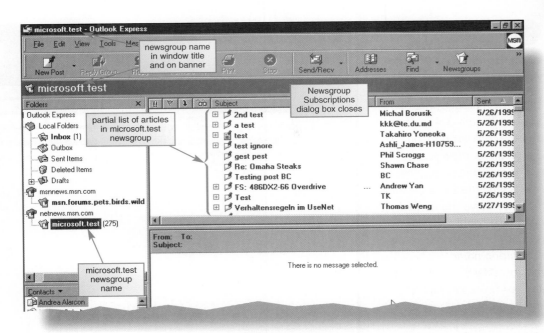

FIGURE 3-39

Posting a Newsgroup Article

After displaying the articles in the microsoft.test newsgroup, post a test article to the newsgroup. Use the words, Test Message, as the subject of the article to indicate that the article is a test and can be disregarded by anyone browsing the newsgroup. Perform the following steps to post a test article.

Other Ways

1. Click news server name in folders list, click Newsgroups button on toolbar

Steps: To Post a Newsgroup Article

1 Point to the New Post button on the toolbar (Figure 3-40).

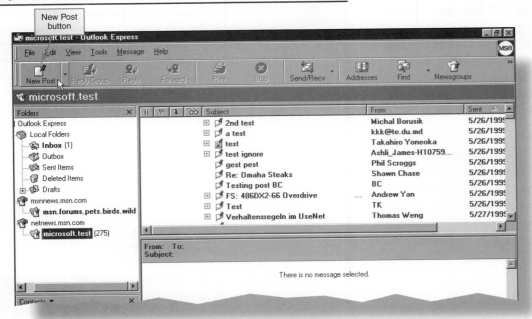

FIGURE 3-40

2 **Click the New Post button and then maximize the New Message window.**

The New Message window displays (Figure 3-41). The window contains a menu bar, a toolbar, four text boxes, and a message pane. The News Server text box contains the news server name (netnews.msn.com), the Newsgroups text box contains the newsgroup name (microsoft.test), and the Subject text box contains the insertion point.

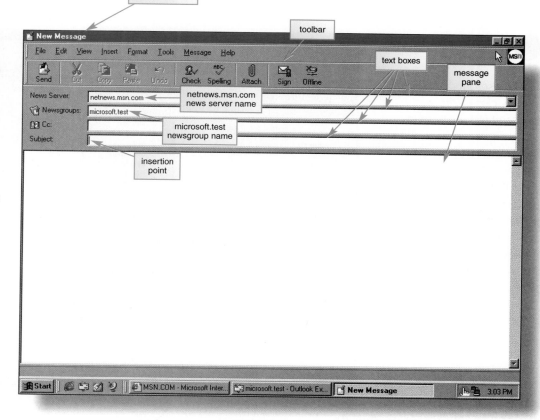

FIGURE 3-41

3 **Type** Test Message **in the Subject text box, press the TAB key, type** Please ignore this message. I am learning to post a message to a newsgroup. **as the message, and then point to the Send button.**

The subject displays in the window title and in the Subject text box and the message displays in the message pane (Figure 3-42). The subject indicates that this is a test message and can be disregarded.

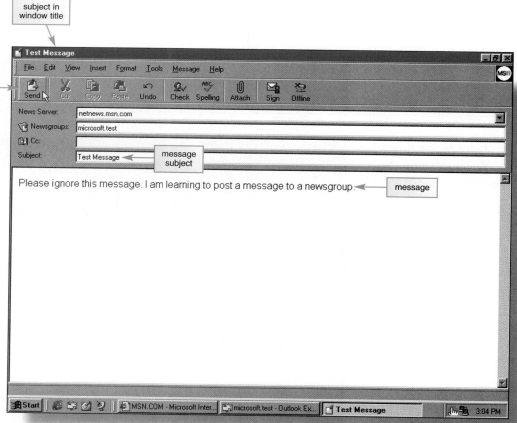

FIGURE 3-42

4 **Click the Send button and then point to the OK button in the Post News dialog box.**

The Post News dialog box displays (Figure 3-43). The dialog box contains a message to indicate the news message is being sent to the news server and may not display immediately in the message list.

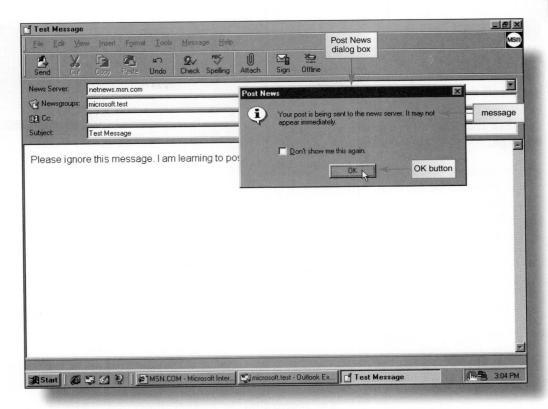

FIGURE 3-43

5 **Click the OK button.**

The Post News dialog box and Test Message window close, and the Microsoft.test - Outlook Express window redisplays (Figure 3-44). You may have to wait several minutes for the article to be posted to the microsoft.test newsgroup.

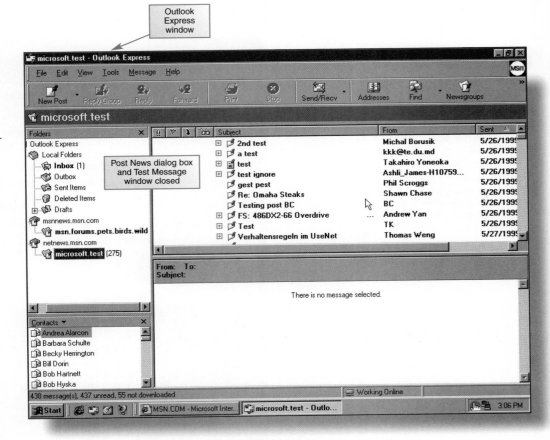

FIGURE 3-44

6 **You may have to wait several minutes before the message displays in the message list. Scroll the message list to display the test message and then click the test message.**

The Test Message article displays in the message list, and the contents of the message display in the preview pane (Figure 3-45).

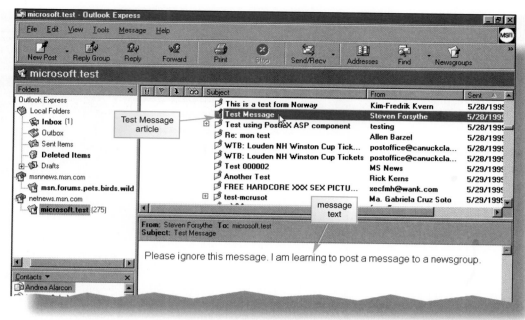

FIGURE 3-45

1. On File menu point to New, click News Message
2. Press ALT+M, press N
3. Press CTRL+N

The buttons on the toolbar illustrated in Figure 3-41 on page IE 3.34 (Send, Cut, Copy, Paste, and so on) are useful when posting a new article. Table 3-8 shows the buttons on the toolbar and their functions.

More About

Newsgroups

Instructors use newsgroups in courses taught over the Internet. An instructor posts a question and students respond by posting an article. Students can read the articles in the thread to be aware of all responses and subscribe to the newsgroup to quickly return to it.

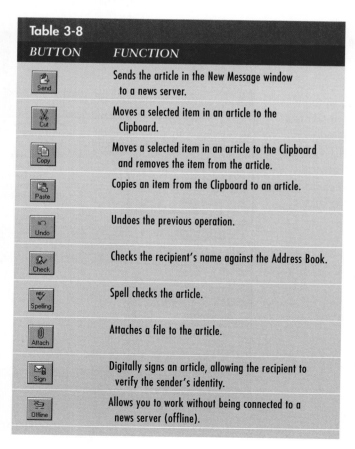

Table 3-8	
BUTTON	**FUNCTION**
Send	Sends the article in the New Message window to a news server.
Cut	Moves a selected item in an article to the Clipboard.
Copy	Moves a selected item in an article to the Clipboard and removes the item from the article.
Paste	Copies an item from the Clipboard to an article.
Undo	Undoes the previous operation.
Check	Checks the recipient's name against the Address Book.
Spelling	Spell checks the article.
Attach	Attaches a file to the article.
Sign	Digitally signs an article, allowing the recipient to verify the sender's identity.
Offline	Allows you to work without being connected to a news server (offline).

Displaying the Articles in a Newsgroup after Subscribing to the Newsgroup

Previously in this project, you subscribed to the msn.forums.pets.birds.wild newsgroup. After subscribing to a newsgroup, you can view the articles in the newsgroup by clicking the newsgroup name in the folders list without having to search or scroll to find the articles in the newsgroup. Perform the following step to view the articles in the msn.forums.pets.birds.wild newsgroup.

 ### To Display the Articles in a Newsgroup

1 **Click msn.forums. pets.birds.wild in the folders list. If the Outlook Express dialog box displays, click the OK button.**

The msn.forums.pets.birds. wild newsgroup name is highlighted in the folders list and the articles in the newsgroup display in the message list (Figure 3-46).

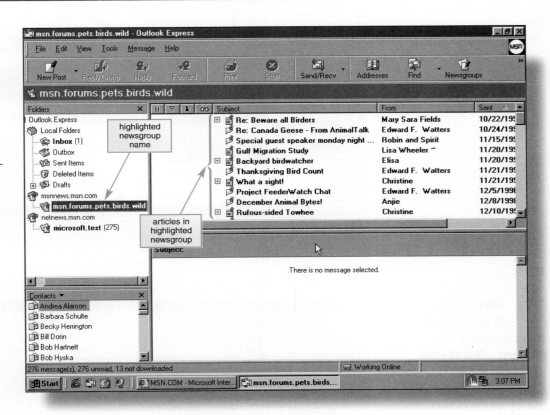

FIGURE 3-46

Unsubscribing from a Newsgroup

When you no longer need quick access to a newsgroup, you can cancel the subscription to the newsgroup, called **unsubscribing**, and remove the newsgroup name from the folders list. Perform the steps on the following page to unsubscribe from the msn.forums.pets.birds.wild newsgroup.

To Unsubscribe from a Newsgroup

1 **Right-click the msn.forums.pets. birds.wild newsgroup name in the folders list and then point to Unsubscribe on the shortcut menu.**

A shortcut menu, containing the Unsubscribe command, displays (Figure 3-47).

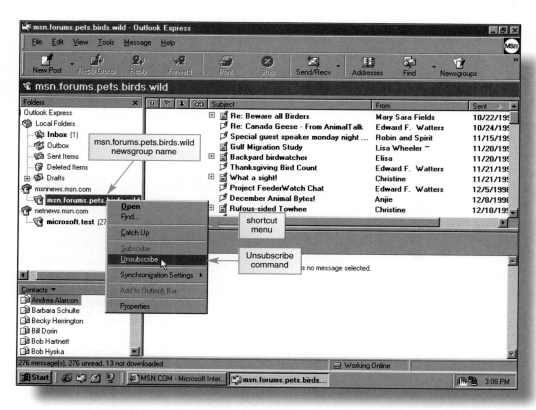

FIGURE 3-47

2 **Click Unsubscribe. If the Outlook Express dialog box displays, click the OK button in the dialog box. If a second Outlook Express dialog box displays, click the No button in the dialog box.**

The newsgroup name is removed from the folders list to indicate the subscription to the newsgroup has been canceled (Figure 3-48).

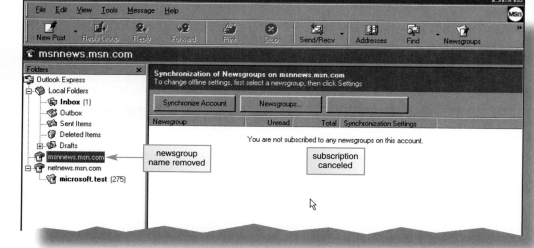

FIGURE 3-48

Other Ways

1. Select newsgroup name in Newsgroup Subscriptions dialog box, click Unsubscribe button
2. Double-click newsgroup name

Quitting Outlook Express

When you have finished working with newsgroups, you should quit Outlook Express.

TO QUIT OUTLOOK EXPRESS

 Click the Close button in the Outlook Express window.

 If the Outlook Express dialog box displays, click the OK button in the dialog box.

The Outlook Express window closes, Outlook Express quits, and the Microsoft Internet Explorer window redisplays.

Live Videoconferences (Microsoft Netmeeting)

Another popular method of communicating with others in business and at home is Microsoft NetMeeting. **Microsoft NetMeeting** allows you to use the Internet to engage in a live videoconference.

You can communicate in several ways using Microsoft NetMeeting. One method of communicating is to use Chat. **Chat** allows users to send text messages to each other and is especially useful when several users are involved in a meeting. When one person in the meeting types a message, the message displays on the desktop of every other person in the meeting.

A second method of communicating is to use Whiteboard. **Whiteboard** is a drawing program that allows all users to sketch and type simultaneously while viewing the results of the other users' efforts. A third method of communicating is to use File Transfer. **File Transfer** allows you to send data files to one or more NetMeeting users.

Using Chat, Whiteboard, or File Transfer to communicate with other NetMeeting users does not require audio devices (microphone, speakers, and headphones) or video devices (video camera). Other methods of communicating require additional devices.

If your computer has a sound card, speakers, and a microphone, NetMeeting allows you to talk and listen to other users without the usual costs associated with long distance telephone calls. If your computer has a video camera, NetMeeting allows you to engage in live, face-to-face meetings by exchanging live video images. In this project, you will be part of a live videoconference and use Chat to exchange text messages.

Internet Addresses and Internet Locator Services

Every computer connected to the Internet has a unique **Internet Protocol address (IP address)** that identifies the computer, and every NetMeeting user must have an e-mail address. To communicate with another NetMeeting user, you must know the IP address of their computer or be able to locate their e-mail address on a computer server maintained by an **Internet Locator Service (ILS)**. The ILS server maintains a **directory list** of personal information (e-mail address, first name, last name, city, state, and personal comments) for each user logged on to the server. The e-mail address, first name, and last name are required by NetMeeting to log on to a server.

When you log on to an ILS server, the server adds your personal information to its directory list and records the IP address of the computer you are using. If someone wants to contact to you, they select your e-mail address from the directory list and the server associates the e-mail address with your computer's IP address, making it possible to contact you. Similarly, when you want to contact another user, you select their e-mail address in the directory list of their ILS server. The server associates their e-mail address with their IP address and makes the connection. Thus, to place a call to another NetMeeting user, you must know the ILS server the user is logged on to and their e-mail address.

More *About*

IP Addresses

You can determine the IP address of your computer by clicking the Start button, clicking Run, typing winipcfg in the Open box, and then clicking the OK button.

More *About*

ILS Servers

Internet locator servers (ILS) will become more prevalent as live conferencing becomes more popular. Use your favorite search engine to locate other ILSs you can use.

WARNING! Not everyone who uses NetMeeting has business purposes in mind, and many people who use NetMeeting are open and frank about the type of communication they want. Some areas may contain violent or sexually explicit content. **Content Advisor,** a program available with Internet Explorer that provides a way to help control the types of content that your computer can access on the Internet, is not available in NetMeeting. Consequently, you may decide you do not want to use NetMeeting.

Launching Microsoft NetMeeting

Before communicating with other NetMeeting users, you must launch Microsoft NetMeeting. Perform the following steps to launch Microsoft NetMeeting and display the Microsoft NetMeeting window.

 To Launch Microsoft NetMeeting

1 **Click File on the Microsoft Internet Explorer menu bar, point to New on the File menu, and then point to Internet Call on the New submenu.**

The File menu and New submenu display (Figure 3-49). The highlighted Internet Call command displays on the New submenu.

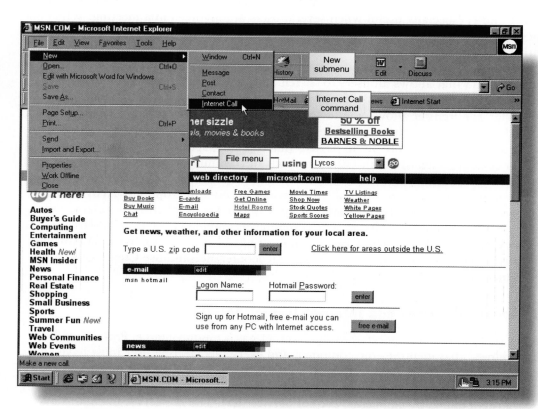

FIGURE 3-49

② Click Internet Call.

Microsoft NetMeeting launches and the maximized Microsoft NetMeeting - No Connections window displays (Figure 3-50). The window contains a menu bar, Directory toolbar, Navigation Icons bar, and Directory sheet.

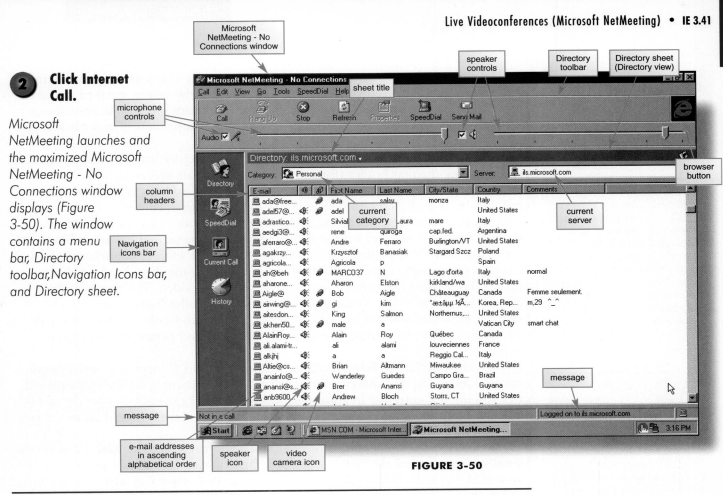

FIGURE 3-50

The Microsoft NetMeeting window shown in Figure 3-50 displays in the default **Directory view**. In Directory view, the Directory toolbar displays below the menu bar. The **Directory toolbar** contains buttons specific to working with NetMeeting (Call, Hang Up, Stop, and so on) and the browser button. Table 3-9 contains the buttons on the Directory toolbar and a brief explanation of their functions. The microphone controls (Audio check box and Microphone Volume slide and slider) indicate the microphone is working and the volume level of the microphone. The speaker controls (Volume check box and Speaker Volume slide and slider) indicate whether the speakers are working and their volume level.

Below the Directory toolbar and slides are the Navigation Icons bar and the Directory sheet. The Navigation Icons bar contains the Directory, SpeedDial, Current Call, and History icons. The **Directory sheet** associated with the Directory icon displays to the right of the Navigation Icons bar. The Directory sheet title (Directory: ils.microsoft.com) indicates the current view is the Directory view and the current ILS server is the ils.microsoft.com server. The current category (Personal) displays in the Category box and the current ILS server name (ils.microsoft.com) displays in the Server box.

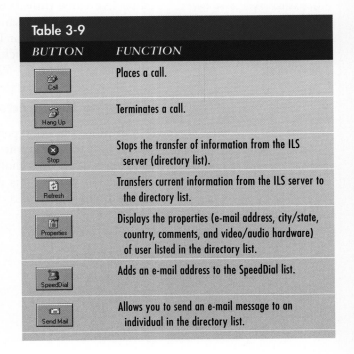

Table 3-9	
BUTTON	**FUNCTION**
Call	Places a call.
Hang Up	Terminates a call.
Stop	Stops the transfer of information from the ILS server (directory list).
Refresh	Transfers current information from the ILS server to the directory list.
Properties	Displays the properties (e-mail address, city/state, country, comments, and video/audio hardware) of user listed in the directory list.
SpeedDial	Adds an e-mail address to the SpeedDial list.
Send Mail	Allows you to send an e-mail message to an individual in the directory list.

Changing the Category

When the default category is Personal, only personal users display in the directory list. You can change the category so that only users in a call (In a Call), users not in a meeting (Not in call), users who have video cameras (With video cameras), or users in your country (In my country) display in the directory list. To change the category, click the Category box arrow and then click a category.

Directory Listings

As you will discover the first time you explore a directory listing, not everyone who uses NetMeeting has business purposes in mind, and many people who use NetMeeting are open and frank about the type of communication they want. Some areas contain violent or sexually explicit content. Consequently, you may decide you do not want to use NetMeeting.

The **directory list** in Figure 3-50 on the previous page contains the personal information for every NetMeeting user who is logged on to the server specified in the Server box (ils.microsoft.com) and who chose the category specified in the Category box (Personal). The directory list displays in ascending alphabetical order based on e-mail addresses.

Eight column markers display at the top of the directory list. The names in the column below the first header (E-mail) indicate the e-mail addresses of the users in the directory list. A computer icon precedes each e-mail address in the E-mail column. If a red star displays on the computer icon, the user is currently in a meeting.

A speaker icon identifies the second header, and a video camera icon identifies the third header. A speaker icon in the column below the second header indicates the user has speakers and a microphone and is able to listen to your communication and respond to it. A video camera icon in the column below the third header indicates the user has a video camera and is able to transmit live video. The names in the columns below the fourth header (First Name), fifth header (Last Name), sixth header (City/State), seventh header (Country), and eighth header (Comments) indicate the first name, last name, city and state, country, and personal comments of each user.

The status bar at the bottom of the NetMeeting - No Connections window contains two messages. The message at the left side of the status bar (Not in a call) indicates you are not currently in a meeting. The message at the right side on the status bar (Logged on to ils.microsoft.com) indicates whether you are logged on to a server and the server name.

The icons in the Navigation Icons bar allow you to change the view. Clicking the **SpeedDial icon** changes the view to the SpeedDial view and displays a list of users you would like to be able to call quickly. Clicking the **Current Call icon** changes the view to the Current Call view, which allows you to view a list of the users currently in the meeting. In addition, you can preview your live video transmission and view their live video transmission in this view. Clicking the **History icon** changes the view to the History view, which allows you to view a list of your callers, your response to their calls (Accepted or Ignored), and the time of each call. If the current view is not the Directory view, clicking the **Directory icon** changes the view to the Directory view illustrated in Figure 3-50 on the previous page.

Changing the Directory Information

If more than one person uses the NetMeeting program on your computer, it is important to change the directory information to your personal information before placing a call. After changing the information, your personal information displays in the directory list and is visible to other NetMeeting users. Perform the following steps to change the directory information.

Steps To Change the Directory Information

1 **Click Call on the menu bar and then point to Change My Information.**

The highlighted Change My Information command displays on the Call menu (Figure 3-51). The Log Off from command contains the server name on to which you are logged.

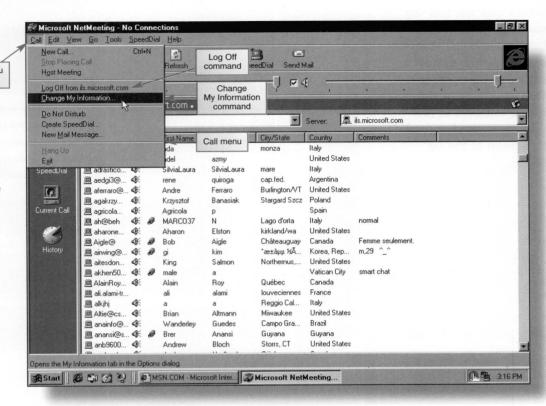

FIGURE 3-51

2 **Click Change My Information.**

The My Information sheet displays in the Options dialog box (Figure 3-52). The Information sheet contains five text boxes. One box is for entering comments. The three option buttons categorize the NetMeeting usage for the server. The insertion point displays in the First name text box and the For personal use (suitable for all ages) option button is selected.

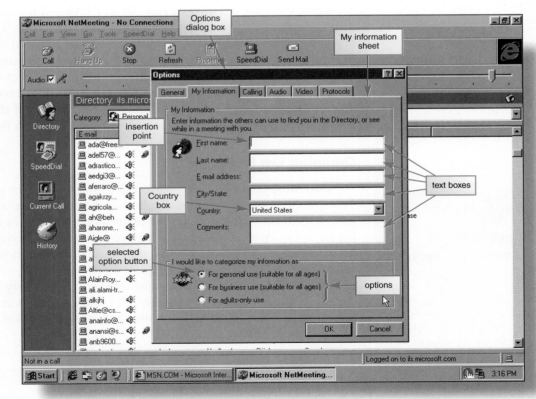

FIGURE 3-52

Type your first name, last name, e-mail address, and city and state in the First name, Last name, E-mail address, and City/State text boxes, respectively. Select your country in the Country box, type a comment in the Comments text box, and then point to the OK button.

The personal information for Steven Forsythe, one of the authors of this book, displays in the My Information sheet (Figure 3-53). Your personal information should display on your computer.

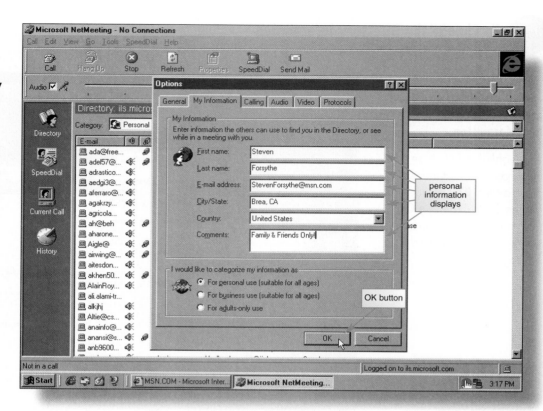

FIGURE 3-53

 **Click the OK button.**

The Options dialog box closes.

Three categories (For personal use, For business use, and For adults-only use) display in the Options dialog box shown in Figure 3-53. The default category is the For personal use category. When you select a category in the Options dialog box, the directory list you view will contain the personal information of only the users who have chosen the same category. For example, if you select the For business use category, only NetMeeting users who have chosen the For business use category will display in the directory list. Users who have selected one of the other categories (For personal use and For adults-only use) will not display in the directory list.

Changing the ILS Server

Currently, you are logged on to the ils.microsoft.com server. The ils.microsoft.com server name displays in the Server box, and a list of all personal users logged on to the ils.microsoft.com server displays in the directory list (see Figure 3-53). Assume you want to place a call to a relative, Jill, who is out of town on business. Jill always logs on to the ils5.microsoft.com server and uses the e-mail address.

Before placing the call, you must display the directory list for the ils5.microsoft.com server and locate Jill's e-mail address in the directory list. Perform the following steps to change to the ils5.microsoft.com server.

More About

Logging On to Another ILS Server

To log on to another ILS server, click Call on the menu bar, click Log Off, click Tools on the menu bar, click Options, click Calling tab, click Server name box arrow, click server name, and then click the OK button.

Steps: To Change the ILS Server

1 Click the Server box arrow in the Directory sheet and then point to ils5.microsoft.com.

The Server list box, containing nine server names, displays (Figure 3-54). The highlighted current server name (ils.microsoft.com) displays in the Server box and the highlighted ils5.microsoft.com server name displays in the Server list box.

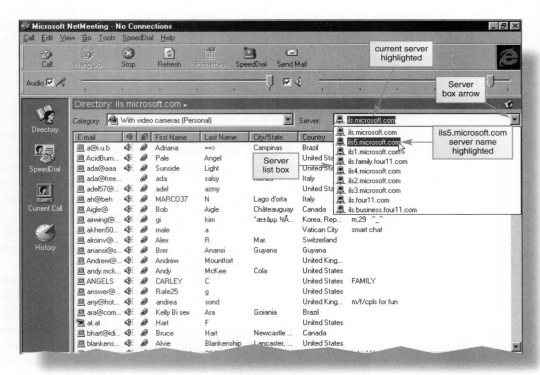

FIGURE 3-54

2 Click ils5. microsoft.com.

The ils5.microsoft.com server name displays in the Server box and the directory list changes to contain only personal users logged on to the ils5.microsoft.com server (Figure 3-55).

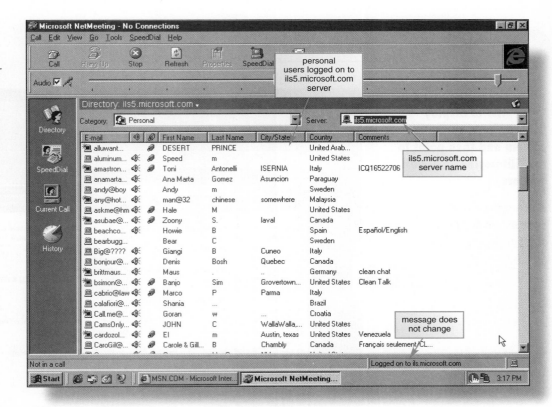

FIGURE 3-55

In Figure 3-55 on the previous page, the server name in the Server box changes to ils5.microsoft.com and the directory list contains the users logged on to the ils5.microsoft.com server. The message at the right side of the status bar does not change. The message indicates you are logged on to the ils.microsoft.com server. Changing the current server does not change the server on to which you are logged. Other users can see your name in the directory list by changing their current server to ils.microsoft.com.

Placing a Call

Currently, you are logged on to the ils.microsoft.com server, your personal information displays in the directory list of the ils.microsoft.com server, and the directory list for the ils5.microsoft.com server displays in the Directory sheet. As such, you can place a call to anyone in the directory list and use any of the NetMeeting tools (Chat, Whiteboard, and File Transfer) to communicate with that user.

The following steps show how to place a call to Jill using her e-mail address (jillforsythe). Because Jill will not be there to accept a call when performing these steps, you must substitute the e-mail address of a person you choose to call in each step that contains the address.

If you are in a computer lab setting, find another student in the lab with whom you can perform these steps. The person you call must enter their personal information, select the For personal use category, click the Calling tab, select the ils5.microsoft.com server name in the Server name box, and then click the Yes button in the Microsoft NetMeeting dialog box. The Logged on to ils5.microsoft.com message must display at the right side of the status bar on their computer.

Perform the following steps to scroll the directory list to display other user's address in the E-mail column and then place a call to Jill.

 To Place a Call

1 **Scroll the directory list to display jillforsythe... in the E-mail column and then point to the jillforsythe... e-mail address.**

Jill Forsythe's partial e-mail address displays in the E-mail column (Figure 3-56).

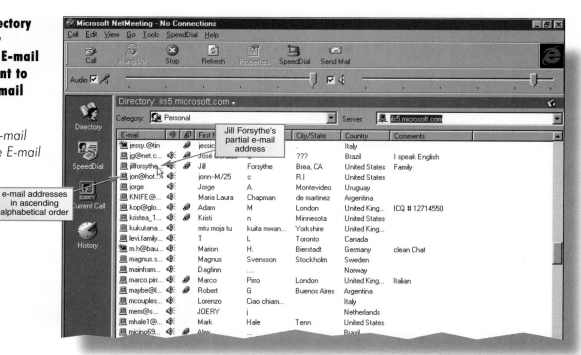

FIGURE 3-56

2 **Double-click the jillforsythe... e-mail address.**

Jill's address is selected in the directory list and two messages display on the status bar while the call is made. When Jill accepts the call, the Current Call toolbar replaces the Directory tool-bar, the Current Call sheet displays, two names display in the sheet, and a message displays on the status bar (Figure 3-57). The My Video window and Jill Forsythe window contain the live video transmissions.

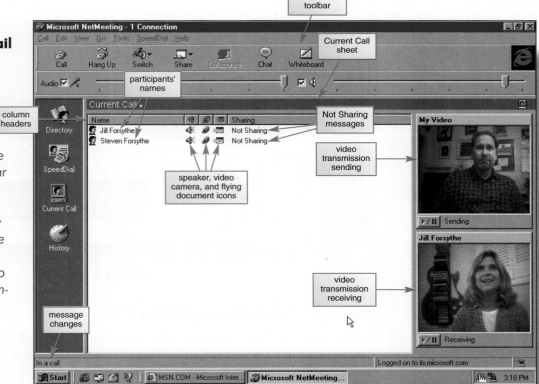

FIGURE 3-57

The Current Call toolbar replaces the Directory toolbar illustrated in Figure 3-57. The **Current Call toolbar** contains buttons specific to participating in a call (Call, Hang Up, Switch, Share, Collaborate, Chat, and Whiteboard). Five column markers display at the top of the Current Call list in Figure 3-57. Names in the column below the first header (Name) indicate the first and last names of the callers. A speaker icon identifies the second header and a video camera icon identifies the third header. A speaker icon in the column below the second header indicates the user has a microphone and speakers and is able to talk with others and listen to their communications.

A video camera icon in the column below the third header indicates the user has a video camera and is able to transmit live video. A flying document icon identifies the fourth header. This icon indicates the user is using a conferencing program, such as NetMeeting, and can share applications (Chat, Whiteboard, and File Transfer). The Not Sharing message in the column below the fifth header (Sharing) indicates neither participant currently is sharing an application.

Two windows display to the right of the Current Call sheet. The My Video window contains the live video transmission sent by the caller (Steven Forsythe). The Jill Forsythe window contains the live video transmission sent by the person that accepted the call (Jill Forsythe). The two windows are larger than their default sizes to improve how you view the video transmission.

In the previous steps, you successfully placed a call to another person using NetMeeting. The person you placed the call to sees the Microsoft NetMeeting dialog box shown in Figure 3-58 on the next page. The dialog box on Jill Forsythe's desk-top contains the message, Incoming call from Steven Forsythe..., and two buttons (Accept and Ignore). Clicking the Accept button accepts the call.

Other Ways

1. Click e-mail address, click Call button on Directory tool-bar, click Call button
2. Click SpeedDial icon, dou-ble-click e-mail address
3. Highlight e-mail address, press ALT+C, press N, press ENTER key

More About

The Video Transmission Windows

To change the size of the Sending and Receiving windows that display in the Current Call sheet, click Tools on the menu bar, click Options, click Video tab, click desired image size button in Send Image size area, and then click the OK button.

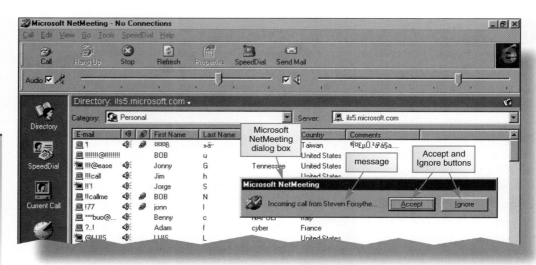

FIGURE 3-58

Sending a Typed Message Using Chat

Using Chat is another method of communicating with other users. Chat allows you to send text messages to other NetMeeting users. Chat is useful when several users are involved in a meeting or the sound quality is not adequate for a meeting. When one person in the meeting types and sends a message using Chat, the message displays on the desktop of every person in the meeting to which the message was sent. Because only two people can use audio and video at the same time, Chat is especially useful when several users are involved in the same meeting.

Assume you have a problem with the microphone, and the sound quality is not good enough to continue the meeting. Steven would then suggest to Jill that they use Chat to complete their meeting. Jill agrees. Perform the following steps to use Chat to send a text message to and receive a text response from Jill.

Steps **To Send a Text Message Using Chat**

1 **Point to the Chat button on the Current Call toolbar (Figure 3-59).**

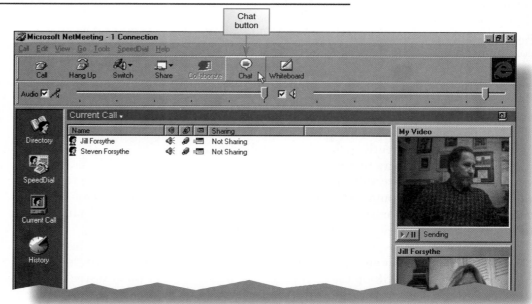

FIGURE 3-59

Click the Chat button, type I hope the weather in Michigan is good. Where are you staying? **in the Message text box, point to the Send button.**

The Untitled - Chat window displays (Figure 3-60). The window contains a display area, Message text box, Send button, Send to box, and message area. The message displays in the Message text box. A similar window displays on the desktop of the other participant.

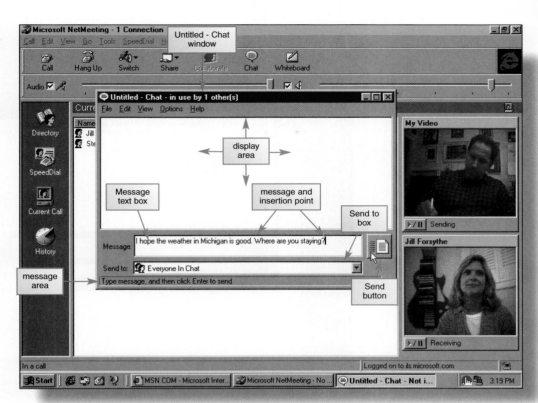

FIGURE 3-60

Click the Send button.

Chat removes the message in the Message text box, displays your name and the message in the display area, and then sends the message to the other participant (Figure 3-61). Your name and message display in the other participant's display area.

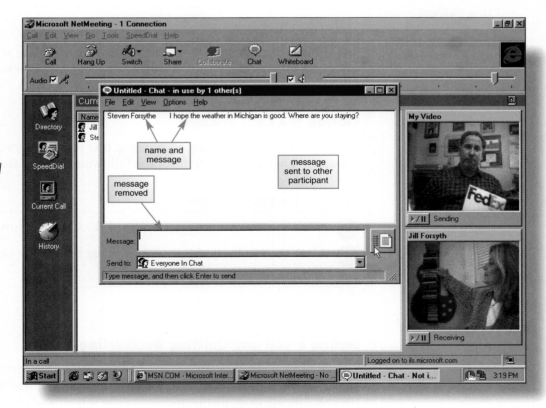

FIGURE 3-61

4 **The other participant (Jill Forsythe) sends a response.**

Jill sends her response (I am staying at the Thomas Edison Inn in Port Huron.), and Jill's name and message display in the display area in the Untitled - Chat window (Figure 3-62).

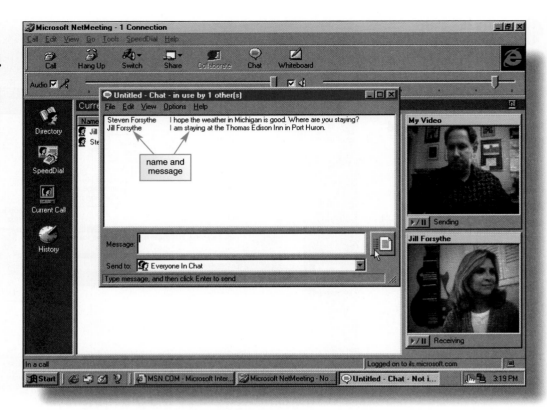

FIGURE 3-62

Other Ways

1. On Tools menu click Chat, type message, click Send
2. Press CTRL+T, type message, press ENTER

You can continue conversing in this manner, reading what the other user has to say and then typing a response. If you wish to send a message to only one person, select the person's name in the Send to list box and then click the Send button.

Closing the Chat Window

When you have finished exchanging text messages, you should close the Untitled - Chat window. Perform the following steps to close the window.

TO CLOSE THE CHAT WINDOW

1 Click the Close button in the Untitled - Chat window.

2 Click the No button in the Chat dialog box to not save the current list of messages.

The Untitled - Chat window closes.

Ending a Call and Quitting NetMeeting

After placing a call and chatting with another NetMeeting user, you decide it is time to end the call and the NetMeeting session. Perform the following steps to end the call, log off from the ils.microsoft.com server, and quit NetMeeting.

TO END A CALL, LOG OFF, AND QUIT NETMEETING

(1) Click the Hang Up button on the Current Call toolbar.

(2) Click Call on the menu bar and then click Log Off from ils.microsoft.com on the Call menu.

(3) Click the Close button in the Microsoft NetMeeting window.

NetMeeting ends the call, logs off from the ils.microsoft.com server, and closes the Microsoft NetMeeting window.

Creating Web Pages (Microsoft FrontPage Express)

With the growing popularity of the Internet, the need to develop a presence on the World Wide Web has become increasingly important for businesses, schools, government, and other organizations. Whether you create a personal Web page to brag about your hobbies and achievements or create a more involved Web site for use in business, the ability to create a Web page has become a popular and profitable skill. In fact, many new employees are expected to have knowledge of the Internet and Web page creation.

Although many software programs, are available today that allow you to create Web pages, all Web pages are created using a special formatting language called **hypertext markup language (HTML)**. HTML consists of special instructions, called **tags** or **markups**, that are used to create a Web page. The instructions indicate to the Web browser software (Internet Explorer) how each Web page should look and how it relates to other Web pages.

Fortunately, you do not have to know the HTML language or its instructions to create a Web page. The capability to create a Web page is available within Internet Explorer using a tool called FrontPage Express.

Microsoft FrontPage Express

Microsoft FrontPage Express is a Web page editor that allows you to use the power of HTML to create and format Web pages. To demonstrate the capabilities of FrontPage Express, you will create a personal Web page in this project. Before creating a Web page, you must launch FrontPage Express using the Edit button on the toolbar in the Microsoft Internet Explorer window. Perform the following steps to launch FrontPage Express.

More *About*

Web Authoring Tools

Other Web page creation programs, such as Hotdog and Hotmetal, are available free from public access FTP sites.

Steps: To Launch Microsoft FrontPage Express

1 **Click the arrow on the Edit button on the Standard Buttons toolbar and then point to Edit with Microsoft FrontPage Editor.**

The Edit menu, containing the highlighted Edit with Microsoft FrontPage Editor command, displays (Figure 3-63). Notice that the MSN.COM home page displays in the Microsoft Internet Explorer window.

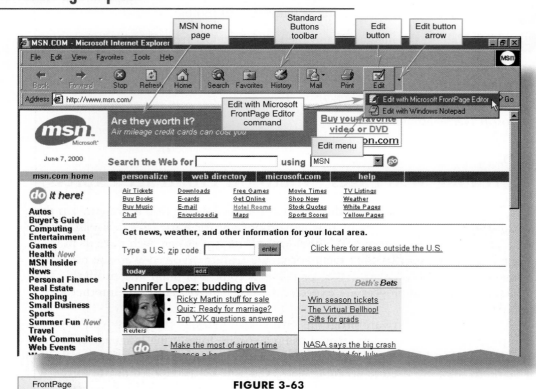

FIGURE 3-63

2 **Click Edit with Microsoft FrontPage Editor.**

The FrontPage Express window displays and the MSN home page displays in a special format in the window to allow FrontPage Express to edit, or change, the elements on the MSN home page (Figure 3-64). Instead of editing a Web page, you will use FrontPage Express to create a new Web page.

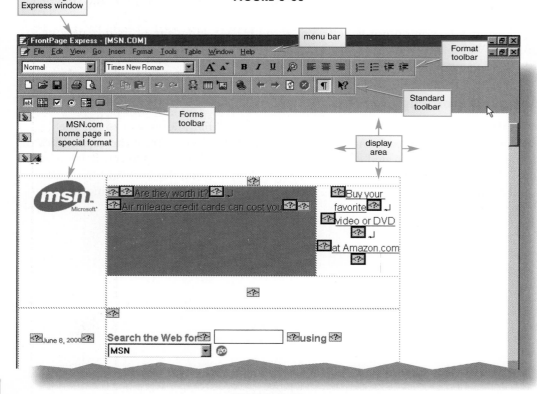

FIGURE 3-64

Other Ways

1. Click Start button, point to Programs, point to Internet Explorer, click FrontPage Express

The FrontPage Express window illustrated in Figure 3-64 contains a menu bar, Format toolbar, Standard toolbar, Forms toolbar, and a display area where the Web page on which you are working displays. Currently, you could use FrontPage Express to edit the elements on the MSN home page. However, you want to create a new personal Web page.

Because designing a Web page can be a complex process, FrontPage Express provides a special automated assistant, called a **wizard**, to help you through the process of creating a Web page. A wizard asks questions and automatically performs actions based on the answers to quickly create a Web page. All of this is accomplished without knowing the HTML language. One wizard, the **Personal Home Page wizard,** makes developing a home page as simple as selecting the sections to display on the home page, selecting the type of information to display, and typing the text you want to display on the page. The following steps show how to start the Personal Home Page Wizard.

More *About*

Wizards

Another FrontPage Express wizard is the Form Page wizard to create a form to collect input from a user and store the information on a Web page or in a text file. Templates include the Confirmation Form template to create a page to acknowledge receipt of user information, New Web View Folder template to create a new Web View folder, and Survey Form template to create a survey to collect information from readers.

 To Start the Personal Home Page Wizard

1 **Click File on the FrontPage Express menu bar and then point to New.**

The File menu displays (Figure 3-65). The highlighted New command displays on the File menu.

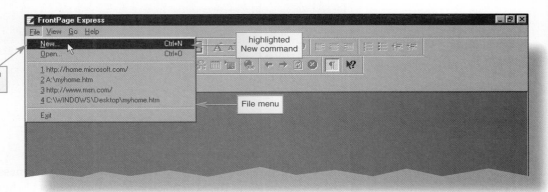

FIGURE 3-65

2 **Click New, click Personal Home Page Wizard in the Template or Wizard list box in the New Page window, and then point to the OK button.**

The New Page window displays (Figure 3-66). The Template or Wizard list box contains a list of six wizards and templates, including the highlighted Personal Home Page Wizard. A message displays in the Description area.

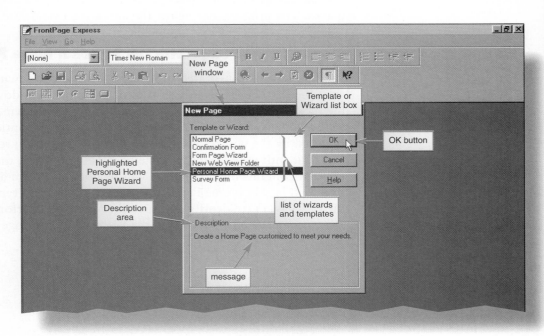

FIGURE 3-66

Click the OK button.

The Personal Home Page Wizard window displays (Figure 3-67).

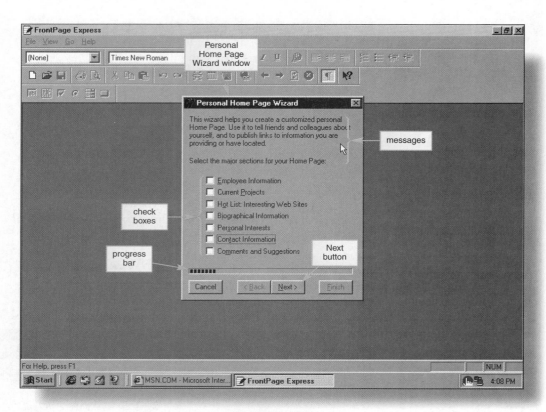

FIGURE 3-67

The window shown in Figure 3-67 contains two messages and seven check boxes, representing the seven sections you can select when you create a personal home page. Because the wizard remembers the options that were selected the last time it was used, some boxes in the window on your computer may contain check marks. The progress bar below the check boxes indicates the progress of the wizard.

Creating a Web Page with the Personal Home Page Wizard

The window illustrated in Figure 3-67 is the first window to display when you start the Personal Home Page wizard. Additional windows display when you click the Next button in the Personal Home Page Wizard window. Read the messages and follow the instructions in each window to select the options or type the text as required by the wizard and then click the Next button to display the next window.

To identify the personal home page being created, the file name of the HTML file that contains the home page will be homepage.htm and the title of the home page will be My Home Page. The wizard asks you to type the file name and title and then uses them to identify and save the Web page. Perform the following steps to create a personal home page using the Personal Home Page wizard.

Steps **To Create a Web Page Using a Wizard**

1 **Remove all check marks from the check boxes in the Personal Home Page Wizard window. Click Employee Information, click Personal Interests, click Contact Information, and then point to the Next button.**

Check marks display in the Employee Information, Personal Interests, and Contact Information check boxes (Figure 3-68). These check boxes represent the three sections the wizard will create in the personal Web page.

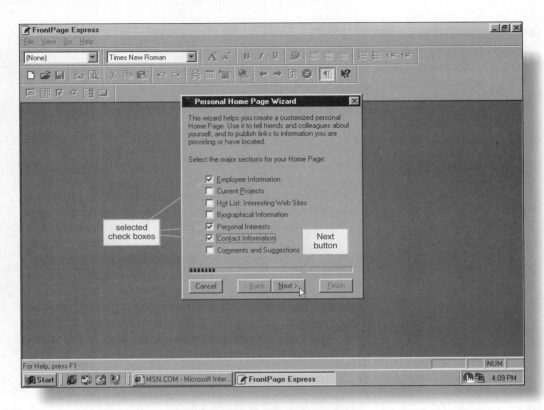

FIGURE 3-68

 2 **Click the Next button.**

The next window contains the Page URL text box and Page Title text box (Figure 3-69). The highlighted default HTML file name (home1.htm) and the insertion point display in the Page URL text box, and the default page title (Home Page 1) displays in the Page Title text box.

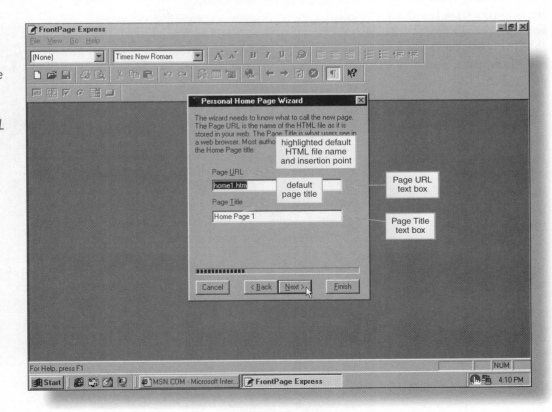

FIGURE 3-69

3 **Type** `homepage.htm` **in the Page URL text box, select the text in the Page Title text box, type** My Home Page **in the text box, and then point to the Next button.**

The homepage.htm entry in the Page URL text box is the name of the HTML file that will contain the home page, and the entry in the Page Title text box (My Home Page) is the title of the Web page (Figure 3-70).

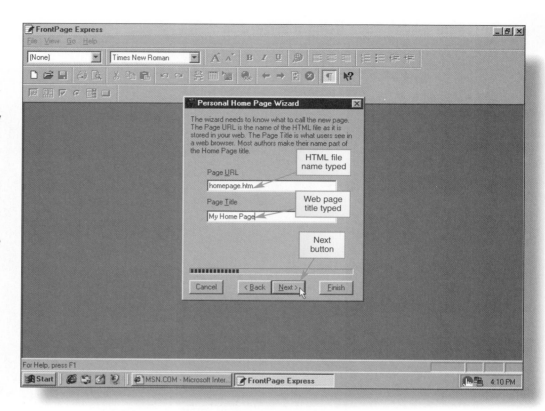

FIGURE 3-70

4 **Click the Next button, remove all check marks from the check boxes in the window, click Job title, click Key responsibilities, and then point to the Next button.**

The next window contains two messages and a note, and check marks display in the Job title and Key responsibilities check boxes to indicate what information will display in the Employee Information section of the home page (Figure 3-71).

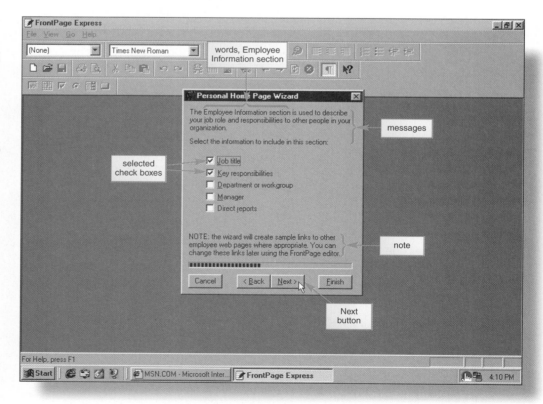

FIGURE 3-71

5 Click the Next button, type `Fishing` **and press the ENTER key, type** `Writing` **and press the ENTER key, type** `Hiking` **as the last entry, click Bullet list, and then point to the Next button.**

The new window contains a message, a text box containing three personal interests, and a selected Bullet list option button to cause a bulleted list of the three personal interests to display in the Personal Interests section (Figure 3-72).

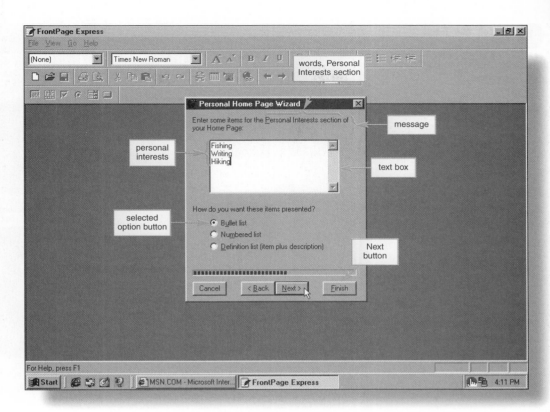

FIGURE 3-72

6 Click the Next button, remove all check marks from the check boxes in the window, click E-mail address, and then point to the Next button.

The new window contains a message and six check boxes and text boxes (Figure 3-73). Selecting the E-mail address check box causes the e-mail address in the associated text box to display in the Contact Information section.

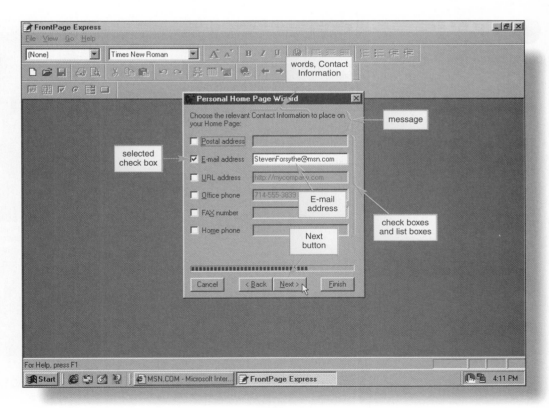

FIGURE 3-73

7 **Click the Next button and then point to the Next button in the new window.**

A message and the Home Page sections list box display in the window (Figure 3-74). The order of the sections in the list box determines the order in which the sections display on the home page. You can change the order by following the instructions in the message.

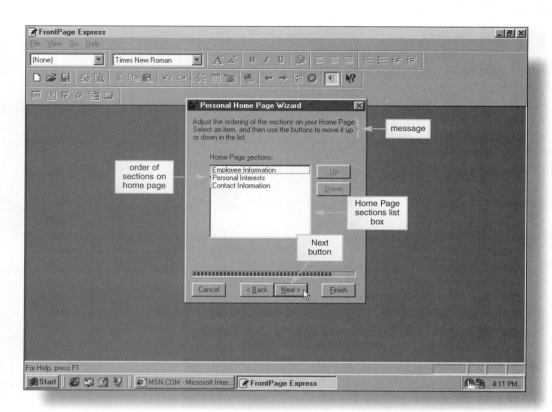

FIGURE 3-74

8 **Click the Next button and then point to the Finish button.**

The new window contains a message (Figure 3-75). The message and progress bar at the bottom of the window indicate the process of supplying information to the wizard is complete and the wizard is ready to create the home page.

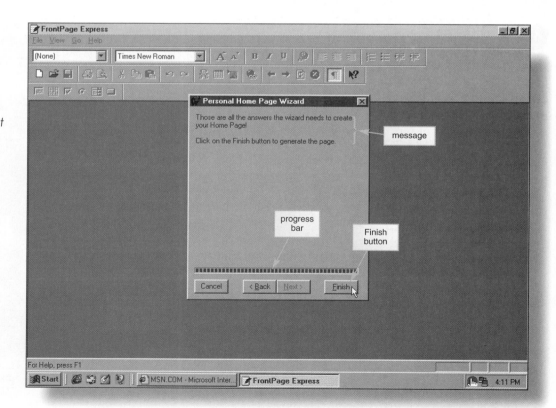

FIGURE 3-75

9 **Click the Finish button.**

The Personal Home Page Wizard window closes, and the wizard creates and displays the home page in the FrontPage Express – [My Home Page] window (Figure 3-76). The home page title (My Home Page) displays at the top of the home page and in the window title.

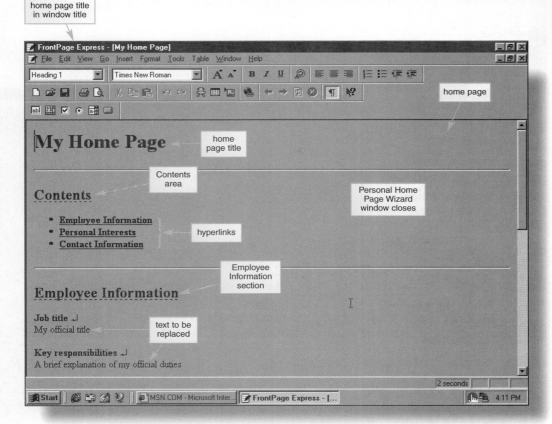

FIGURE 3-76

The home page consists of a title (My Home Page), a Contents area, and three sections (Employee Information, Personal Interests, and Contact Information). The Contents area contains hyperlinks to the three sections on the home page. The first section in the home page (Employee Information) is visible in Figure 3-76. This section contains two headings (Job title and Key responsibilities). The text below the Job title heading should be replaced with the job title and the text below the Key responsibilities heading should be replaced with the key responsibilities of the job. To replace this text, you must edit the home page.

Editing a Web Page Using FrontPage Express

Before publishing the home page to the World Wide Web, the text below the Job title heading should be replaced with the job title (Writer) and the text below the Key responsibilities heading should be replaced with the key responsibilities of the job (Writing about Internet Explorer). Perform the step on the next page to edit the home page and replace the text.

To Edit a Web Page

1 **Select the text, My official title, below the Job title heading and then type** `Writer` **as the job title. Select the text, A brief explanation of my official duties, below the Key responsibilities heading and then type** `Writing about Internet Explorer` **as the job responsibilities.**

The word, Writer, replaces the words, My official title, and the words, Writing about Internet Explorer, replace the words, A brief explanation of my official duties (Figure 3-77).

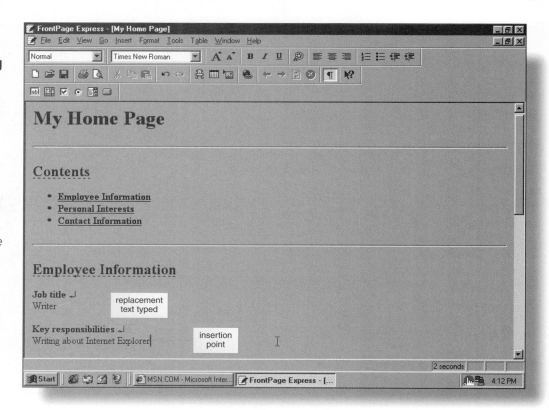

FIGURE 3-77

Creating a Hyperlink in a Web Page

The Personal Home Page wizard created three hyperlinks in the home page (Figure 3-76 on page IE 3.59). Clicking a hyperlink causes the home page to scroll and the associated section to display. In addition to hyperlinks within the same Web page, many Web pages contain hyperlinks to other Web pages on the World Wide Web.

Assume you want to include a hyperlink on the home page to your employer's Web site and the URL for the home page is http://www.scseries.com. Some Web page designers suggest that the text of a hyperlink on a Web page should be mnemonic, meaning it should be descriptive of the Web page it displays. After creating a hyperlink to your employer's Web site using the URL for the site, you may want to replace the less meaningful URL with more meaningful text, like the employer's name (Course Technology). Perform the following steps to use the Create or Edit Hyperlink button on the Format toolbar to create the hyperlink using the URL as the hyperlink, and then replace the URL with the words, Course Technology.

Hyperlinks

You can create a hyperlink to a Web page on another computer connected to the Web, to a Web page on the same computer, or to a location within the same Web page.

Steps **To Create a Hyperlink in a Web Page**

1 **Verify the insertion point displays following the words, Writing about Internet Explorer. Press the ENTER key to move the insertion point to the beginning of the next line of the home page, and then point to the Bold button on the Format toolbar.**

The insertion point displays at the beginning of a blank line (Figure 3-78).

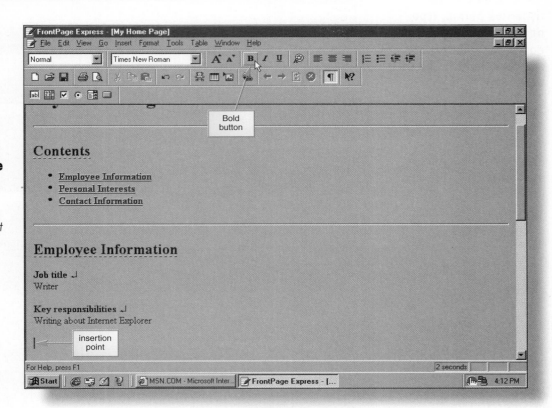

FIGURE 3-78

2 **Click the Bold button, type** Employer **as the heading, press the ENTER key, and then point to the Create or Edit Hyperlink button on the Standard toolbar.**

The word, Employer, displays on the Web page in bold text (Figure 3-79). A blank line and insertion point display below the heading.

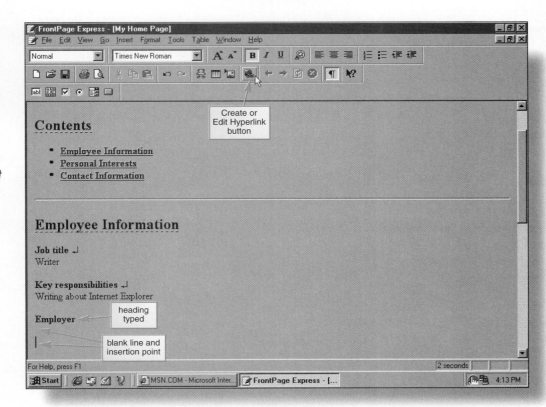

FIGURE 3-79

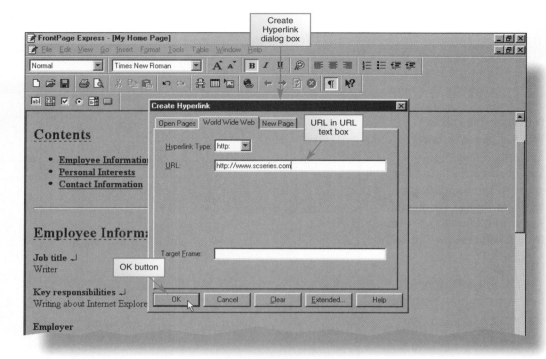

FIGURE 3-80

3 Click the Create or Edit Hyperlink button, type http://www.scseries.com in the URL text box, and then point to the OK button.

The Create Hyperlink dialog box displays and the URL for the employer (http://www.scseries.com) displays in the URL text box (Figure 3-80).

4 Click the OK button.

The Create Hyperlink dialog box closes and the http://www.scseries.com hyperlink displays below the Employer heading in the home page (Figure 3-81).

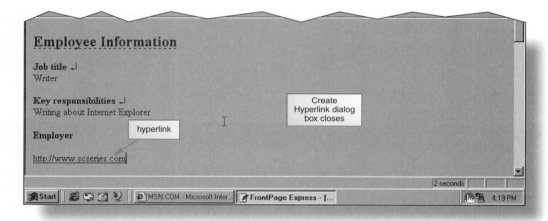

FIGURE 3-81

5 Click anywhere within the text of the URL to move the insertion point into the text and then type Course Technology as the company name.

The text, Course Technology, displays within the hyperlink text (Figure 3-82).

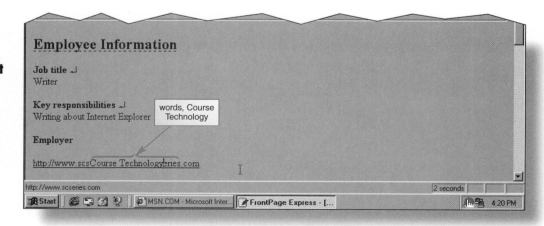

FIGURE 3-82

6 Using the DELETE key and ARROW keys, delete the text of the http://www.scseries.com hyperlink. Do not delete the text, Course Technology.

The text, Course Technology, displays as the hyperlink (Figure 3-83).

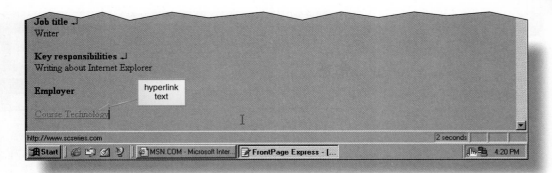

FIGURE 3-83

The awkward process of inserting the words, Course Technology, in the URL text and then deleting the original URL text was necessary to preserve the connection to the Course Technology Web page. If you delete the http://www.scseries.com text and then type the words, Course Technology, the connection to the Web page represented by the URL you typed in the Create Hyperlink dialog box will be lost and the hyperlink will not display the associated Web page. You can determine if the hyperlink works when the text you type to replace the URL text is the same color as the original hyperlink, and the new text is underlined.

Saving a Web Page

Once you have finished editing the Web page, you should save it on disk. Perform the following steps save the Web page on a floppy disk in drive A.

Other Ways

1. On Edit menu click Hyperlink
2. Press ALT+E, press K
3. Press CTRL+K

More About

Saving Web Pages

FrontPage Express allows you to place a new Web page on a Web server immediately. The Page Location text box in the Save As dialog box contains the path of the Web server where FrontPage Express will publish (store) the Web page. Once published, it is available instantly for viewing on the Web.

 To Save a Web Page on a Floppy Disk

1 Insert a formatted floppy disk into drive A.

2 Click File on the menu bar, click Save, and then point to the As File button.

The Save As dialog box displays (Figure 3-84). The Page Title text box contains the home page title and the Page Location text box contains the Web server location where this document can be stored. Clicking the As File button in the dialog box saves the home page on a disk file.

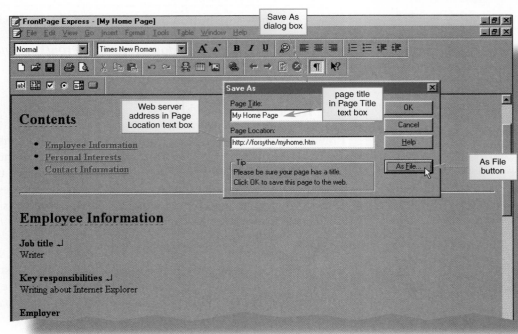

FIGURE 3-84

3 **Click the As File button.**

The Save As File dialog box displays (Figure 3-85). The Desktop folder name displays in the Save in box and the file name, myhome, displays in the File name text box.

4 **Click the Save in box arrow, click 3½ Floppy [A:], and then click the Save button in the Save As File dialog box.**

The home page is saved in a file called myhome on the floppy disk in drive A.

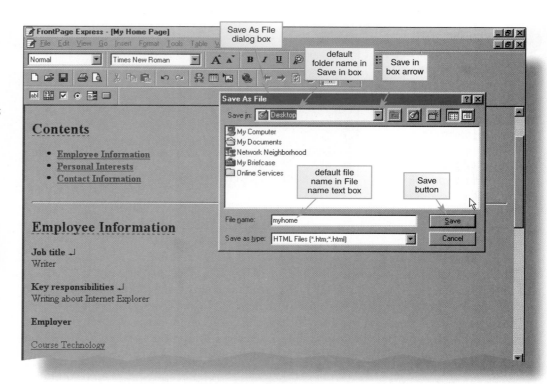

FIGURE 3-85

Other Ways

1. Press ALT+F, press S
2. Press CTRL+S

More About

The Radio Toolbar

If, when you right click a blank area on any of the toolbars in the Microsoft Internet Explorer window, the word, Radio, does not display on the shortcut menu, you must download and install the Windows Media Player software from the Microsoft Web site (www.microsoft.com) if you wish to listen to radio stations.

Quitting FrontPage Express

When you have finished using FrontPage Express, perform the following step to quit FrontPage Express.

TO QUIT FRONTPAGE EXPRESS

1 Click the Close button in the FrontPage Express window.

The FrontPage Express window closes and FrontPage quits.

The Radio Toolbar

Previously in this book, three toolbars (Standard Buttons, Address bar, and Links bar) were shown in the Microsoft Internet Explorer window. The **Radio toolbar**, a new feature of Internet Explorer 5, allows you to listen to more than three hundred talk and music radio stations located in the United States and around the world. The radio toolbar is available when you install **Windows Media Player**, a program included with Internet Explorer that allows you to play multimedia files (audio, video, and animation).

After displaying the Radio toolbar, you can select a station based on station format (Classical, Country, Modern Rock, and so on), state, country, or zip code. You can play and pause the music, control and mute the volume, and display the name of your favorite radio stations on the Radio toolbar. Perform the following steps to display the Radio toolbar.

To Display the Radio Toolbar

1 **Right-click a blank area on any toolbar in the Microsoft Internet Explorer window and then point to Radio on the shortcut menu.**

A shortcut menu, containing the highlighted Radio command, displays (Figure 3-86).

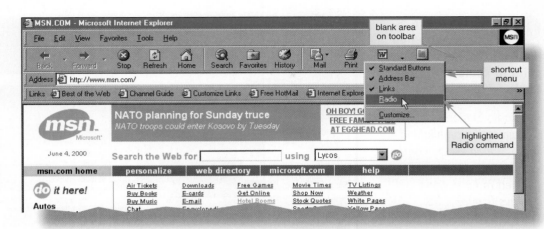

FIGURE 3-86

2 **Click Radio.**

The Radio toolbar displays below the Links bar in the Microsoft Internet Explorer window (Figure 3-87). The Radio toolbar contains a Play button, Mute button, Volume Control slide and slider, Radio Stations button, and message area. The message area contains the name of a previously selected radio station (Kiss Country WKIS). Other station names may display in the message area on your computer.

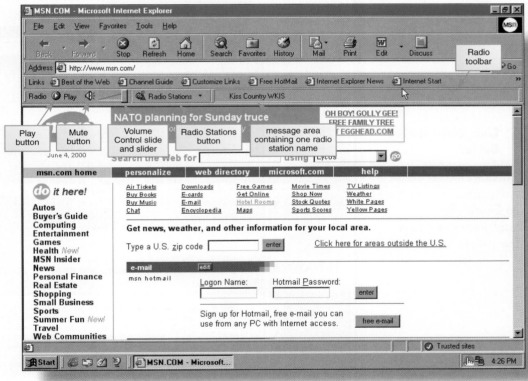

FIGURE 3-87

Using the Radio Station Guide

The **radio station guide,** located on the Windows Media Guide Web page, allows you to search for radio stations based on US zip code, state, country, or station format. The Radio Stations button on the Radio toolbar displays the radio station guide in the Microsoft Internet Explorer window. Perform the following steps to display the radio station guide.

To Display the Radio Station Guide

1 **Click the Radio Stations button on the Radio toolbar, and then point to Radio Station Guide.**

The Radio Stations menu, containing the highlighted Radio Station Guide command, and a list of previously selected radio stations displays (Figure 3-88).

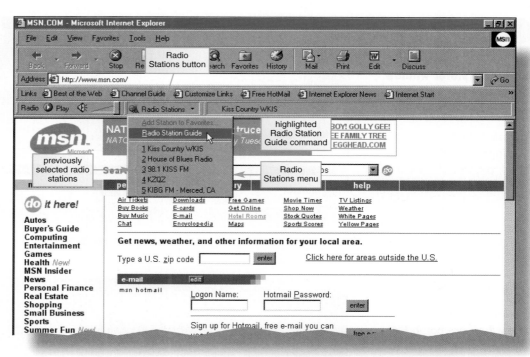

FIGURE 3-88

2 **Click Radio Station Guide.**

The Windows Media Guide page displays in the Windows Media Guide - Radio - Microsoft Internet Explorer window (Figure 3-89).

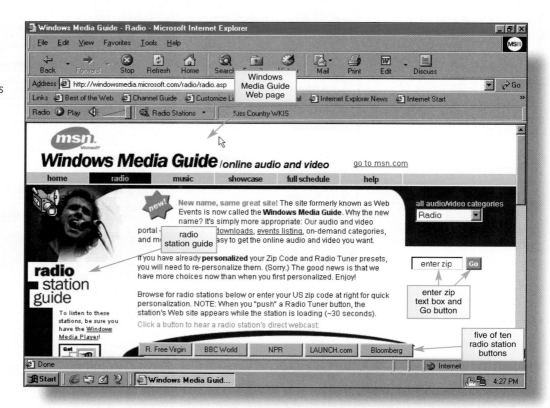

FIGURE 3-89

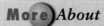
The Windows Media Guide page illustrated in Figure 3-89 contains the Enter Zip box and Go button that allows you to enter a US zip code and display a listing of radio stations within that area. Although not completely visible in Figure 3-89, ten radio station buttons display in the radio station guide that allow you to select one of ten radio stations. In addition, three option buttons and the Browse radio stations or personalize your tuner list box that are not visible in Figure 3-89 allow you to browse radio stations based upon state, country, or station format (Country, Rock, Talk, Classical, and so on).

Selecting a Radio Station

Currently, only five radio station buttons display in the radio station guide. To view all radio station buttons and the Browse radio stations or personalize your tuner list box, you must scroll the Web page. Perform the following steps to scroll the Web page and select the House of Blues radio station.

 To Listen to a Radio Station

1 Scroll the Windows Media Guide page to display the radio station buttons and the Browse radio stations or personalize your tuner list box, and then point to the House of Blues button.

Ten radio station buttons and the Browse radio stations or personalize your tuner list box display (Figure 3-90). The list box contains three option buttons and the Format box that allow you to select the state, country, or station format.

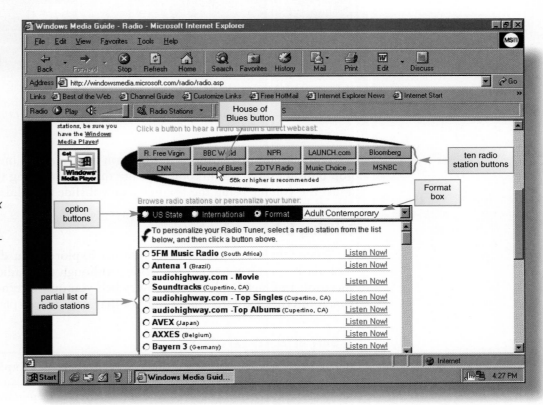

FIGURE 3-90

2 **Click the House of Blues button.**

The House of Blues Internet Radio page displays in the Microsoft Internet Explorer window and the message, Buffering, displays in the message area on the Radio toolbar while the computer prepares to receive the radio transmission from the House of Blues station. When the buffering of information is complete, various messages from the House of Blues display in the message area (Figure 3-91).

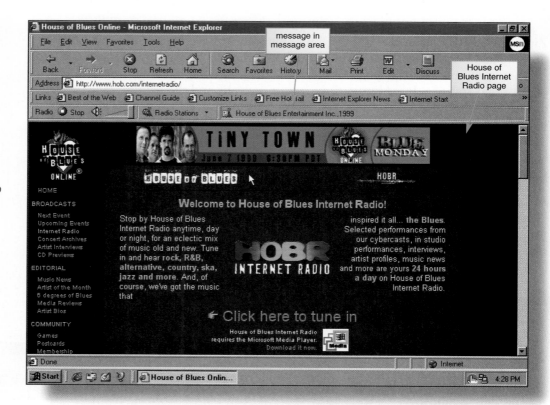

FIGURE 3-91

While listening to a radio station, you may stop the music temporarily using the Stop button on the Radio toolbar, mute the volume using the Mute button, and adjust the volume using the Volume Control slide and slider.

Quitting Internet Explorer

When you have finished using Internet Explorer, you should quit Internet Explorer by performing the step below. Although the Radio toolbar displays in the Microsoft Internet Explorer window, when you quit Internet Explorer and then launch Internet Explorer, the Radio toolbar does not display.

TO QUIT INTERNET EXPLORER

 Click the Close button in the Microsoft Internet Explorer window.

Internet Explorer quits, Microsoft Internet Explorer window closes, and Windows desktop displays.

Project Summary

In this project, you learned to use Outlook Express to read, reply to, delete, compose, send, and format e-mail messages. You also used Outlook Express to search for and display newsgroups, read and post newsgroup articles, expand and collapse a thread, and subscribe and unsubscribe to a newsgroup. Using NetMeeting you learned to place a call, send a typed message, and change directory information and the ILS server. You used FrontPage Express and a wizard to create a Web page and then edited the Web page. Finally, you displayed the Radio toolbar and used the radio station guide to select and listen to radio stations over the Internet.

What You Should Know

Having completed this project, you now should be able to perform the following tasks.

▶ Change the Directory Information *(IE 3.42)*
▶ Change the ILS Server *(IE 3.45)*
▶ Close an E-Mail Message *(IE 3.11)*
▶ Close the Chat Window *(IE 3.50)*
▶ Collapse a Thread *(IE 3.28)*
▶ Compose an E-Mail Message Using Stationery *(IE 3.16)*
▶ Create a Hyperlink in a Web Page *(IE 3.61)*
▶ Create a Web Page Using a Wizard *(IE 3.55)*
▶ Delete an E-Mail Message *(IE 3.15)*
▶ Display the Articles in a Newsgroup *(IE 3.25, IE 3.37)*
▶ Display the Newsgroups on Another News Server *(IE 3.32)*
▶ Display the Newsgroups on the Default News Server *(IE 3.22)*
▶ Display the Radio Station Guide *(IE 3.66)*
▶ Display the Radio Toolbar *(IE 3.65)*
▶ Edit a Web Page *(IE 3.60)*
▶ End a Call, Log Off, and Quit NetMeeting *(IE 3.51)*
▶ Expand a Thread *(IE 3.27)*
▶ Format an E-mail Message *(IE 3.19)*

▶ Launch Microsoft Internet Explorer *(IE 3.4)*
▶ Launch Microsoft FrontPage Express *(IE 3.52)*
▶ Launch Microsoft NetMeeting *(IE 3.40)*
▶ Launch Microsoft Outlook Express *(IE 3.6)*
▶ Listen to a Radio Station *(IE 3.67)*
▶ Place a Call *(IE 3.46)*
▶ Post a Newsgroup Article *(IE 3.33)*
▶ Print a Newsgroup Article *(IE 3.29)*
▶ Print an Opened E-mail Message *(IE 3.10)*
▶ Quit Outlook Express *(IE 3.21, IE 3.39)*
▶ Quit FrontPage Express *(IE 3.64)*
▶ Quit Internet Explorer *(IE 3.68)*
▶ Open (Read) an E-Mail Message *(IE 3.9)*
▶ Read a Newsgroup Article *(IE 3.27)*
▶ Reply to an E-mail Message *(IE 3.13)*
▶ Save a Web Page on a Floppy Disk *(IE 3.63)*
▶ Send a Text Message Using Chat *(IE 3.48)*
▶ Send an E-mail Message *(IE 3.20)*
▶ Start the Personal Home Page Wizard *(IE 3.53)*
▶ Subscribe to a Newsgroup *(IE 3.31)*
▶ Unsubscribe from a Newsgroup *(IE 3.38)*

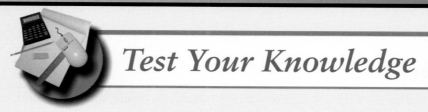

Test Your Knowledge

1 True/False

Instructions: Circle T if the statement is true or F if the statement is false.

T   F   1. FrontPage Express allows you to receive and store incoming e-mail messages, compose and send e-mail messages, and read and post messages to Internet newsgroups.

T   F   2. The Drafts folder is the destination for incoming mail.

T   F   3. Stationery allows you to add a colorful background image, unique text sizes and colors, and custom margins to an e-mail message.

T   F   4. A news server is a collection of news and discussion groups that you can access via the Internet.

T   F   5. A thread is the original newsgroup article and all subsequent related replies to the article.

T   F   6. Subscribing is the process of posting an article to a newsgroup.

T   F   7. An Internet Locator Service (ILS) maintains a computer server that contains electronic mail addresses.

T   F   8. Hypertext markup language (HTML) is the language used to create a Web page.

T   F   9. A hyperlink is a special automated assistant that helps you through the process of creating a Web page.

T   F   10. The radio station guide allows you to search for radio stations based on zip code, state, country, and station format.

2 Multiple Choice

Instructions: Circle the correct response.

1. The place where e-mail messages are stored until you read them is the _____ folder.
   a. Inbox   b. Sent Items   c. Outbox   d. Drafts

2. An opened envelope icon to the left of an e-mail message in the message list indicates you have _____ the message.
   a. sent   b. replied to   c. composed   d. read

3. A bolded message heading indicates you have not _____ the e-mail message.
   a. replied to   b. sent   c. read   d. printed

4. Alt, comp, news, rec, and sci are examples of _____.
   a. threads   b. prefixes   c. subgroup names   d. suffixes

5. The msnnews.msn.com and netnews.msn.com names are examples of _____.
   a. threads   b. newsgroup articles   c. news servers   d. subscriptions

6. Selecting a newsgroup you wish to visit frequently is called _____.
   a. unsubscribing   b. subscribing   c. posting   d. saving

7. Which of the following is not a method of communicating using NetMeeting?
   a. File Transfer   b. Chat   c. Whiteboard   d. Wizard

Test Your Knowledge

8. While using NetMeeting, clicking the Current Call icon allows you to view a list of _____.
   a. users currently in a meeting
   b. your callers, your response to their calls, and the time of each call
   c. users you would like to be able to call quickly
   d. users on a ILS
9. The software you use to create a Web page is _____.
   a. Outlook Express   b. NetMeeting   c. FrontPage Express   d. Internet Explorer
10. The _____ toolbar contains a play button, mute button, and volume slide and slider.
    a. Format   b. Radio   c. Standard Buttons   d. Forms

3 Opening and Reading an E-Mail Message

Instructions: Figure 3-92 illustrates the Inbox - Outlook Express window. In the spaces provided, list the steps to open and read the new e-mail message from Juan Benito and then send a reply to him. The return e-mail should contain a subject (Re: Golf Tournament Information) and a message (I put together a foursome for the golf tournament. Sign us up and I will send you a check for the tournament entry fee in the mail. Please call me if you have any questions).

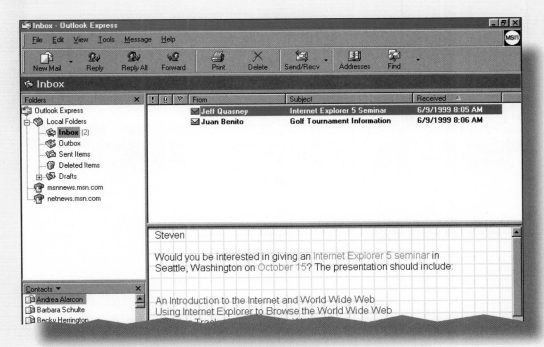

FIGURE 3-92

Step 1: _____

Step 2: _____

Step 3: _____

Step 4: _____

Test Your Knowledge

4 Searching For and Subscribing to a Newsgroup

Instructions: Figure 3-93 shows the Outlook Express window that displays when you click the Read News command on the Mail menu. In the spaces provided, write the steps to select the net.news.msn.com server, search for newsgroups containing the word, rabbits, subscribe to the rec.pets.rabbits newsgroup, and display the newsgroup articles in the rec.pets.rabbits newsgroup.

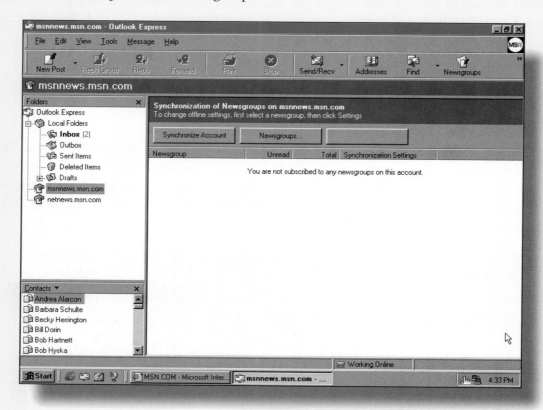

FIGURE 3-93

Step 1: _____

Step 2: _____

Step 3: _____

Step 4: _____

Step 5: _____

Step 6: _____

Use Help

1 Using Outlook Express Help

Instructions: Use Help and a computer to perform the following tasks.

1. Launch Internet Explorer, click the Mail button, and then click Read Mail.
2. Click Help on the menu bar of the Inbox - Outlook Express window.
3. Click Contents and Index on the Help menu and maximize the Outlook Express Help window (Figure 3-94).

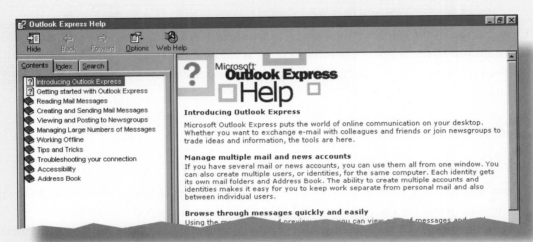

FIGURE 3-94

4. Click the Index tab.
5. Using the Index tab, answer the following questions.
   a. According to the instructions in Outlook Express Help, how do you insert a file into an e-mail message?
   _____
   _____
   b. How do you save a file attached to an e-mail message you receive?
   _____
   c. If an e-mail message displays in the preview pane, how do you save a file attached to the e-mail message?
   _____
6. Click the Contents tab in the Outlook Express Help window.
7. Using the Contents tab, answer the following questions.
   a. How do you read messages offline?_____
   b. What are the keyboard shortcuts to perform the following Outlook Express tasks? *Hint:* Look in Tips and Tricks.
   Send and receive mail _____
   Open or post a new message _____
   Go to the Inbox _____
   Download news for offline reading _____
   Check spelling _____

(continued)

Use Help

Using Outlook Express Help *(continued)*

8. Using the Contents tab, answer the following questions.
   a. How do you open the Address Book from the Inbox - Outlook Express window? _____
   _____

   b. What is a business card? _____
   _____

   c. What does the business card allow you to exchange? _____
   _____

9. Click the Close button in the Outlook Express Help window.
10. Click the Close button in the Inbox - Outlook Express window.
11. Clicke the Close button in the Microsoft Internet Explorer window.

2 Setting Newsgroups Properties

Instructions: Use Help and a computer to perform the following tasks.

1. Launch Outlook Express. Use Outlook Express Help and the Contents tab to answer the following questions. Write your name on the printouts and then hand them in to your instructor.
   a. Print the Help topic that answers the question: How do you add a signature to outgoing messages?
   b. Print the Help topic that answers the question: How do you insert a file?
   c. Print the Help topic that answers the question: How do you insert a business card in all e-mail messages?
   d. Print the Help topic that answers the question: How do you insert a sound in an e-mail message?
2. Launch NetMeeting. Use NetMeeting Help to answer the following questions.
   a. When would you want to send a text message to another participant? _____
   _____

   b. Under what two conditions is a user's name added to the SpeedDial list? _____
   _____

   c. How do you manually add a name to your SpeedDial list?_____
   _____

   d. How do you find a file sent to you by another participant? _____
   _____

3. Launch FrontPage Express and answer the following questions?
   a. What is a WebBot? _____
   _____

   b. Name three things a WebBot adds to a Web page? _____
   _____

   c. What is the difference between FrontPage and FrontPage Express?_____
   _____

4. Close all open windows.

In the Lab

1 Sending E-mail Messages

Instructions: Launch Internet Explorer and perform the following tasks with a computer.

1. Click the Address bar. Type www.house.gov and then press the ENTER key to retrieve the Web page shown in Figure 3-95.

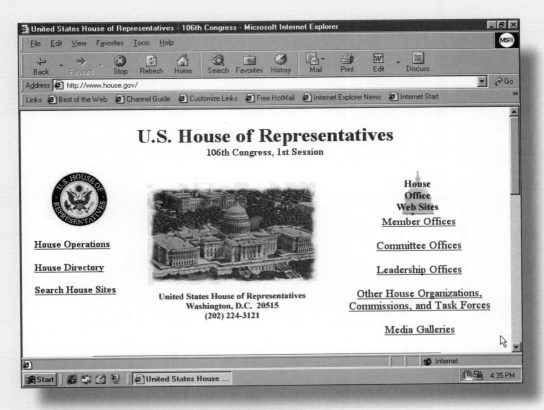

FIGURE 3-95

2. Find and display the e-mail address of the member of the House of Representatives from your district. If your representative is not listed, select the name of one you recognize.
3. Click the Mail button, click Read Mail, and then click the New Mail button to display the New Message window.
4. Using the e-mail address of the U.S. House of Representative member you obtained in Step 2, compose a mail message to your representative about some issue that is important to you.
5. Ask your instructor for his or her e-mail address and type it in the Cc text box. Send a carbon copy of the message to your instructor. Print the copy you receive and then hand it in to your instructor.
6. Close all open windows.

In the Lab

2 Reading Newsgroup Articles

Instructions: Launch Internet Explorer and perform the following tasks with a computer.

1. Click the Mail button and then click Read News on the Mail menu.
2. Click the Newsgroups button on the toolbar to display the list of all the newsgroups in the default news server (Figure 3-96).

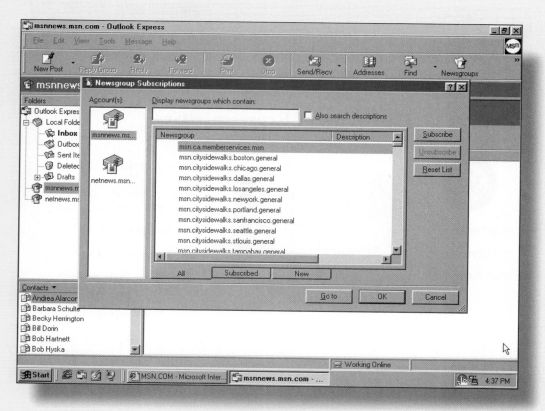

FIGURE 3-96

3. Search for or scroll to find a newsgroup of interest to you. Click the newsgroup and then click the Go to button.
4. Find a thread that contains the original article and at least three replies.
5. Read and print each article in the thread. Write your name on each printout and then hand them in to your instructor.
6. Close all open windows.

In the Lab

3 Posting Newsgroup Articles

Instructions: Launch Internet Explorer and perform the following tasks with a computer.

1. Click the Mail button and then click Read News on the Mail menu.
2. Click the Newsgroups button on the toolbar to display the list of all the newsgroups in the default news server.
3. Search for or scroll to find a newsgroup of interest to you. Click the newsgroup and then click the Go to button.
4. Click the New Post button to display the New Message window (Figure 3-97).

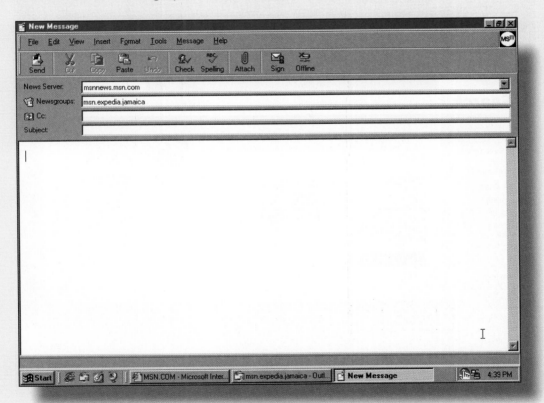

FIGURE 3-97

5. Compose and send a message to the newsgroup.
6. Find your message in the message list.
7. Print the message, write your name on it, and then hand it in to your instructor.
8. Close all open windows.

In the Lab

4 Finding E-Mail Addresses

Instructions: Start Internet Explorer and perform the following tasks with a computer.

1. Click the Address bar in the Microsoft Internet Explorer window, type www.msn.com, and then click the Go button.
2. Find and click the White Pages hyperlink that displays on the MSN home page. The MSN search page displays (Figure 3-98).

FIGURE 3-98

3. Use the search form on the MSN search page to search for your name. Print the resulting page, write your name on the printout, and then hand it in to your instructor.
4. Use the search form to search for one of your friends. Print the resulting page, write your name on the printout, and then hand it in to your instructor.
5. Use the search form to search for someone famous or someone whom you admire. Print the resulting page, write your name on the printout, and then hand it in to your instructor.
6. Close all open windows.

In the Lab

5 Using NetMeeting

Instructions: Perform the following tasks on the computer using Microsoft NetMeeting.

WARNING! Not everyone who uses NetMeeting has business purposes in mind and many people who use NetMeeting are open and frank about the type of communication they want. Some areas may contain violent or sexually explicit content. Content Advisor, a program available with Internet Explorer that provides a way to help control the types of content that your computer can access on the Internet, is not available in NetMeeting. Consequently, you may decide you do not want to use NetMeeting.

Part 1: *Launch NetMeeting*

1. If necessary, launch Internet Explorer.
2. Click File on the menu, point to New, and then click Internet Call (Figure 3-99).

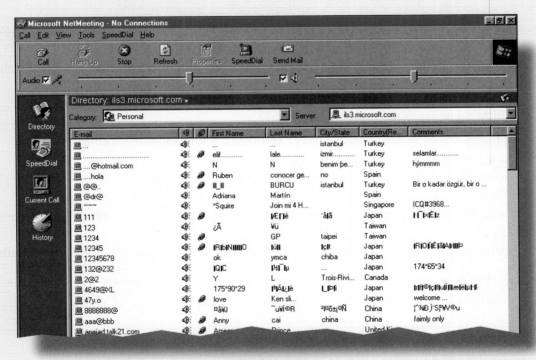

FIGURE 3-99

Part 2: *Enter Your Directory Information*

1. Click Call on the menu bar and then click Change My Information.
2. Type your first name in the First name text box. Type your last name in the Last name text box. Type your e-mail address in the E-mail address text box. Type your city and state in the City/State text box.
3. Select your country in the Country box. Type a comment in the Comments text box.
4. Click the For personal use (suitable for all ages) option button.
5. Click the OK button in the Options dialog box.

(continued)

In the Lab

Using NetMeeting *(continued)*

Part 3: *Placing a Call to Someone Who Lives in Your State*

1. Click the Server box arrow in the Directory sheet and then click ils3.microsoft.com.
2. Click the City/State column header button to sort the names in the directory list by city/state.
3. Scroll the directory list until you find an individual who lives in your state.
4. Double-click the name.
5. If the person accepts your call, begin the conversation by explaining who you are, where you live, and why you placed the call.
6. In the spaces provided, record interesting information about the individual to whom you are talking.

_____

_____

_____

_____

7. When you have finished talking, click the Hang Up button on the Current Call toolbar to end the conversation.

Part 4: *Place a Call to Someone in a Foreign Country*

1. Click the Server box arrow in the Directory sheet and then click ils5.microsoft.com.
2. Click the Country header button to sort the names in the directory list by country.
3. Scroll the directory list until you find an individual who lives in Canada.
4. Double-click the name.
5. If the person accepts your call, begin the conversation by explaining who you are, where you live, and why you placed the call.
6. In the spaces provided, record interesting information about the individual to whom you are talking.

_____

_____

_____

_____

7. When finished talking, click the Hang Up button on the Current Call toolbar to end the conversation.
8. Click the Close button in the Microsoft NetMeeting - No Connections window.
9. Click the Close button in the Microsoft Internet Explorer window.

6 Creating a Web Page Using FrontPage Express

Instructions: Start Internet Explorer and perform the following steps with a computer.

1. Click the arrow on the Edit button on the Standard Buttons toolbar and then click the Edit with Microsoft FrontPage Editor command.
2. Using the Personal Home Page wizard (Figure 3-100), create a Web page that contains some of your personal interests and contact information. Make sure you type your name somewhere in the Web page.

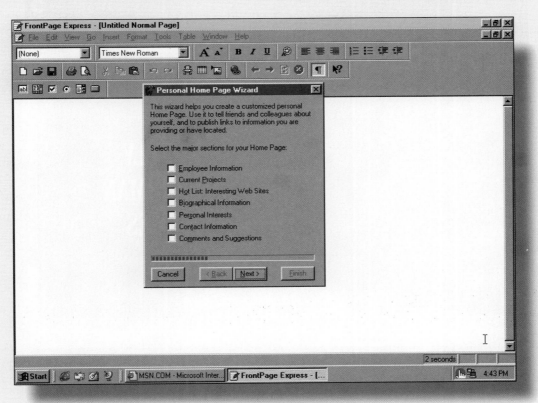

FIGURE 3-100

3. Using the Create or Edit Hyperlink button on the FrontPage Express Standard toolbar, add a hyperlink to your college, university, or organization's home page.
4. Save the Web page on a floppy disk.
5. Print the Web page and hand it in to your instructor.
6. Close all open windows.

In the Lab

7 Connecting to the Shelly Cashman Series Web Site

Instructions: Perform the following steps.

1. Start Internet Explorer and then click the Address bar.
2. Type www.scseries.com and then press the ENTER key (Figure 3-101).

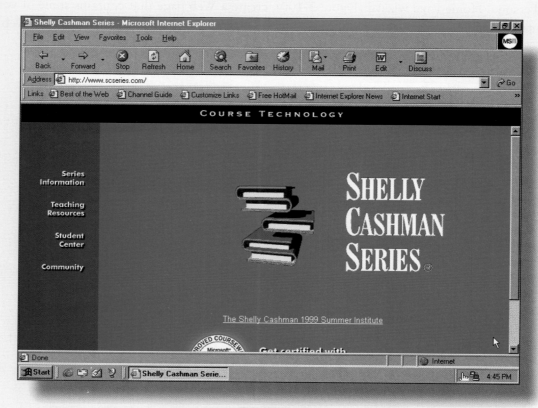

FIGURE 3-101

3. Click the Student Center link.
4. Scroll down and then click Microsoft Internet Explorer 5: An Introduction.
5. Scroll down and then click Project 3. Complete the activities listed.

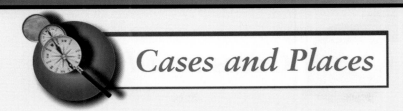

Cases and Places

The difficulty of these case studies varies:
▶ are the least difficult; ▶▶ are more difficult; and ▶▶▶ are the most difficult.

1 ▶ Several Web sites are available that allow you to enter a person's name and search for information about the individual. Using a search engine, locate three of these sites. Use your name, a friend's name, and a relative's name to search for information using all three sites you find. Print the information you find, write your name on the printouts, and then hand them in to your instructor.

2 ▶ Many software products such as Microsoft Word and Microsoft FrontPage Express contain a library of images, graphics, pictures, and other clip art. Libraries of clip art also are available for you to download on the Web. Using the Web search engine of your choice, search for five sites that offer clip art for use on Web pages. Print a few of the images from each site.

3 ▶▶ Using computer magazines, advertising brochures, the Internet, or other resources, compile information about the latest version of Microsoft Outlook. In a brief report, compare Microsoft Outlook and Microsoft Outlook Express. Include the differences and similarities, how to obtain the software, the function and features of each program, and so forth. If possible, test Microsoft Outlook and then add your personal comments.

4 ▶▶ NetMeeting allows you to log on to and display the directory for nine ILS servers. Microsoft owns and operates six of those servers. Conservative users have expressed concerns that some users try to disguise their identities by displaying false information in the First Name, Last Name, City/State, and Comments columns. In a brief report, summarize the reasons for correctly identifying yourself on the Internet, problems that result when users disguise their identities, who you think is responsible, and how to prevent this problem.

5 ▶▶ Using computer magazines, advertising brochures, the Internet, or other resources, compile information about the latest version of FrontPage. In a brief report, compare FrontPage and FrontPage Express. Include the differences and similarities, how to obtain the software, the functions and features of each program, and so forth. If possible, test Microsoft FrontPage and then add your personal comments.

6 ▶▶▶ Many colleges and universities maintain their own news servers containing school related newsgroups. Locate a school that has a news server. Explore the news server, determine how many newsgroups are on the server, locate five newsgroups that are of interest to you, determine the number of articles in each newsgroup, and read several articles in each newsgroup. Write a brief report summarizing your findings. Hand the report in to your instructor.

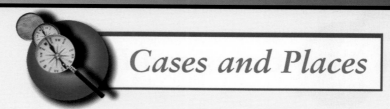

Cases and Places

7 ▶▶▶ Many schools provide you with disk space to store personal Web pages and publish them on the Web. Using FrontPage Express wizards design three separate Web pages. Obtain the instructions to place the Web pages on the Web and then place them on the Web. Include personal and contact information, interests and hobbies, links to useful Web resources, and your school's home page. Link the pages together using hyperlinks. Print each page and then hand the pages in to your instructor.

APPENDIX A
Internet Explorer Options

Internet Options Dialog Box

When you use Internet Explorer to browse the World Wide Web, learn about Web research techniques, and communicate over the Internet, default settings control your interaction with Internet Explorer. You can view and modify many of these settings by using the **Internet Options dialog box** shown in Figure A-1.

The Internet Options dialog box contains six tabs (General, Security, Content, Connections, Programs, and Advanced) that allow you to view and modify the Internet Explorer default settings. Using these settings, you can change the home page that displays when you launch Internet Explorer; delete temporary Internet files; assign a Web site to a security zone; control the Internet content to which a computer can gain access; and select the programs to send and receive e-mail, read and post articles to a newsgroup, and place internet calls.

To display the Internet Options dialog box, click Tools on the Internet Explorer menu bar, and then click Internet Options on the Tools menu. The remainder of this appendix explains the contents of the six sheets in the Internet Options dialog box.

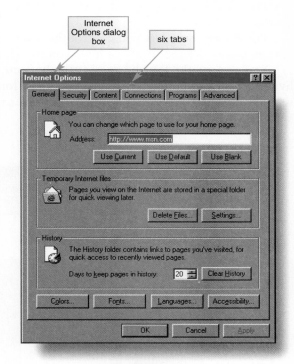

FIGURE A-1

The General Sheet

The **General Sheet** illustrated in Figure A-2 contains the Home page area, Temporary Internet files area, and History area. The **Home page area** allows you to change the **home page**, which is the Web page that displays when you launch Internet Explorer. The home page should be the Web page that contains the information you use most frequently. The Address box in the Home page area contains the URL for the current home page. The three buttons below the Address box allow you to use the Web page that currently displays in the Microsoft Internet Explorer window as the home page (Use Current), use the default Web page (Use Default), or display no Web page (Use Blank).

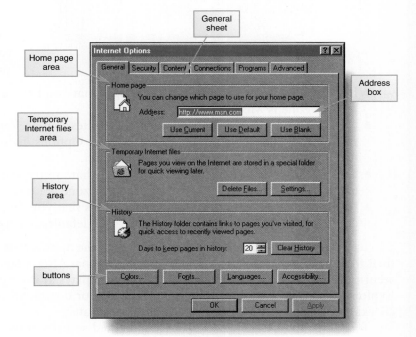

FIGURE A-2

The **Temporary Internet files area** permits you to delete the files in the Temporary Internet Files folder on the hard drive or change the settings of the folder. When you display a Web page in the Microsoft Internet Explorer window, a file called a **temporary Internet file** is stored in the Temporary Internet Files folder on the hard disk. The next time you display that Web page, the page displays quickly because Internet Explorer retrieves the page from the Temporary Internet Files folder instead of the Internet.

The Delete Files button in the Temporary Internet files area allows you to delete all files in the Temporary Internet Files folder. The Settings button allows you to view a list of the temporary Internet files, change the amount of disk space reserved to store the files, and move the Temporary Internet Files folder to another location on the hard disk.

The **History area** lets you control the number of days the Web pages in the History list are kept before being automatically deleted. It also allows you to delete the contents of the History list.

You can use the four buttons at the bottom of the General sheet to change the default text, background, and hyperlink colors (Colors); change the default fonts used to display a Web page (Fonts); specify the language to use when displaying Web pages (Languages); and cause the color and font settings you select to override the settings specified by a Web page (Accessibility).

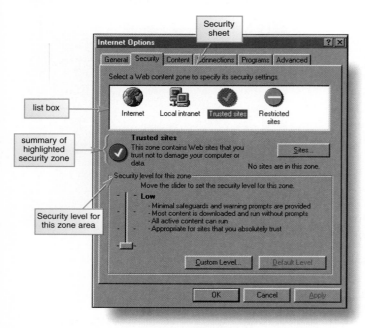

FIGURE A-3

The Security Sheet

The **Security sheet** shown in Figure A-3 contains a list box, which contains an icon for each security zone available on the computer (Internet, Local intranet, Trusted sites, and Restricted sites), a summary of the highlighted security zone, the Sites button, and the Security level for this zone area. The Trusted sites icon is highlighted; a summary of the Trusted sites zone displays below the list box; and the **Security level for this zone area**, which indicates the security level of the zone, displays at the bottom of the Security sheet. The Security level can be changed as needed.

Internet Explorer divides the Internet into four zones of content to which you can assign a security setting. These zones are called **security zones** (Internet, Local intranet, Trusted sites, and Restricted sites), and Explorer allows you to assign a Web site to a zone with a suitable security level. An explanation of the four security zones appears below:

- **Internet:** This zone contains all Web pages that you have not placed in other zones. The default security level for this zone is Medium.
- **Local intranet:** This zone contains all Web sites that are on an organization's intranet, including sites specified on the Connections sheet in the Internet Options dialog box, network paths, and local intranet sites. The default security level for this zone is Medium.
- **Trusted sites:** This zone contains Web sites that are trusted not to damage the computer or the data on the computer. The default security level for this zone is Low.
- **Restricted sites:** This zone contains Web sites that you do not trust because they could possibly damage the computer or the data on the computer. The default security level for this zone is High.

To assign a Web site to a security zone, click the appropriate icon in the list box, click the Sites button, and then follow the instructions to assign a security zone. After assigning a Web page to a security zone, the icon of the security zone to which the Web site is assigned displays at the right side of the status bar in the Microsoft Internet Explorer window. Each time you attempt to open or download content from that Web site, Internet Explorer checks the security settings and responds appropriately.

To change the security level of the highlighted security zone, move the slider along the slide in the Security level for this zone area to display the different security level.

The two buttons at the bottom of the Security level for this zone area allow you to customize the settings for a security zone (Custom Level) and reset the security level to the default level for the security zone (Default Level).

The Content Sheet

The **Content sheet** illustrated in Figure A-4 contains three areas: Content Advisor area, Certificates area, and Personal information area. The **Content Advisor area** permits you to control the types of content (violent content, sexual content, and so on) that a computer can access on the Internet. The **Certificates area** allows you to positively identify yourself, agencies that grant certificates, and certificate publishers. In the **Personal information area**, you can modify the AutoComplete settings, modify private information used to conduct private transactions over the Internet, and modify your personal information (name, e-mail address, telephone numbers, and so on).

Content Advisor provides a way to help you control the types of content that your computer can access on the Internet. After turning on Content Advisor, content that does not meet or exceed the chosen criteria will not display. Initially, Content Advisor is set to the most conservative (least likely to offend) setting. The two buttons in the Content Advisor area allow you to turn on Content Advisor (Enable) and modify the Content Advisor ratings for Internet sites (Settings).

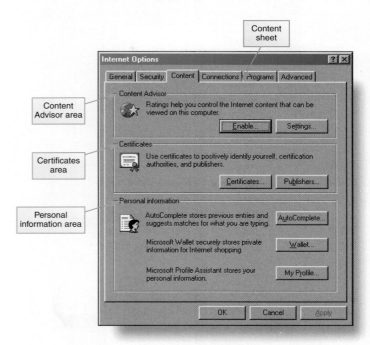

FIGURE A-4

A **certificate** is a statement guaranteeing the identity of a person or the security of a Web site. The **Personal certificate** guarantees your identity to Web sites that require certification. The **Web site certificate** guarantees that a Web site is secure and no other Web site has falsely assumed the identify of the Web site. The left button in the Certificates area allows you to require a Web site to send a security certificate to you before sending them information (Certificates), and the right button displays a list of trusted software publishers whose software can safely be placed on the computer (Publishers).

The three buttons in the Personal information area permit you to modify the settings of the AutoComplete feature, modify the confidential information maintained by Wallet, and modify a user profile. The AutoComplete button lets you use AutoComplete to display Web addresses, forms, and user names and passwords. **Microsoft Wallet** is a software program that stores personal credit card and shipping address information on your computer. The Wallet button in the Personal information area allows you to add, edit, or delete payment methods, addresses, and other information stored by Wallet. You can use the My Profile button to modify the personal information stored on the computer (name, e-mail address, home and business addresses, birthdays, NetMeeting settings, and Digital IDs).

The Connections Sheet

The **Connections sheet** shown in Figure A-5 on the next page allows you to use the Internet Connection wizard to create a new Internet connection, control dial-up networking connections, and modify local area network (LAN) settings. The Setup button at the top of the sheet lets you create a new Internet connection. The **Dial-up settings area** contains a list box displaying the current dial-up settings. The buttons in the area allow you to add, remove, and modify dial-up networking connections. The options buttons control the method to connect to the Internet, allow you to select the default dial-up networking connection, and perform security checks before dialing. The **LAN settings area** permits you to edit the local area network (LAN) settings if the computer is connected to a local area network.

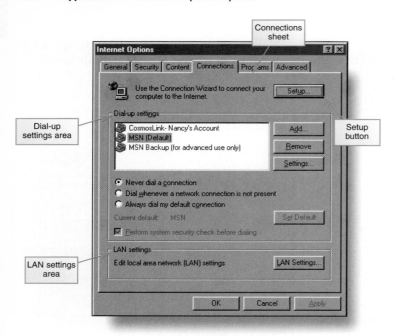

FIGURE A-5

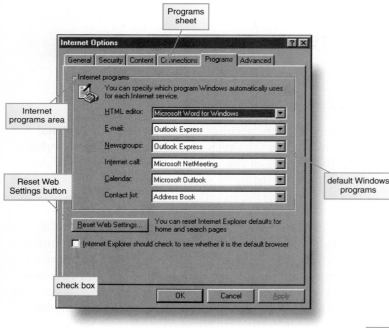

FIGURE A-6

The Programs Sheet

The **Programs sheet** in Figure A-6 allows you to select the Microsoft Windows program to use to edit Web pages, send and receive e-mail, read and post articles to a newsgroup, place an internet call, manage appointments and tasks, and maintain contact information. The **Internet programs area** contains six boxes that contain the default program for each of the following Internet services: HTML editor, E-mail, Newsgroups, Internet call, Calendar, and Contact list.

The Reset Web Settings button below the Internet programs area lets you restore the default settings for the six Internet services listed in the Internet programs area. You can use the check box below the button to select Internet Explorer as the default Web browser.

The Advanced Sheet

The **Advanced sheet** in Figure A-7 contains the Settings list box and the Restore Defaults button. The **Settings list box** contains check boxes for each Internet Explorer setting. The settings are organized into categories: Accessibility, Browsing, HTTP 1.1 settings, Java VM, Multimedia, Printing, Search from the Address bar, and Security. A check mark in a check box indicates the setting is selected. The **Restore Defaults button** returns all settings in the Settings list box to their original (default) settings.

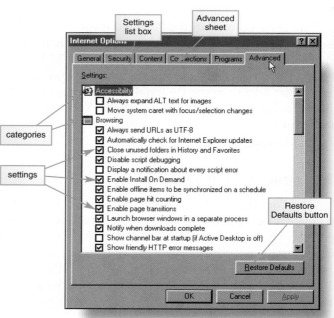

FIGURE A-7

Index